This book is outstanding! I've read many Christian books in my thirty-eight years of being born again. I have a library full of books by just about every notable Christian author and I was blown away with *Called to Christlikeness, Not Christianity*. Many believers, including many Pastors, will receive it with gladness and gratitude. Whether it be lay people, Pastors, Sunday School teachers, or Bible Study teachers, I can see this book becoming their "Go To" reference for applicable sermon preparation, Bible study presentations, and also as a personal study guide.

—Jim Johnson, Associate Pastor
United Community Church – Macon, GA

In recent decades, much of the evangelical world has been flooded with "cheap grace"—defined by Dietrich Bonhoeffer as "forgiveness without discipleship." The tragic result has been acceptance of converts who are grateful for a ticket to heaven, but who display little interest in being transformed while here on earth. This timely book, *Called to Christlikeness, Not Christianity*, sounds an urgent alarm, masterfully confronting the troubling spectacle of professing Christians who aren't on the pathway to Christlikeness. You will find yourself both challenged and encouraged by his much-needed message.

—Jim Buchan, Director of Discipleship
Mission Community Church – Charlotte, NC

This book brought me to my knees in conviction and reflection regarding my walk with Christ. *Called to Christlikeness, Not Christianity* made me stop and consider some hard truths. The Holy Spirit used it to convict me regarding holiness, consecration, and sanctification—whew! When I read this part, it brought me to tears. It made me realize there are some things I need to "tighten up" on this journey. As the apostle Paul says, "Let every man examine himself," so here I am examining some things in my walk.

—Rev. Charles Maldon – Raleigh, NC

Called to Christlikeness, not Christianity is a powerful and useful guide to faith in Christ and subsequent spiritual growth by focusing not only on the "how," but also the "who," the "why" and the "what." With plain and focused language, not theologian-ese, this book leads readers deep into the character and nature of God. It describes in gripping detail the incredible price Jesus paid for sin on the cross of Calvary. Lastly, it charts a clear path toward spiritual maturity. Seekers, new believers, and those who, like me, have followed Jesus Christ for over half a century, will discover amazing insights and practical steps toward a closer and more fulfilling walk with our precious Lord and Savior!

—Thomas Mayhew – Simi Valley, CA
Retired Navy Captain; former Silicon Valley Tech Executive

CALLED TO CHRISTLIKENESS, NOT CHRISTIANITY

Also by Nate Stevens

Matched 4 Life (book and workbook)
Deck Time with Jesus
Transformed: Until Christ is Formed in You
Conformed: Into the Likeness of Christ
Informed: Living by God's Absolute Truth
Surrendered: Yielding to God's Perfect Will
God's Secret Place
Accelerate Your Destiny

Called to Christlikeness, not Christianity

Nate Stevens

Called to Christlikeness, not Christianity
Copyright © 2024 by Nate Stevens

All rights reserved. No part of this publication may be reproduced, stored in a retrieval system or transmitted in any way by any means, electronic, mechanical, photocopy, recording or otherwise without the prior permission of the author except as provided by USA copyright law. For permission requests, contact the author at www.natestevens.net.

Unless otherwise indicated, Scripture quotations are from The New King James Version (NKJV), Thomas Nelson Publishers, Nashville: Thomas Nelson Publishers. Copyright © 1982. Used by permission. All rights reserved.

Scripture quotations marked (AMP) are from the Amplified Bible, Copyright © 2015 by The Lockman Foundation, La Habra, CA 90631. All rights reserved.

Scripture quotations marked (CEV) are from the Holy Bible; Contemporary English Version, Copyright © 1995, Barclay M. Newman, ed., American Bible Society. Used by permission. All rights reserved

Scripture quotations marked (KJV) are taken from the Holy Bible, King James Version, Public Domain.

Scripture quotations marked (MSG) are taken from The Message, Copyright © 1993, 1994, 1995, 1996, 2000, 2001, 2002. Used by permission of NavPress Publishing Group. All rights reserved.

Scripture quotations marked (NLT) are taken from the *Holy Bible*, New Living Translation, copyright © 1996, 2004, 2015 by Tyndale House Foundation. Used by permission of Tyndale House Publishers, Inc., Carol Stream, Illinois 60188. All rights reserved.

Scripture quotations marked (TLB) are taken from The Living Bible Copyright © 1971 by Tyndale House Foundation. Used by permission of Tyndale House Publishers Inc., Carol Stream, Illinois 60188. All rights reserved.

Cover design: Christine Dupre, www.vidagraphicdesign.com
Photo: iStock courtesy of redtea
Book design: Russel Davis, Bravo Book Design, www.BravoBookDesign.com

This book is designed to provide accurate and authoritative information with regard to the subject matter covered. This information is given with the understanding that neither the author nor publisher is engaged in rendering legal, professional advice. Since the details of your situation are fact dependent, you should additionally seek the services of a competent professional.

Soft Cover ISBN: 978-1-7376825-4-7
eBook ISBN: 978-1-7376825-5-4

Contents

Acknowledgment vii
Introduction...ix

Section 1: Following Jesus the Christ

Chapter One: Defining Christlikeness.................................... 3
Chapter Two: Practical Christlikeness.................................... 9
Chapter Three: Clearing Our Vision 17
Chapter Four: All of God Does All that God Does................ 25

Section 2: Identifying the Christ of Infinity

Chapter Five: Infinity: How Big is God and Why Should We Care?.... 35
Chapter Six: Omnipresence: Dwelling in the Eternal Present Tense..... 41
Chapter Seven: Omniscience: Perfect Knowledge of Everything 49
Chapter Eight: Omniscience: What God Reveals to Us 59
Chapter Nine: Omnipotence: Absolute and Unbounded Power 67
Chapter Ten: Sovereignty: Absolute Authority..................... 77
Chapter Eleven: Sovereignty: Divine Orchestration............. 87

Section 3: Embracing the Christ of Calvary

Chapter Twelve: Calvary: Why Did Jesus Die? 99
Chapter Thirteen: Calvary: Why Blood?............................... 107
Chapter Fourteen: Calvary: God's Holiness......................... 115

Chapter Fifteen: Calvary's Enormous Cost 121
Chapter Sixteen: Calvary's Unimaginable Horror 127
Chapter Seventeen: Calvary's Unmatched Love 135
Chapter Eighteen: Calvary's Blessings and Victory............................ 141
Chapter Nineteen: Calvary: A Personal Choice 153
Chapter Twenty: Calvary: What It Expects from Us 157

Section 4: Glorifying the Christ of Eternity

Chapter Twenty-One: The Call to Newness of Life............................ 171
Chapter Twenty-Two: Called to Holiness 181
Chapter Twenty-Three: Disciplines of Holiness 191
Chapter Twenty-Four: The Priority of Eternal Significance................ 203
Chapter Twenty-Five: Personal Accountability for Eternity................ 213
Chapter Twenty-Six: The Waste of Insignificant Things 227
Chapter Twenty-Seven: Hindrance of Worldly Influence 237
Chapter Twenty-Eight: Hindrance of Worldly Associations 243
Chapter Twenty-Nine: Satisfied at Last in His Likeness 251

About the Author 257
Endnotes 259

Acknowledgment

How incredible yet humbling to know God made each of us to be conformed into Christlikeness. He has revealed Himself to us, given us His Word and Holy Spirit, and provided Jesus as our sacrificial Substitute and Example. He then purposed us to become like Jesus through the power of His blood and the Holy Spirit's indwelling. Oh, may we commit to the journey toward Christlikeness. Then let's passionately pursue it.

Thank You, Infinite, Eternal, Omni-Everything God, for Your unspeakable, unchanging, unsearchable, incomprehensible desire to create, call, choose, and commission us. Thank You for extending Your everlasting attributes toward us so liberally and graciously. Thank You for empowering us to be conformed into the likeness of Jesus Christ.

Thank you, Andrea Merrell, for your editing expertise and encouragement. I appreciate and value your literary investment in me and this effort.

Thank you to all my draft readers (Barbara, Charles, Eddie, Jim B., Jim J., Miriam, and Tom) who caught my mistakes, challenged me for further clarity, and shared insightful grasps of Christlikeness. God has blessed me with a "great cloud of witnesses"! What a team!

Thank you, Christine Dupre, for yet another superb cover concept. What an incredible gift to conceptualize and design the "narrow, difficult path" of Christlikeness.

Thank you, Russel Davis and Bravo Book Design, for your illustrative layout, formatting, and every other effort. May God continue to bless you and your ministry.

Thank you, Karen Stevens, for inspiring and encouraging me as we pursue Christlikeness together. I'm grateful you're patiently walking the journey with me. I love you fiercely!

Introduction

When asked, "Are you a Christian?" two-thirds of Americans say, "Yes."[1] Though this response is still a majority, it's much lower than the early 90s when about 90 percent identified as Christians. However, if we changed the question to, "Are you Christlike?" I suspect many would struggle to answer—myself included.

I try to be.
I guess I am in certain situations.
Sunday morning is probably when I'm most like Him.
Can you clarify the question?

It may even seem sacrilegious or blasphemous to have such a title for a book. But I've come to realize the unfortunate need to distinguish between Christlikeness and what passes for Christianity today.

What is today's Christianity missing? Scriptural newness of life. Holy separation from the world. The fruit or evidence of the Spirit. "Believers" energized by the victory available to them. Spiritual development and maturity.

In essence, today's Christianity is missing Christlikeness.

Modern Christianity has fallen a long way from the first century Christ followers. And it isn't Christ, His Word, His message, or His Spirit that have changed. Progressive Christianity has become so tolerant of and aligned with the world that the cause of Christ and the "offense of the cross" (Galatians 5:11) have ceased.

A. W. Tozer says modern-day Christians "have imitated the world, sought popular favor, manufactured delights to substitute for the joy of the Lord, and produced a cheap and synthetic power to substitute for the power of the Holy Ghost."[2] Unfortunately, in today's progressive, modern Christianity, salvation is cheap, sanctification is ignored, and separation to God is missing.

> The devil isn't fighting religion. He's too smart for that. He's producing a counterfeit Christianity, so much like the real one that good Christians are afraid to speak out against it.[3]

Here's a crazy thought. Jesus wasn't a Christian. He was and is the Christ who calls us to believe on, follow, and be like Him.

In all likelihood, the term *Christian* wasn't invented by Christ followers. The book of Acts refers to the first century believers and followers of Christ as "the Way" (Acts 9:2; 19:9, 23; 22:4; 24:14, 22). This may be because Jesus said He is the only way to God the Father (John 14:6). Being part of "the Way" identified a person as a Christ follower.

Some people think the term *Christian* was later invented by the unbelieving, mocking world (Acts 11:26). King Agrippa seems to imply this when he told the apostle Paul, "In such a short time do you think you can talk me into being a Christian?" (Acts 26:28, CEV). This derogatory nickname marginalized those who followed Christ and shared His gospel wherever they went. Even today, what should be a badge of honor, carries a confusing, insulting, or foolish stigma in the world. But as the apostle Peter said, there is no shame in being insulted or persecuted for being called by Christ's name (1 Peter 4:14, 16, NLT).

The term *Christian* should define a disciple or follower of Christ. By action, thought, belief, mindset, characteristics, values, and priorities, a person is a Christian because he represents the Christ we find in Scripture. His life becomes an echo of the life Jesus lived while He was here on earth. Because of this distinction, followers of Christ should devote themselves to becoming Christlike.

Unfortunately, such a pursuit is rare in our current cultural and social environments. Much of what passes for modern or progressive Christianity falls far short of Christlikeness.

> Christianity has been watered down until the solution is so weak that if it were poison it wouldn't hurt anyone, and if it were medicine, it wouldn't cure anyone.[4]

For some, being a Christian has devolved to opposing God's Word and conflicting with what Jesus said and claimed to be. Today's eroding, perverse, blindly tolerant and accepting, preferential norms challenge, change, or ignore God's moral standard as expressed in His Word, the Bible.

Immoral behaviors and unholy lifestyles are championed as respecting everyone's voice or allowing everyone to be their true selves. Such an environment, with no moral boundaries, guarantees complete moral decay. It promotes perversion and acceptance—along with the marginalization of anyone who challenges such filth.

We expect such moral ignorance and perversion from unbelievers. Jesus explained, "You do not hear, because you are not of God" (John 8:47). The sinful world and its wicked systems naturally produce perverse outcomes. As Jesus clarified, they're simply acting like their father, the Devil.

Unfortunately, professing Christians fade into consenting silence instead of calling people to repent. A growing number of believers and churches accept immorality under the guise of tolerance and love. They do so to attract people at the expense of doctrinal soundness. To remain relevant, and to support their enormous budgets, such churches modify Christianity. Instead of lifting up Jesus—His life, death and resurrection, His salvation, His holiness and call to self-denial, taking up the cross, and following Him—they promote a feel-good *experience*.

Instead of repentance, they soften the gospel. "God loves you. Jesus died for you. If you simply believe—poof! You're a Christian! Now go enjoy your life. Have fun. Push the boundaries of grace. And be sure to share the *experience* with others." This approach is the gateway to apostasy and directly opposes the narrow, difficult way that transforms us into Christlikeness.

> Christianity isn't worth a snap of your finger if it doesn't straighten out your character.[5]

Many people believe *religion* is a matter of the mind—a choice similar to joining a civic club. But after more than forty years of studying the Bible, I've found Christlikeness to be a matter of the heart. A person may *think* many Christlike thoughts, yet his heart remains unchanged. But once God transforms a person's heart, his mindset changes.

A transformed heart leads to a renewed mind (Romans 12:2). The Bible commands us to, "be renewed in the spirit of your mind" (Ephesians 4:23). The resulting transformed heart and renewed mind no longer want to conform to the world or tolerate sin. This transformation and renewal lead to Christlikeness.

The pursuit of Christlikeness is scriptural. In 1 Timothy 6:11 Christ followers are instructed to "pursue righteousness, godliness, faith, love, patience, gentleness." The word translated *pursue* means to run, follow, or chase after.

What does such pursuing involve? The nature of Jesus. His characteristics and disposition. His mindset.

Yet many people view Christlikeness as something old fashioned. Out of style. Politically incorrect. Not inclusive. Fanatical. Offensive. Inflammatory. Insensitive. Some radicals fume that it violates manmade laws—at the expense of God's holy standard. True followers of Christ who exhibit Him in lifestyle, conduct, views, beliefs, convictions, and morals are at odds with society as a whole (2 Timothy 3:12).

Our current culture considers such Christlikeness a threat to their promiscuity. Modern society is hellbent on marginalizing, silencing, and eradicating it. With crooked media outlets, corrupt politicians, controlled organizations, and compromised religious affiliations, all facets of life are subtly infiltrated and influenced by those who hate everything Christlike.

And yet Christlikeness is the specific identity, disposition, mindset, and lifestyle to which Jesus calls His followers.

- Let this mind [mindset; affections; lifestyle] be in you which was also in Christ Jesus. (Philippians 2:5)
- … until Christ be formed in you. (Galatians 4:19)
- Christ in you, the hope of glory. (Colossians 1:27)

Christianity has been and continues to be manipulated to the whims of man. In the name of Christianity wars have been fought, people tortured and martyred. Christianity even ebbs and flows with societal standards and cultural preferences. But Christlikeness never wavers.

So we encounter a conflict, a "great gulf fixed" (Luke 16:26). And this impassable divide offers every person the decision to truly follow Christ or not. On this decision hangs not only the fortunes of this life but also the next.

Throughout this book, I've included thoughts and quotes from stellar preachers and teachers from times past. Their voices remind us of truth long since forgotten, ignored, or pushed aside. You get the benefit of their insight without reading their extensive works. For those who wish to pursue such reading, I reference their works in the endnotes. May they inspire you as much as they inspired me.

I've also included many Scripture references. This is intentional because the Bible is my source of absolute truth. With today's moral relativity, many people have opinions about what they *think* the Bible says. Or they take verses out of context to fit their preferred agendas and narratives. I saturate my writings with Scripture, along with many contextual cross references, to validate the message I share. I encourage you to research the Scriptures I've listed in your personal studies.

At the end of most chapters, the *Personal Reflection* questions are intended as solemn self-examination. These aren't self-righteous, in-your-face finger pointers. I'm simply sharing the questions I faced in my research and writing. As the Holy Spirit brought them to mind, I examined myself first, then captured them to motivate others.

May this book motivate those who claim Christ as Lord and Savior to become more like Him each day. May it help us better represent Him to a lost world and prepare us to hear Him say, "Well done, good and faithful servant."

To those who don't know, or merely *profess* to know, Christ as personal Lord and Savior, I pray it creates an urgency to do so in sincerity and truth. Time is short. Death is certain. God loves you and has done all He can to forgive your sin, transform you, and give you eternal life. But He awaits your decision.

Whatever your path, walk with me now to discover why those who would follow Christ are *Called to Christlikeness, not Christianity*.

SECTION 1

Following Jesus the Christ

Chapter One

Defining Christlikeness

Narrow is the gate and difficult is the way which leads to life, and there are few who find it. (Matthew 7:14)

What exactly is Christlikeness? Who came up with such a concept? What does it look like? What does it believe? How does it behave? Once I understand the concept, how can I get better at it?

The purpose of following Christ is to become like Him.

Think that's impossible?

Not according to God. He created us for that purpose and empowers us to do it.

We Can Do This!

To imitate or become like someone, I must know him intimately.

Younger siblings sometimes imitate older siblings. Groupies want to dress, act, and sing like celebrities. Professional impersonators and comedians spend hours studying the objects of their attention. They watch films. Study pictures. Analyze mannerisms. They scrutinize everything—mindset, disposition, habits, characteristics, gait, gestures, facial expressions, tone—until they can mimic the person accurately and believably.

With the Holy Spirit's help, genuine Christ followers give the same research and effort to Jesus. Hebrews 12:2-3 offers valuable insight on how to accomplish this. Two phrases demand attention. "Looking unto Jesus" and "consider Him." The first phrase uses the Greek word *aphorōntes (ἀφορῶντες)* that means to look at exclusively or study intently. It implies looking away from everything else to focus solely on Jesus. A human tendency is to become like what we dwell or fixate on. So let's look to Jesus.

The second phrase uses the Greek word *analogisasthe (ἀναλογίσασθε)*. It means to contemplate or estimate. Using an accounting approach, it's similar to balancing a checkbook to the bank statement.[6] It implies aligning my life to Jesus. I study Him, comparing and aligning myself to what I find Him to be.

Since the beginning of time, before God created us, He planned to make us in His image, after His likeness (Genesis 1:26). God had a specific purpose in mind when He decided to make us. The apostle Paul, through the inspiration of God's Holy Spirit, said, "[God] chose us in Him before the foundation of the world, that we should be holy and without blame before Him in love" (Ephesians 1:4).

What a comforting thought. We were made for this and can do it!

Modeling Jesus

A model is a miniature representation of something.

Christlikeness is the process whereby we represent Christ.

Before He made you and me, God chose us and designed us for Christlikeness. We aren't products of random, evolutionary acts over billions of years. God's creation was a deliberate act of the "determined purpose and foreknowledge of God" (Acts 2:23).

In order to *choose* us, God had to *know* us beforehand. This is called foreknowledge. Since God knows all things, He foreknew and foreordained us. Here again, Paul, with spiritual inspiration, took this concept a step further.

> For whom He [God] foreknew, He also predestined [purposed] to be conformed to the image of His Son. (Romans 8:29)

Think about that for a moment.

God the Father, Jesus, His Son, and the Holy Spirit (the Holy Trinity) had a meeting somewhere in the cosmic halls of eternity past. They decided to create a fantastic world filled with gorgeous scenery, incredible discoveries, and amazing creatures. All life pulsated with vibrant energy of Almighty power. At the pinnacle of it all, this Triune God handmade humans to populate this Edenic environment.

Since God knows and sees the "end from the beginning" (Isaiah 46:10), He saw each person—you, me, all of us. We all passed before God Almighty's inspection before we were born. God saw "my substance, being yet unformed. And in Your book they all were written, the days fashioned for me, when as yet there were none of them" (Psalm 139:16). He knows us better than we know ourselves because He foreknew, foresaw, and chose us before creating us.

- God from the beginning chose you for salvation through sanctification by the Spirit and belief in the truth, to which He called you. (2 Thessalonians 2:13)
- [God] called us with a holy calling ... according to His own purpose and grace which was given to us in Christ Jesus before time began. (2 Timothy 1:9)
- The LORD of hosts has sworn, saying, "Surely, as I have thought, so it shall come to pass, and as I have purposed, so it shall stand." (Isaiah 14:24, 27)

From before the world or time began, far back into eternity past, God chose us and called us before creating us. Then He made it all happen. That, my friend, is divine foreknowledge. It is creative genius, omnipotent power, and sovereign orchestration all wrapped into one Triune God.

Knowing this, some natural questions arise. Humans have asked them for centuries. *For what purpose did God do all this? Why are we here? Why would God create beings with the freedom to choose for or against Him? What's the point of Him sovereignly coordinating all things, including circumstances, events, and people?*

These are all great questions that deserve solid answers.

Human Free Will

God granted humans free will so they could, of their own accord, make choices.

He didn't want automated robots with programmed affection and allegiance. He loves us so much that He gave each person the freedom of choice—to love Him in return or reject Him outrightly. He had the creative and sovereign *right* to program us to love and serve Him. However, He didn't want programmed love any more than we want anyone forced to love us.

If I discovered people loved me because they *had to*, I'd quickly release them from that obligation. No thank you. If someone is to love me, or if I am to love someone, I want that to be a free-flowing expression from a heart consumed by the object of affection. Loving out of obligation loses its compelling dearness and appeal.

In the same way, God wants us to willingly *choose* to love Him. He places His love in our hearts so we can experience it and reciprocate it.

God's Eternal Purpose

Regardless of how we exercise our free will, it was (and still is) God's eternal purpose that each person know Him intimately, establish a personal relationship with Him through His Son, Jesus, and develop increasingly into Christlikeness.

God foreknew some would reject Him and be eternally lost. That breaks His heart because He's "not willing that any should perish" (2 Peter 3:9). But it has always been His heart's desire that we spend eternity with Him.

How do we do that?

We turn once again to Jesus.

We accept what Jesus did on Calvary and claim Him as personal Lord and Savior. We surrender lordship of our lives to Him. We allow His Spirit to influence our lives. When we do this, we are born into God's family, bearing His resemblance.

This brings us back to the purpose of modeling Jesus.

Children usually look and act like their parents. In addition to their shared DNA and gene pool, children see the modeled behavior and begin to act and talk like mom and dad—both good and bad. In the same way, true born-again followers of Christ exhibit His modeled behavior and bear His family resemblance.

> If anyone is in Christ, he is a new creation; old things have passed away … all things have become new. (2 Corinthians 5:17)

Supernatural Transformation

The loving desire and mission of God's Holy Spirit is to supernaturally transform every person who wholeheartedly chooses to accept and follow Jesus Christ.

Yeah but Nate, I'm a pretty good person already. Why would I need to be transformed?

God created man in His image or likeness (Genesis 1:26). But Adam's sin distorted that image. That distortion was passed along to every person (Romans 5:12). Only through salvation, made possible by Jesus' death and resurrection, can that image be restored. Once a person is spiritually reborn (John 3:3, 7), God begins His supernatural transformation.

Slowly but surely, in proportion to how we yield to the Spirit's work in our lives, we become transformed into Christlikeness. We allow the Holy Spirit to stamp His image upon our nature, thus reflecting His likeness in our characteristics and conduct. Here again, God foreknew His purpose of such transformation.

> But we ... are being transformed into the same image ... by the Spirit of the Lord. (2 Corinthians 3:18)

We are to become just like Jesus.

Submission Versus Conformity

Becoming like Jesus is a freewill choice.

But some people confuse submitting to God with conforming to Christ. I can submit to someone out of fear, coercion, or manipulation. But that doesn't mean I desire to become like him. There's a big difference between mere submission to God and conformity to Christlikeness.

> Conformity, to live one with God, is a far higher and diviner life than to live simply in submission to God. Submission is non-rebellion ... which is good, but not the highest. Conformity means ... to delight to do God's will, to run with eagerness and ardor to carry out His plans. Conformity to God's will involves submission, patient, loving, sweet

submission. But submission in itself falls short of and does not include conformity. We may be submissive but not conformed. Conformity means to be one with God, both in result and in processes. Submission may be one with God in the end. Conformity is one with God in the beginning and the end. Conformity is the only true submission, the most loyal, the sweetest, and the fullest.[7]

By becoming like Jesus, we develop the same mindset and disposition of Jesus. His love. His righteousness. His compassion for others. His self-denial and obedience to take up His cross. His self-sacrifice and surrender to the will and purpose of His Father. His response to every aspect of life. As Spiros Zodhiates explained, "We make the righteousness and holy life of Christ the object of our trust as well as our walk and practice."[8]

This is the eternal purpose for each person.

By imitating [Jesus], by sharing His experiences, by living life as He lived it, allowing the Holy Spirit to shape you ... from the inside out, you will become more like Him.[9]

Make no mistake, this isn't something we fully achieve in this life. But it should be our life's pursuit. Our passion. Our overarching endeavor that colors all other interactions. Our goal should be, "Till we all come ... to a perfect man, to the measure of the stature of the fullness of Christ" (Ephesians 4:13). Jesus said, "Be ye therefore perfect, even as your Father which is in heaven is perfect" (Matthew 5:48, KJV).

Increase in piety is ever presented as a growth, which should be as normal and natural as the orderly progression in human life from infancy to full stature and power.[10]

A Christ follower's lifelong pursuit and consuming passion is to consistently and constantly yield to the transformation into Christlikeness. To pursue spiritual maturity (Hebrews 6:1). To be complete in Him (Colossians 2:10). To fulfill God's purpose. "As He is, so are we in this world" (1 John 4:17).

What is Christlikeness? It's a purposeful, intentional, lifetime journey to become like Jesus. And we can do this!

Chapter Two

Practical Christlikeness

*Oh! to be like Thee, blessed Redeemer—
stamp thine own image deep on my heart.*[11]

It's great to conceptualize something, yet quite another to put it into practice. If we are to increasingly become like Jesus, what does that look like? What human traits and characteristics did He exhibit? In His humanity, how did He interact as our example to follow? What practical steps can we take based on what we find about Jesus from the Bible? We know the *Who* and *what* about Jesus. But we must look closer at *how* He lived.

The challenge in trying to describe Jesus and His essence is like trying to capture the brightness of the sun. How do we adequately describe Omniscient, Omnipresent, Omnipotent, Infinite Jesus in His deity and humanity? It's impossible without the Bible and the Holy Spirit. Thankfully, both reveal how He lived and how we must live to become like Him.

Before we look at how Jesus lived and His disposition, let's first look at what Christlikeness is not.

Christlikeness isn't Legalism

Strict rule-followers and those who detest religious *dos* and *don'ts*, don't worry. Christlikeness isn't about holding fast to rigid religious rules. That's legalism, not Christlikeness. I know what legalism looks and feels like.

As a child of missionary parents with a Mennonite-Brethren influence, Sunday was sacred in our family. Other than attending church and Bible reading, nothing was allowed that day. Shopping, yard work, or employment were strictly forbidden. It was a holy day to the Lord. Never mind that we aren't of Jewish heritage and it wasn't Saturday (Sabbath).

Even later in life, as part of an independent, fundamental, fire-breathing, heaven-is-high, hell-is-hot, turn-or-burn denomination, I maintained an unhealthy, unholy, condescending judgmentalism toward others who didn't "measure up" to my religious standards. But the best cure for a legalistic Pharisee is when he falls into sin and personally experiences the sting of such judgmentalism. Legalism doesn't appear so righteous from that standpoint.

Yes, there is a day of rest set aside by God, yet Jesus challenged the legalistic approach to the Sabbath. "The Sabbath was made for man, and not man for the Sabbath" (Mark 2:27). He also challenged the religious leaders who prided themselves in following strict religious rules yet missed the whole point.

> Woe to you … hypocrites! For you pay tithe … and have neglected the weightier matters of the law: justice and mercy and faith. These you ought to have done, without leaving the others undone. [You] strain out a gnat and swallow a camel! (Matthew 23:23-24)

Our best intentions and strict rules are hinderances to becoming like Christ. We aren't called to a set of religious rules. We are called to Christlikeness (Romans 8:29).

Religious legalism replaces Christlikeness with our religious preferences. We hold others accountable to our personal sense of right and wrong. Then we point out the flaws in others or self-righteously judge them to make ourselves look better than we are. Instead of allowing the Holy Spirit to transform, we try to conform others to our religious rules.

Its most obvious form is when we self-righteously judge others. *Joe, you drink alcohol. You need to repent or I'll have to break fellowship with you.* However, its more subtle form is more harmful. Even well-intentioned people fall into this legalistic trap by disguising their judgmentalism with a thin layer of pseudo righteousness. *Let's pray for Mary. I heard she's sleeping with three different men in the church.* This is merely gossip wrapped in a prayer request.

But guess what? There's no job vacancy in the role of Holy Spirit. He's still actively doing His transforming work. We just need to get out of His way and surrender to His influence.

Legalism doesn't please God and only causes harm to all involved. It harms believers by unholy thoughts and actions. It turns unbelievers away with its loveless arrogance. It stagnates the legalistic person's spiritual growth while also inviting God's discipline.

Religious rules blind self-righteous and *churchy* people against their own need for God's righteousness (John 3:3,7). They cloud the real transformation of becoming "a new creation" (2 Corinthians 5:17). People try so hard to *do* things, *act* as they think Christians should, and *mandate* the same in everyone else. But they miss the new life in Christ. Being complete in Him. Allowing Him to perform His inner transformation. Sadly, our self-righteous efforts fall short of God's standards and alienate others in the process.

Finally, religious legalism hides the truth of God's transforming grace and liberty. Christ followers have "… liberty by which Christ has made us free" (Galatians 5:1). Christ came to set us free (John 8:36) and give us His abundant life (John 10:10). He brought liberty from "the curse of the Law" (Galatians 3:13), from required works, from anything we create as additional religious burdens for others.

To be clear, avoiding legalism doesn't remove accountability for ourselves or our fellow believers. There's a scriptural, loving way to confess our faults to each other (James 5:16), support each other, and hold each other accountable to God's moral standard and holy living. But legalism isn't it.

Christlikeness isn't trying to imitate Christ in our own strength. Following rigid religious rules and trying to live up to certain moral standards only get us so far—and not far enough. Yes, Christlikeness does have an external process. Scripture identifies several *put off, put on,* and *put away* actions for us to do. However, the more intricate work of becoming Christlike is internal.

Christlikeness isn't Sinless Perfection

We can't achieve sinless perfection in this life.

But we should strive to become as Christlike as possible. We have become "partakers of the divine nature" (2 Peter 1:4). With the Holy Spirit dwelling inside and doing His supernatural work internally, we partner with Him by working on the outside. We protect our sphere of holiness by keeping ourselves "unspotted by the world" (James 1:27).

We *put off* the old, sinful, pre-salvation habits. We *put on* the new, Christlike habits. We *put away* every non-Christlike influence, mindset, preference, desire, habit, and action (Ephesians 4:22-32). Transformation is difficult in an unchanged environment.

As a crude analogy, the Holy Spirit is the antidote and my *putting on, putting off* and *putting away* is the antihistamine. The Holy Spirit cures me from the inside while I yield to His transformation, fight the good fight of faith (1 Timothy 6:12), and resist sin outwardly. This ongoing, lifelong, deliberate transformation, in partnership with the Holy Spirit, helps us live God-honoring lives here on earth. It also positions us to hear God say, "Well done, faithful servant" (Matthew 25:21) when we stand before Him one day.

> Every real believer, every truly converted soul, every one who has received the Spirit of adoption, does *follow* holiness, and longs for the time when, at the coming again of our Lord Jesus Christ … we shall have become absolutely and forever holy.[12]

Christlikeness is more than joining a church and following religious rules. It's more than choosing a preferred religious denomination, being acquainted with Jesus, or appreciating the moral concepts of the Bible. It's more than the societal perception of what Christianity should be or how it should behave. It's more than flirting with Jesus—it's the lifelong commitment to a personal relationship with Him. Christlikeness, not Christianity, is the eternal purpose for each person. Christlikeness is why we were created.

With that in mind, let's set our sights on Jesus and learn from Him.

Looking to Jesus

The earthly life of Jesus provides a perfect example to follow.

While here, He exhibited a broad range of healthy characteristics. And He did it all without sin (Hebrews 4:15). He was approachable, courteous, loving, and purposeful. He was bold, yet compassionate, humble, and forgiving. He bonded with His followers, yet still took time to be alone—usually with God the Father in prayer. From what we find in Scripture, He is far from the stoic, weak, demure person depicted in books and movies.

Jesus didn't champion social justice issues or advocate changing the political landscape. He clearly stated, "My kingdom is not of this world" (John 18:36). Instead, He met people at their individual points of need and changed them one heart at a time. He was comfortable interacting with people from all stages and statures of life. He said what He meant and meant what He said.

Ever in control, He loved fully, exuded confidence in the face of adversity, and remained calm in overwhelming chaos. He challenged leaders when they were wrong, even though it placed Him in danger. Never losing sight of His identity, He fulfilled His purpose with unwavering determination. As a leader, He stood for what was right without compromising His moral standards—disregarding public appeal and personal gain.

With a topic as large as Christlikeness, it helps to break it down into practical steps. In Mark 12:30, we find the four main aspects of life.

> Love the LORD your God with all your heart [spiritual], with all your soul [emotional], with all your mind [intellectual], and with all your strength [physical].[13]

Looking at Jesus from these four aspects helps dissect and digest the goal of Christlikeness.

Spiritually

Jesus knew Scripture, quoted it, and lived by it. He often spent entire nights in prayer. He was anointed by the Holy Spirit (Matthew 3:16) and lived in agreement with Him.

In John 3, He met Nicodemus, a religious leader, at his point of spiritual need. Jesus listened intently, asked engaging questions, and revealed the way to true salvation.

Yet in John 4, we find Him talking with the five-times-divorced Samaritan woman at her point of emotional and spiritual need. He was flexible, attentive, and interested in her wellbeing. He wasn't influenced by her history or distracted by His disciples.

Intellectually

Being omniscient, Jesus knows everything. He can talk with anyone on any given topic.

Although we aren't omniscient, we can ask God for His wisdom. He promises to give it to us abundantly (James 1:5). We can also learn all we can on topics within our reach. Doing so gives us common ground with those

God brings within our sphere of influence. Scripture encourages us to be prepared to share with everyone who asks the "reason for the hope" that we have (1 Peter 3:15).

As a conversationalist, Jesus challenged people's intellectual needs (John 7:15). He also spoke with complete wisdom and unquestioned authority with humans (Matthew 7:29), demons (Luke 4:36), and forces of nature (Mark 4:39-41).

Emotionally

Jesus modeled a wide variety of healthy emotional interactions.

He wept at Lazarus' grave and mourned for Jerusalem. He grew impatient with His disciples. He angrily drove out the money changers in the Temple. His charisma and affection drew children to Him. Large crowds were attracted to His healthy personality and message.

In John 8, with the adulterous woman, He was just, yet compassionate, merciful, protective, and forgiving.

He consistently modeled healthy, sinless relational behavior.

Physically

In John 5 Jesus met the physical need of the disabled man at the Pool of Bethesda. He challenged him with, "Do you want to be made whole?" He didn't ask if the man wanted healing. He knew the man's core need and looked beyond the disability and targeted the man's will.

In John 6, Jesus met the physical needs of the masses by providing food.

Jesus became physically fatigued and needed rest, yet without impatience and anger. Never do we find Him lashing out at the people He came to save. No, He came lovingly, caringly, and sacrificially.

Character Traits

If we began to list the characteristics Jesus exhibited, it would be endless.

The most observable immediately come to mind. Love. Mercy. Grace. Forgiveness. Humility. Courage. Honesty. Truthfulness. Generosity. Patience. Holiness. Respect. Tenderness. Encouragement. Meekness. Wisdom.

Empathy. Compassion. Thoughtfulness. Kindness. Discretion. Peace. Righteousness. Hospitality. Selflessness. Servant leadership. Sincerity. Surrendered to His Father's will. Committed to His redeeming purpose.

Then we see the kingdom principles Jesus outlined in His Sermon on the Mount (Matthew 5-7).

> Love your enemies, bless those who curse you, do good to those who hate you, and pray for those who spitefully use you and persecute you. (Matthew 5:44)

These are just the tip of the iceberg.

As His followers, all these characteristics, traits, principles, and more are what the Holy Spirit wants to develop in us. Remember, we were made for this!

Yeah but Nate, how's it possible for me to develop all these? I'm lucky if I exhibit two or three of them on a good day!

It's humanly impossible to emulate the character traits of Jesus in our own strength. Only by being born into God's family, with the Holy Spirit living inside, do we have the capacity and power to reflect the family resemblance. As we surrender to the Holy Spirit's transformation, as we *put off* our old traits and *put on* spiritual virtues (Ephesians 4:20-32), we begin to bear spiritual fruit. This *fruit* is the evidence of our new spiritual *root* (Matthew 7:16-20).

Fruit of the Spirit

The fruit of the Spirit is love, joy, peace, longsuffering, kindness, goodness, faithfulness, gentleness, self-control (Galatians 5:22-23). Unpacking each one helps us understand the depth of transformation the Holy Spirit performs in us if we allow Him to do so. Not only are these Christlike traits, they're also personally beneficial.

- *Love* – out-serving, sacrificial, unconditional love; a distinguishing characteristic of a Christ follower (John 13:35; John 15:13; John 3:16; 1 John 3:1).
- *Joy* – overflowing, abundant, inner joy that supersedes the temporary, often fickle feelings of happiness (John 15:11; John 17:13).

- *Peace* – inner tranquility and contentment in spite of adversity and unfavorable circumstances (John 14:27; John 16:33; Colossians 3:15; Philippians 4:7).
- *Patience* – inner tolerance, fortitude, and acceptance in difficult situations without getting angry or making demands (Romans 12:12; James 1:3-4).
- *Kindness* – benevolence, courtesy, and hospitality (Ephesians 4:32).
- *Goodness* – integrity, honesty, compassion, and doing the right thing (Romans 2:4; Romans 11:22).
- *Faithfulness* – steadfastness, reliability, and accountability (Matthew 25:21, 23; 1 Corinthians 15:58; Colossians 1:23).
- *Gentleness* – calmness, meekness, and tenderness with others (Matthew 11:29; Philippians 4:5; 2 Timothy 2:24).
- *Self-Control* – discipline, restraint, and obedience to God (2 Peter 1:6).

These lists are nowhere near exhaustive. But we can begin our journey today by surrendering to God and allowing Him to complete His good work in us (Philippians 1:6).

May we become just like Jesus. Let's study, research, and model Him. May we apply to our lives what we learn about Him in Scripture. Most importantly, let's surrender to the Holy Spirit's transformation into His likeness.

As we explore the critical differences between Christlikeness and Christianity, let's first discover as much as we can about Jesus Christ. If we are to become like Him, we need to know who He is. What He did in ages past. What He knows and when He knew it. What He's doing now. And what future events may intersect His life with ours.

To do this, we need to clear our vision.

Personal Reflection

Although the journey of Christlikeness is a lifelong process, it should show a continual, incremental increase toward spiritual maturity. We should periodically evaluate whether we are truly becoming more like Jesus. As you examine your life, can you see progress in your growth toward Christlikeness? Are you willing to take the next step of the journey?

Chapter Three

Clearing Our Vision

*Look with your eyes ... Hear with your ears ...
Set your heart on all that I am going to show you.
(Ezekiel 40:4, AMP)*

To learn something new, we must first consider the sources available to us.

In today's age of false narratives, fake news, and online sources that offer various *versions* of truth, it's wise to question and validate who and what we believe. The topic of Jesus—who He was during His earthly life, who He is now in His heavenly life, and what He offers to us—is too important to trust to questionable or unreliable sources.

Clearing our vision enables an accurate picture of who He is, His attributes, His salvation, and His purpose for us. And let's resist the urge to think, *I already know all about Him,* or respond with a, *Yeah but ...*

To truly learn something new, listen to absorb—not to argue, defend existing perceptions, or justify current perspectives. If we're talking, we're not learning anything new. Now is an opportune time to open our minds, clear our vision, and prepare ourselves to learn something new.

Yeah but Nate, why must we clear our vision?

Take a moment to consider some candid questions. Are you comfortable where you are in your walk of faith? Are you seeking a deeper understanding? Do you want to walk closer to God? Do you want to see things more clearly and love Him more dearly?

Instead of defending your existing mindset and beliefs, are you open to God showing you something new, refreshing, and powerful? Are you open to God revealing something that enlightens your journey, strengthens your faith, and enables you to walk in spiritual power and victory?

Then the first step is to clear your vision.

The deeper the dissatisfaction with what is wrong and deficient in our spiritual lives, the stronger the longing to be really delivered from sin, the more lively the desire to have unbroken [interaction] in the presence of God.[14]

Partial and Biased Truth

We need God to clear our vision because we are impressionable by various people at different times in our lives.

What most of us learned about Jesus came from people with their own misconceptions, biases, prejudices, denominational nuances, and homegrown spirituality. We're the sum total of all our experiences, both good and bad.

I grew up attending churches with pastors who believed only the King James Version of the Bible was inspired. According to them, all other versions or translations were heresy. I've since grown to appreciate the variety of other versions, the depth behind the Hebrew and Greek meanings, and contextual study.

I also heard one youth pastor say, *Guys, anytime any part of your body enters any part of the female body, you're committing intercourse and sinning against God.* By implication, he included passionate kissing. Although I appreciate his intense concern for teenage purity, what he said was incorrect. His protective intensity was biased.

Preachers speak from personal knowledge and experience. Most (not all) youth pastors—usually young, inexperienced, and right out of Bible college or seminary—are generally the product of their professors and textbooks. Authors and speakers don't have to establish authority and credibility on what they write or say. Online social media is filled with varying *degrees* of truth as people see it.

So where do we go for an accurate, clear picture of Jesus?

Here's our first opportunity to resist the urge to think we already know all about Him.

In addition to the possibility that someone along the way may have given us partial or biased truth, we face an internal danger. Familiarity breeds contempt.

When we hear a familiar Bible story, it's easy to tune it out, take it for granted, and rush on. We know the ending, so why pay close attention, even though we may encounter something brand new, completely unbiased, and totally accurate. That's how spiritual complacency infects our hearts and freezes our minds.

A crisis of faith helped clear my vision.

Crisis of Faith

Heaven was silent. God seemed distant.

After many years in the pigpen of sin, I rededicated my life to God and committed to a closer walk with Him. I confessed my sins, repented, asked God's forgiveness, and accepted it by faith. I read the Bible more, prayed more earnestly, and tried to live in a way that pleased God.

Yet something was off. My prayers sounded hollow. I sensed a disconnect. But I didn't know what was wrong.

I followed all the steps I knew. I did all the things I thought God wanted me to do. Reading the Scriptures cover to cover almost thirty times in my life, studying it intensely, I figured I'd done what it outlined.

Born in a Bible-believing home, check.

Christian upbringing, check.

Salvation prayer and experience, check.

Baptized, check.

Christian high school, check.

Bible College, check.

Church attendance, check.

Deacon, finance committee member, choir member, consistent tither, Sunday School teacher, pastor's prayer partner, backslidden sinner, repentant saint, reformed mindset, walking in newness of life—check, check, check.

Still, I sensed an undeniable nagging in my soul.

Finally, in complete brokenness, I lay flat out on the floor before God. I asked Him to show me what was missing. I cried out, "I don't even know what to say, God, but I'm tired of feeling this way. I'm tired of the coldness and distance in our relationship. I'm tired of faking it until I make it. I'm tired of empty platitudes and religious clichés. Whatever is causing this, I give up. I'm tired and I yield. I surrender myself completely to You, Lord."

Then I prayed something life-changing. "God, please remove everything I've learned about You from all the preachers, youth pastors, Bible teachers, and college professors. Yes, even from my parents. It may all be good and accurate, but something is hindering a closer, more intimate walk with You. Take it all. Help me from this day forward to learn only from You. Teach me from Your Word and from Your Holy Spirit."

It's difficult to describe the inner peace and comfort that descended on me. I realized God didn't want all my religious *stuff*. He wanted me. An undivided, undistracted, emptied-of-all-religious-nonsense me. His Word says, "The sacrifices of God are a broken spirit, a broken and a contrite heart—these, O God, You will not despise" (Psalm 51:17). That was me. Finally. Because I was done. Done with my knowledge. Done with my understanding. Done with my effort. Done with spiritual powerlessness and defeat. Simply, done.

God is completely and forever awesome. From that moment, I've barely been able to keep up with what He shows me. My quiet time is vibrant. Prayers are more intimate and ongoing. Insight into God's Word is phenomenal. Tears roll unexpectedly when I think of Who He is and what He's done and is doing in me.

I can't explain what happened in that moment. But I'm coming to understand that when I get rid of everything associated with self, when I stop playing games with God, and empty myself completely, God begins His supernatural work.

When God clears my vision, along with my preconceived ideas, He then reveals more of Himself. What I'm seeing, hearing, and discovering anew, makes me love Him all the more. I wonder what took me so long to arrive at this place. God is good, faithful, and righteous in all His ways.

Yeah but, Nate, isn't it okay to have my own comfortable feelings about God? Why are you emphasizing the importance of an accurate view of who Jesus is?

Because life is too short. Jesus is coming soon. And eternity is too long to get wrong.

I firmly believe we are living in the end times described in Bible prophecy. Global events and nations are positioning precisely as God said they would. Moral erosion, cultural perversion, and lawlessness are increasing at frightening levels (2 Timothy 3:13).

This sinful world, with its deception and "strong delusion" (2 Thessalonians 2:11), pulls at us with insatiable appeal. We must guard against its friendly yet betraying call. To be who God calls His followers to be, to live the spiritual life of power and victory He offers, we must allow Him to wipe from our eyes all impurities and spiritual sawdust. Only then can we begin to see Him clearly.

It's important to get an accurate view of who Jesus is because we are commissioned to faithfulness. Jesus asked, "When the Son of Man comes, will He really find faith on the earth?" (Luke 18:8). He also said, "Blessed is that servant whom his master will find so doing when he comes" (Luke 12:43).

Oh, may He find us faithful! Faithful to Him and faithfully engaged in our Father's business. Faithfully allowing Him to transform us into His likeness.

A Renewed Mental Image

What comes to mind when you think about God?

Aside from religious notions, denominational nuances, or homegrown spirituality, what's your mental image of God? Is He The Man upstairs? The Good Lordy? A cuddly grandpa who winks at our indiscretions? Or maybe He's an invisible, distant God who doesn't really have much influence in the events, circumstances, or affairs of life. He just sits in a huge, white rocking chair, waiting for things to blow up down here before actually getting involved.

What about Jesus? Is He merely the Savior who keeps you from going to hell? Or maybe a great prophet, incredible teacher, or wise guru with some profound life principles? Perhaps you view Him as Someone who extends so much mercy that you can't out-sin His grace.

Maybe you unknowingly separated God's attributes by accepting His love, grace, and mercy while ignoring His holiness, transformation, and moral standard. Perhaps you misunderstood that Jesus' crucifixion was a random act of murder by an angry, frenzied, uncontrolled mob. Maybe He was just in the wrong place at the wrong time.

Such thoughts and mindsets are based on inaccurate, unreliable, and misinformed sources. Manmade philosophies, counterfeit beliefs, false religions, and skewed portrayals of Jesus are all reasons why we must base our information on accurate, reliable, and unchanging sources.

Several verses in God's Word encourage us to clear our vision and get our information from Him. Two in particular identify how to eliminate falsehood and find the truth.

> For the weapons of our warfare are not carnal but mighty in God for pulling down strongholds, casting down arguments and every high thing that exalts itself against the knowledge of God, bringing every thought into captivity to the obedience of Christ. (2 Corinthians 10:4-5)

The apostle Paul, who wrote these verses, encouraged us to resist and reject any argument, philosophy, religion, mindset, strongly held and defended positions, and anything else conflicting with the true knowledge of God. To find the absolute truth, we must surrender all these to the authority of Jesus Christ.

If God said it, it's true; if He didn't, it doesn't matter.

Our feelings don't matter. Neither do our opinions and preferences. Our progressive culture doesn't get to say who God is, how He acts, or what He does. He alone maintains that sovereign right.

Along with eliminating everything false about the true knowledge of God, we must also increase our knowledge of His truth (2 Peter 3:18). No human knows it all nor can anyone know everything about Him until eternity. Until then, may we continue to increase and expand our knowledge of Him from His reliable sources.

> The Christian is strong or weak depending upon how closely he has cultivated the knowledge of God. Progress in the Christian life is exactly equal to the growing knowledge we gain of the Triune God in personal experience.[15]

Over time, we've lost our sense of awe of God's majesty.

Somehow, we've replaced the passion of the first century believers with *churchy* traditions. The sanctuary morphed into a darkened theater. Worship devolved into staged entertainment. The sacred became a circus.

We serve Him out of ritual and obligation instead of pure love and gratitude. We base our mental image of God on unreal and false information. We downgrade Him to our frame of reference. We conveniently place Him in a box to control and manipulate according to our preferences instead of acknowledging Who He truly is.

By replacing the Almighty with our own thoughts and perceptions, we've lost our spiritual identity, spiritual testimony, spiritual power, and reverent meditation.

A shallow view of God leads to a shallow life. Cheapen God and you cheapen life itself. Treat God superficially and you become superficial. But hold God in profoundest respect and it is remarkable how deep the roots of your spiritual life grow.[16]

We need fresh eyes. We need clean ears. We need renewed, receptive minds. We need transformed hearts.

Oh, that we would discover who God is from verified, reliable, truthful sources. May God give us a clear vision of who He is—from His Word, His Son, and His Spirit. May He grant us His wisdom and open the eyes of our understanding (Ephesians 1:17-18).

Let's discard everything we think we know about Him and discover anew what He discloses about Himself. Doing so draws us into His loving, holy, eternal, infinite presence.

Father God, let us know You as You are that we may adore You as we should.[17]

Personal Reflection

Are you prepared to see God with clear eyes? Are you willing to accept a maybe-I-missed-something approach to your faith? If God reveals a new reality or refreshed truth, are you willing to discard your current mindset and embrace what He shows you?

Chapter Four

All of God Does All that God Does

Your view of God will shape every aspect of your spiritual life.[18]

Our pursuit of Christlikeness involves discovering Who He is.

The Merriam-Webster dictionary defines the holy Trinity as, "the unity of Father, Son, and Holy Spirit as three persons in one Godhead."[19] The Council of Nicaea defined the Triune God as the "equality of the Father, the Son, and the Holy Spirit in the Holy Trinity." This same council declared "only the Son became incarnate as Jesus Christ."[20]

Over the years, scholars, teachers, preachers, and commentators have shared their input on the topic of God. We benefit greatly from their thoughtful insight and hours of Bible study. But one of the things I love about God's Word is that it often explains itself.

When I was learning to read, I'd get in a hurry and make up or substitute words. My dad said something that still resonates today as I study God's Word. "Son, just read what's there."

There's no substitution for God's Word. Just read what's there.

What does the Bible say about the Holy Trinity, the complete Godhead, the great Three-in-One? Let's look at several verses that plainly describe the three Persons as well as their roles or functions.

Who God Is

The first verse in the Bible doesn't explain God—it starts with the assertion that He is.

> In the beginning God … (Genesis 1:1)

Throughout the Creation account, God didn't explain Himself to Adam and Eve. They knew He existed because He was their Creator and often spoke with them.

Over the years, God spoke with humans in different ways. He spoke to Cain after he killed his brother, Abel (Genesis 4:9). God enjoyed talking with Enoch so much that after three hundred years of walking and talking together, "God took him" (Genesis 5:24). I imagine their last earthly conversation went something like this. "Enoch, we've walked a long way today. We're closer to My place than we are to yours. Just come home with Me."

Years later, God spoke with Noah regarding mankind's global wickedness. He revealed His plan to destroy everyone and everything with a worldwide flood. He would start over with Noah and his family (Genesis 6:13).

God then spoke at length with Abram (known later as Abraham), promising to make of his descendants a mighty nation (Genesis 12:1-2) through a promised son, Isaac. From this promise, the people and nation of Israel were born.

God appeared in a dream to Jacob (Genesis 28:12-13) and later had a nighttime wrestling match with him (Genesis 32:24-30).

About twenty-five hundred years after creating Adam, God identified precisely who He is in a conversation with Moses. Previously, God revealed Himself as "The God of Abraham, Isaac, and Jacob." But this time, when Moses asked God's identity, God said "I AM WHO I AM" (Exodus 3:14). Some translators state, "I AM who I AM going to be" or "I am the Existing One." Either way, that's all God said. He just is.

Fast forward approximately fifteen hundred years to the small village of Bethlehem. The angel Gabriel told Mary she would have a son (Luke 1:28-34). He told her to "call His name Jesus. He will be great, and will be called the Son of the Highest" (Luke 1:31-32). When Mary questioned him because she was still a virgin, Gabriel replied, "The Holy Spirit will come upon you, and the power of the Highest will overshadow you ... that Holy One who is to be born will be called the Son of God" (Luke 1:35). Scripture later identified this same baby boy as, "Immanuel, which is translated, 'God with us'" (Matthew 1:23).

Now it's about to get fun.

Jesus Revealed

The apostle John began his gospel similar to how Genesis starts. "In the beginning …" However, John introduced something new.

> In the beginning was the Word, and the Word was with God, and the Word was God. He was in the beginning with God. All things were made through Him, and without Him nothing was made that was made. (John 1:1-3)

This Word (*Logos*) means a spoken intelligence or a word as the expression of that intelligence. Greek scholar Spiros Zodhiates clarified, "Jesus Christ in His preincarnate state is called the Word (*ho logos*; in the Greek ὁ Λόγος), meaning immaterial intelligence and then the expression of that intelligence in speech that humans could understand."[21]

John further explained, "The Word became flesh and dwelt among us, and we beheld His glory, the glory as of the only begotten of the Father, full of grace and truth" (John 1:14).

This is none other than Jesus Christ. Immanuel. God with us. The Lamb of God who takes away the sin of the world (John 1:29).

Echoing the divine "I AM WHO I AM" expression from Exodus 3:14, Jesus made several "I am" statements. For example,

- I am the bread of life. (John 6:35)
- I am the light of the world. (John 8:12)
- Before Abraham was, I AM. (John 8:58)
- I am the resurrection and the life. (John 11:25)
- I am the good shepherd. (John 10:11)
- I am the way, the truth, and the life. No one comes to the Father except through Me. (John 14:6)

John's deliberate repetition of the "I am" phrase helps us understand Jesus' timeless present tense existence of eternity.[22] In most instances, the meaning behind the Greek *egō eimi* (ἐγὼ εἰμί) is "I exist" or simply parallels the Old Testament's "I AM." Jesus declared Himself to be the second Person in the Triune Godhead. The religious elite of that day knew what Jesus meant. They wanted to kill Him because He challenged their religious beliefs and made Himself equal with God (John 5:18).

Then there's the powerful statement in the Garden of Gethsemane. When Judas and the mob came to arrest Jesus, He asked for whom they were seeking. Hearing, "Jesus of Nazareth," Jesus said, "I am He" (John 18:5). The power released from that statement knocked the entire mob to the ground. The interesting thing is that many English versions of the Bible place the "He" in italics or brackets as an added word to help it makes sense in English. But in the Greek, all Jesus said was "I am." Wow!

Finally, during His mockery of a trial, the high priest said, "Tell us if You are the Christ, the Son of God!" (Matthew 26:63). In the face of certain death, Jesus acknowledged His identity with, "I am" (Mark 14:62). He admitted He is the Great I AM.

Since "God is Spirit" (John 4:24), and no one has seen God at any time (John 1:18), humans needed a visible expression of God. So Jesus came as God in the flesh (1 John 4:2). In Him "dwells all the fullness of the Godhead bodily" (Colossians 2:9). This means the entire, infinite, eternal, unmeasurable immensity of the Triune God was compressed into the Incarnate Jesus. He is "the express image [mirror image] of His person" (Hebrews 1:3).

In other words, when God looks in a mirror, Jesus looks back.

As further confirmation about His divine identity, Jesus said, "I and My Father are one" (John 10:30) and "He who has seen Me has seen the Father" (John 14:9). In heaven, "the Father, the Word, and the Holy Spirit" are one in essence and existence (1 John 5:7).

Even in the last book of the Bible we find evidence of Jesus' deity. "These things says the Son of God … I am He who searches [examines] the minds and hearts" (Revelation 2:18, 23). This ties in to Hebrews 4:12 that describes God's Word as "a discerner of the thoughts and intents of the heart." He knows us inside and out. That being the case, it's a wonder why we try to hide things from Him instead of being instantly and completely honest.

Going back to the Creation story in Genesis chapter 1, God spoke everything into existence. "Let there be light." "Let there be a firmament." "Let the earth bring forth grass." "Let there be lights in the firmament of the heavens to divide the day from the night." "Let the earth bring forth …" By coupling those divine commands with what we've discovered about Jesus being the Word of God, we see more clearly what Paul said about Jesus.

He is the image of the invisible God … By Him all things were created that are in heaven and that are on earth, visible and invisible … All things were created through Him and for Him.
(Colossians 1:15-16)

Jesus is the eternal, infinite, living, creative Word.

Now that we've discovered what God's Word reveals about God the Father and Jesus, God the Son, let's turn our attention to God the Holy Spirit.

The Holy Spirit Revealed

Jesus confirmed the existence, presence, and work of the Holy Spirit. He said,

I will pray the Father, and He will give you another Helper, that He may abide with you forever—the Spirit of truth, whom the world cannot receive, because it neither sees Him nor knows Him; but you know Him, for He dwells with you and will be in you.
(John 14:16-17)

Several times Jesus clarified the work of the Holy Spirit.

- He will teach you all things, and bring to your remembrance all things that I said to you. (John 14:26)
- He will testify of Me [Jesus]. (John 15:26)
- He will guide you into all truth … and He will tell you things to come. (John 16:13)

The ability to know and disclose things in the future is clear evidence of omniscience.

We wouldn't have the Holy Spirit except by Christ's death, resurrection, and ascension. When Jesus explained His pending death, resurrection, and departure from this world, He told the disciples, "It is to your advantage that I go away; for if I do not go away, the Helper will not come to you; but if I depart, I will send Him to you" (John 16:7).

At some point between His death and ascension, Jesus walked into the throne room of heaven and, with nail-scarred hands, sprinkled His blood on the altar in God's presence as proof of His finished work (Hebrews 9:24, 12:24). I can imagine Him turning to God the Father and saying, "I've completed the work you sent Me to do. I promised My followers We would send the Holy Spirit to not just dwell *on* or *with* them but *within* them. Let's do that now."

Before His ascension, Jesus told His followers "not to depart from Jerusalem, but to wait for the Promise of the Father, which … you have heard from Me" (Acts 1:4). True to His promise, the Holy Spirit of God arrived at Pentecost (Acts 2:1-4).

In Peter's impassioned Pentecost sermon, he said, "Therefore being exalted to the right hand of God, and having received from the Father the promise of the Holy Spirit, He poured out this which you now see and hear" (Acts 2:33).

Jesus also revealed the real, active presence of the Holy Spirit.

> "He who believes in Me, as the Scripture has said, out of his heart will flow rivers of living water." But this He spoke concerning the Spirit, whom those believing in Him would receive; for the Holy Spirit was not yet given, because Jesus was not yet glorified. (John 7:38-39)

Here's a practical point about the Holy Spirit. By name, identity, and disposition, He is holy. He's not just a Spirit—He's the *Holy* Spirit. When He indwells a person, He brings a holy designation. Meaning, He doesn't tolerate or overlook anything unholy. His primary goal is to make us holy—to transform us into the likeness of Christ Jesus.

The journey of holiness involves our minute-by-minute surrender to the Holy Spirit's work inside. We become Christlike as we yield to the Holy Spirit's cutting through our excuses and justifications for unholy habits, thoughts, and actions.

Holy Trinity Revealed

Clearing our vision with God's disclosure of Himself as the Almighty Triune God helps us better understand the plurality of some verses.

- Then God said, "Let Us make man in Our image, according to Our likeness." (Genesis 1:26)

- Jesus answered and said to him, "If anyone loves Me, he will keep My word; and My Father will love him, and We will come to him and make Our home with him." (John 14:23)

The plurality confirms the Holy Trinity. As we continue, all references to God, unless distinguished by role or function, mean all of God.

As we will see, the call to Christlikeness is a call to holiness. To closer nearness to God. To a more intimate level of fellowship with Him. It involves trusting God the Father, accepting Jesus, and surrendering to the Holy Spirit.

Within the Holy Trinity, there are no separate agendas. There is complete unity in everything (1 John 5:7). One doesn't act separately from the others. To claim Jesus Christ is to claim all Three. To become Christlike is to recognize and surrender to the authority and transforming work of all Three.

All of God does all that God does.

Personal Reflection

What sense of familiarity may have subtly crept into your mind regarding God the Father, Jesus, or the Holy Spirit? Do you accept who God's Word reveals all Three to be? Since Jesus is God, how does that change your interaction with Him? As divine, do you hold Him in awe and reverence? As the Spirit of truth, are you willing to listen and surrender to the Holy Spirit's influence and illumination?

SECTION 2

Identifying the Christ of Infinity

Chapter Five

Infinity: How Big is God and Why Should We Care?

How great is our Lord! His power is absolute! His understanding is beyond comprehension! (Psalm 147:5, NLT)

The challenge with understanding infinity is that it has no starting point or ending.

We have trouble imagining infinity because we have no frame of reference. We are created, temporal, time-bound, finite, dying beings with limited comprehension. Much lies beyond our scope of reason that we simply don't know.

It's impossible to understand what we have no capacity to know. For example, what keeps planets and stars hanging in space? There's nothing above or below to support them. Why does space have no oxygen? Earth is tiny in comparison to the expansive universe, so why all that uninhabitable space? Where are heaven and hell located? Being visual creatures, if we saw the splendor of heaven and horror of hell, those sights might prompt quicker, wiser decisions regarding our eternal destinations. Then again, God may not explain everything because, "We walk by faith, not by sight" (2 Corinthians 5:7).

There's much about God we don't know. But God, through His Word, His Son, and His Spirit, reveals enough for us to understand what He wants us to know.

God's Holy Spirit is "the Spirit of truth" who guides us into all truth (John 16:13).

God's *written* Word is "living and powerful, and sharper than any two-edged sword, piercing even to the division of soul and spirit ... and is a discerner of the thoughts and intents of the heart" (Hebrews 4:12). The *living* Word, Jesus, "became flesh and dwelt among us, and we beheld His glory, the glory as of the only begotten of the Father, full of grace and truth" (John 1:14).

With these as our truthful, reliable sources, we find God to be infinite, limitless, and measureless.

How Big is God?

In the pursuit of Christlikeness, it's important to get and maintain an infinite view of God.

- His infinite genius created us.
- His infinite power redeems us.
- His infinite wisdom enlightens us.
- His infinite love overwhelms us.
- His infinite grace saves us.
- His infinite blood cleanses us
- His infinite Spirit empowers us.

If He were an omni-everything yet impersonal God, we would know nothing of His immense and eternal love for us. If He didn't disclose Himself and encourage us to increase our understanding of Him, we wouldn't know He created us in His image. We wouldn't know how to reconcile ourselves back to Him. We wouldn't know how to live in a way that pleases Him. We would know nothing of the blessings and favor He has for those who draw close to Him.

Oh, we know about our badness, failures, and shortcomings as a result of our negative interactions with other humans. But without His disclosure, we would know nothing about how such sinfulness prevents a personal relationship with Him and diminishes fellowship with Him. If God didn't reveal Himself to us, we wouldn't know of Jesus' redeeming sacrifice to enable us to live in His newness of life.

Thankfully, God has revealed and continues revealing Himself.

Although His thoughts and wisdom are far above ours (Isaiah 55:8-9), He still sympathizes with, understands, and calls us to Himself. He explains His majesty and eternal existence so we may reverence Him and turn from our sin (Exodus 20:20). He discloses His unconditional love, unmerited grace, and undeserved mercy so we come to Him fully assured that He won't reject us (John 6:37).

Because God is infinite, limitless, and measureless, so are all His attributes. "From everlasting to everlasting" He is God (Psalm 90:2). That describes infinity as a vanishing point in eternity past to a vanishing point in eternity future. No matter how far we travel, the vanishing point remains beyond our grasp.

The Great I AM always has been, always is, and always will be who He is. Think about that for a moment.

All His attributes—omnipresence, omniscience, omnipotence, love, mercy, grace, truth, righteousness, holiness, justice, forgiveness, goodness, compassion, etc.—have no beginning or end. They are all present, undiminished, in all their fullness, all the time. There is no deviation depending on our feelings, thoughts, or actions. All remain eternally the same.

I am the LORD, I do not change. (Malachi 3:6)

Even His life is abundantly infinite (John 10:10). Amazingly, He offers this infinite, eternal, glorious life to us to accept or reject.

Human Relatability

God wants to relate to us and help us relate to Him too.

To help us get a better picture of this infinite, limitless, measureless God, He reveals Himself through His Word, His Son (Jesus), and His Holy Spirit. What we find in Scripture is a far cry from what we see in Bible pictures, sacred murals, church stain-glassed windows, and movies.

Several times in history, Jesus showed Himself through visions or theophanies. A theophany is normally a pre-Incarnate, physical appearance in tangible or sensed form. These help us understand His infinite power, majesty, and sovereignty. Here are some examples that cover a period of 2,200 years.

- To Abraham, He showed Himself as Melchizedek, the King of Salem (Genesis 14:18-20) and as a Man with two angels (Genesis 18).
- To Jacob, He showed Himself standing at the top of the ladder with angels ascending and descending between heaven and earth

(Genesis 28:12-13). He also appeared in their all-night wrestling match (Genesis 32:22-30).
- To Joshua, He appeared as a mighty warrior with a drawn sword in hand (Joshua 5:13-15).
- To Samson's parents, He appeared as a nameless, "terrible" [frightening; awesome] messenger of God (Judges 13, KJV).
- To Michaiah, He was seated on His majestic throne surrounded by the host of heaven (1 Kings 22:19-22).
- To Isaiah, He appeared on a throne "high and lifted up," dressed in a royal robe, surrounded by mighty seraphim, with incredible rumblings and blinding incense (Isaiah 6:1-5).
- To Ezekiel, He appeared seated on a heavenly throne, surrounded by a bright rainbow. From His waist up, He was the color of fiery amber; from His waist down, He looked like bright fire (Ezekiel 1:26-28).
- To Daniel, He was robed in linen garments, with a belt of purest gold around His waist and glowing, lustrous skin. From His face came blinding flashes like lightning, His eyes were pools of fire. His arms and feet shone like polished brass and His voice roared like a large crowd of people (Daniel 10:4-6, TLB).
- To John the Revelator, He had many crowns on His head and wore a robe dipped in blood. His eyes were like a flame of fire; a sharp sword went out of His mouth (Revelation 19:11-15).

Can you see Him?

This is Jesus, the incredible One we follow. The Lamb of God who sacrificed His life to reconcile us back to Himself. The One His true followers surrender to and obey. The Lion of the tribe of Judah. The soon coming King of kings and Lord of lords!

To become like Christ, I must have a personal relationship with Him. I must discover who He is. Realize what He's done for me. Become intimately associated with Him. Appropriate fully His sacrifice. Surrender fully to Him.

Let's look at a few of His attributes while keeping in mind that all of God does all that God does.

Personal Reflection

How does acknowledging God's infinity affect your view of Him? Does His unchangeable nature prompt a deeper sense of trust in who He is and what He says in His Word? How can you incorporate the descriptions of His theophanies into your everyday life? Knowing you can't outlast His infinite attributes, how does that affect you?

Chapter Six

Omnipresence: Dwelling in the Eternal Present Tense

*Christ is the unseen guest of every meal,
the silent listener to every conversation.*[23]

In my childhood home, I remember a plaque with this impressionable message. I think about it often. It reminds me of God's constant presence.

The journey of Christlikeness begins with knowing Who He is. Wrapping our brains around the *Who* helps direct us toward the *what* (what we need to do) and the *how* (how we can accomplish it). The more we know Him, the more amazing He becomes to us.

In our discovery, we find God is infinitely, eternally omnipresent. That means He exists in all places equally and simultaneously. This is how He is a "present help in trouble" (Psalm 46:1).

To explore this further, let's dissect the word. *Omni* is a prefix that means all—in all ways, all things, all places. For example, an omnibus legislative bill includes many, possibly unrelated, provisions at the same time. An omnivorous animal eats everything edible. *Presence* is "the state of being present; something (such as a spirit) felt or believed to be present; the position close to a person."[24]

How comforting to know the One we follow is always present.

Human Restraints

Omnipresence is difficult to understand because we can't be everywhere at the same time.

As physical beings, we're bound, limited, and restricted by time, space, and matter. We can't alter time or travel backward or forward in time. Time is a non-renewable, depreciating yet precious resource. We can't add to it, relive it, or stop it. We only choose how to invest it. Our time eventually ends. Sooner or later, time ushers us into eternity. The only time we have is this moment.

We're also bound by space. The laws of gravity and motion keep us from existing at more than one place at a time. Thankfully, gravity keeps us from floating off into space. But by keeping us earthbound, it takes time and effort to move from one place to another.

In our physical state, we cannot transcend matter. But this ability would be an awesome superpower! Imagine being able to whoosh out of traffic jams, boring meetings, horrible dates, and long-distance travel. But our molecules won't cooperate. Yet even this has its benefits. We expect a cup of coffee to stay where we place it and not slip through and crash to the floor.

Our boundaries, though restrictive, are also beneficial.

Simultaneous Present State

God isn't bound by time, space, and matter restrictions.

Jesus declared, "God is Spirit" (John 4:24). As such, we know God the Father is invisible. Paul confirmed this by saying Jesus "is the image of the invisible God" (Colossians 1:15). Although unseen, God's presence remains everywhere. King David, exclaimed, "Where can I go from Your Spirit? Or where can I flee from Your presence?" (Psalm 139:7). He also sang, "In Your presence is fullness of joy" (Psalm 16:11) and encouraged everyone to "come before His presence with thanksgiving" (Psalm 95:2).

From the I AM identification in Exodus 3:14, we discover God simply *is*. Everywhere. Simultaneously. He dwells in the eternal present tense of *is*.

There are only two possible places where it seems God restricts His presence. One is the human heart—which He accesses by invitation only (Revelation 3:20). The other is the place of eternal damnation. In 2 Thessalonians 1:8-9, Paul warned those who "do not know God" and those who "do not obey the gospel of our Lord Jesus Christ" that the fiery judgment awaiting them includes "everlasting destruction from the presence of the Lord." Being eternally absent *from* the loving, comforting, and peaceful presence of God is one of the horrors of eternal judgment.

Other than these two apparent self-restrictions, God's omnipresence floods everything, everywhere. This is another demonstration of God's sovereign power and control. He's not only everywhere, He also dictates where everywhere is.

Remember this when you're feeling lonely or abandoned. Though unseen and possibly silent, God is still there.

To consider just one aspect of God's omnipresence, look at what happened to Moses. After committing murder and fleeing into the wilderness, he encountered the holiness of God's omnipresence (Exodus 3:1-5). Picture him in the middle of a desert on the back side of nowhere. Tending his father-in-law's flock. Minding his own business.

Then he saw something strange—a burning bush that wasn't burning up. Understandably, the desert is a hot place, and dried bushes could burst into flames under the right conditions. But this bush kept burning. So Moses did what anyone would do. He decided to get closer and check it out.

That's when God stopped him.

Do not draw near this place. Take your sandals off your feet, for the place where you stand is holy ground. (Exodus 3:5)

God's presence was in that burning bush. That made it holy ground. Asking Moses to remove his sandals wasn't because they were dirty. As a loving, holy, omnipresent God, He wants us in His presence. But He wants nothing between Him and us, no matter how seemingly insignificant.

How cool is that!

God's holiness and omnipresence turn every spot in the universe into holy ground. We're always in His holy presence—everywhere. And nothing should ever come between Him and us.

Infinite, Expansive Existence

How big is God?

In 1977, NASA launched the spacecraft Voyager into deep space. After traveling forty-seven years, it's approximately 14.7 billion miles from earth. Along with that spacecraft, several others have been launched, most notably, the Hubble Space Telescope (1990) and the James Webb Telescope (2021). Both have recorded and returned many stunning images from deep space. How incredible to see all that beauty in the expansiveness of nothing.

Yet what takes us years to see and explore, God is already there.

God holds the expansive outer boundaries of space in the palm of His hand. Zechariah said God "stretches out the heavens" and "lays the foundations of the earth" (Zechariah 12:1). Isaiah also rhetorically asked,

> Who has measured the waters in the hollow of His hand, measured heaven with a span and calculated the dust of the earth in a measure? Weighed the mountains in scales and the hills in a balance? (Isaiah 40:12)

Yeah but Nate, what does all this have to do with becoming like Christ?

Jesus, the One we follow and want to become like, spoke it all into existence (John 1:1-3). "For of Him and through Him and to Him are all things" (Romans 11:36).

If we are to model our lives after anyone, this is that Person!

As the Light of the world (John 8:12), Jesus commands the speed of light that travels 186,262 miles per second.[25] Imagine the speed of creation when He said, "Let there be light." As further proof of His deity, Jesus walked on water, passed through walls and locked doors, healed countless people instantly, and raised Himself from the dead. More on that later.

Omnipresence is also the inability to be absent. God promises, "I will never leave you nor forsake you" (Hebrews 13:5). He can't leave or be absent from anyone or anywhere. We're never alone. He sees all (Psalm 33:13-14). He knows all. He is present in every event, every circumstance, every tragedy, every sin, and every surrender.

This can be both comforting and frightening depending on our spiritual status. His constant presence is comforting because we know He's always near, seeing everything. But it can also be frightening, knowing He sees when we stray from Him and wander into sin.

The fact that He is everywhere and nothing is hidden from Him should motivate us to obey His Word, surrender to His Spirit, and pursue Christlikeness every day.

God is Near and Personally Accessible

Since Triune God has no origin, no beginning, and no end, He is self-existent, self-sustaining, self-dependent, and self-sufficient.

God needs nothing from anyone. He can't be dismissed. He doesn't walk off in a huff when we disobey Him. He doesn't unfriend us on social media when we ignore Him. He doesn't gaslight us when we sin against Him. He remains the same.

His presence doesn't depend on our feelings. Even when it *feels* like He is distant and our fellowship with Him is strained, He's still present. Feelings of distance and disconnect don't come from His removal or absence. We feel distant when we separate our hearts or minds, either by sin or willful ignorance, from intimate fellowship with Him. But in reality, we can't leave His presence. Unsurrendered hearts and minds merely create the illusion or imagination that He's abandoned us.

We have several assurances of God's faithful presence. He is near:

- The brokenhearted because they need his comfort. (Psalm 34:18)
- Those who passionately seek Him. (Jeremiah 29:13)
- Those who genuinely, truthfully seek Him. (Psalm 145:18)
- Those with humble and repentant hearts. (Isaiah 57:15)

Even when people disbelieve Him or His existence, He can't and won't deny Himself (2 Timothy 2:13).

Since God is omnipresent, He remains accessible to everyone. We don't need a pilgrimage to some distant land, a holy relic to caress, or any religious middleman to access God's presence. Although He exists everywhere, He still awaits a personal invitation to enter each person's heart. This moves His omnipresence to intimate presence.

He even told us how this happens. Jesus said, "I am the way, the truth, and the life. No one comes to the Father except through Me" (John 14:6). There's no other way.

> God also has highly exalted Him and given Him the name which is above every name, that at the name of Jesus every knee should bow …

and that every tongue should confess that Jesus Christ is Lord, to the glory of God the Father. (Philippians 2:9-11)

Although God is everywhere, Jesus Christ is the only way into God the Father's intimate presence.

Knowing we have access to God is one thing. It's quite another to place our faith, trust, and reliance on Jesus and claim Him as personal Lord and Savior. This is the first step on the journey toward Christlikeness.

Knowing and believing is far different than accepting and surrendering. We can *know* and even *believe* many things about Jesus. But until we confess Him as Lord, believe He was raised from the dead, and invite the Holy Spirit into our lives through spiritual rebirth (John 3:3), we simply have a head full of knowledge.

Sadly, there will be *knowers* and *believers* in the place of eternal damnation. Some people call this hell. Scripture calls it the lake of fire (Revelation 20:15).

During Jesus' ministry, He encountered several demon-possessed people. These demons *knew* and *believed* who Jesus was. They even recognized His authority over them. James 2:19 says, "You believe that there is one God. You do well. Even the demons believe—and tremble!" But there will be no demons in heaven.

Simply *knowing* and *believing* keep people out of heaven. They also keep people from the journey toward Christlikeness.

A New Birth Grants Access to God

We can't theorize the spiritual birth.

Either a person has been born from above—born again, reborn spiritually with a noticeable transformation in his life—or there's been no new birth. No birth, no baby.

Without a personal relationship with Jesus Christ, there's no spiritual rebirth. Without spiritual rebirth, there's no indwelling Holy Spirit. Without the indwelling Holy Spirit, there's no transformation, no conforming to the image of Christ.

We're not believers simply by claiming we are—any more than the neighborhood kids can claim to be mine. Nor do they have unrestricted access to my home—or pantry. Only birth makes a child mine. Birth grants access to me and my resources. Spiritual rebirth is the only way to belong to Jesus and access His power and resources.

As a caution, spiritual rebirth doesn't happen based on our preconceived ideas. Jesus warned of this misconception.

> Many will say to Me in that day, "Lord, Lord, have we not prophesied in Your name, cast out demons in Your name, and done many wonders in Your name?" And then I will declare to them, "I never knew you; depart from Me." (Matthew 7:22-23)

Some Bible expositors say the word *many* should actually be translated as *most*. "Most will say to Me …" This should frighten every person. It should also motivate every professing follower of Christ to confirm their hope of salvation rests solely on Jesus, that spiritual rebirth has truly occurred, and the transforming Holy Spirit is evident in their lives.

By declaring, "I never knew you," Jesus revealed the absence of a personal, intimate relationship. The word *knew* doesn't mean simply knowing about Him or having factual head knowledge. The Greek word for factual or head knowledge is *eido (εἴδω)*. But the Greek word Jesus used is a derivative of *ginōskō (γινώκσω)*. This word often describes the experiential knowledge involved in a personal, intimate relationship. It's also used in reference to sexual relations between a husband and wife. This is knowing and being known intimately and experientially. It's a heart knowledge that goes far deeper than head knowledge.[26]

In essence, Jesus warned that group of self-boasters that they knew much *about* Him and even did many things in His name. But He wasn't in relationship with them. They had much religious interaction, but no relationship with Jesus.

Thankfully, when we call on Jesus in childlike faith and complete trust, He's always near. We have His assurance that He won't reject us (John 6:37). Hallelujah!

Once the miracle of salvation happens, the Holy Spirit takes up residence inside a person's heart. Just as Infinity came as Incarnate Jesus, so God's infinite, eternal, sanctifying Spirit makes His home inside every true believer (1 Corinthians 3:16).

And so the journey toward Christlikeness begins.

Knowing God's presence is everywhere simultaneously is a blessing. But that's *head* knowledge. Experiencing His inner presence is lasting joy. That's *heart* knowledge. Christlikeness is a matter of the heart. A transformed, surrendered heart longs to be like Jesus.

Why is Understanding God's Omnipresence Important?

It's important to understand God's omnipresence because we need to know we can find Him. To know we can invite Him into our hearts and lives. To know He won't reject or abandon us. He encourages every person to find Him.

- You will seek the LORD your God, and you will find *Him* if you seek Him with all your heart and with all your soul. (Deuteronomy 4:29)
- You will seek Me and find *Me*, when you search for Me with all your heart. (Jeremiah 29:13)
- They should seek the Lord, in the hope that they might … find Him, though He is not far from each one of us. (Acts 17:27)

Jesus said, "Come to Me … and I will give you rest" (Matthew 11:28). He invites us into His intimate presence through salvation, sanctification, self-denial, and surrender. May we not only enter His presence but lovingly embrace it.

Becoming like Christ involves undistracted quality time alone in His presence. It involves learning of Him, emulating His characteristics and disposition, and *putting on* His mindset (Philippians 2:5). It's a constant awareness. An intimate fellowship. Unbroken communion with Him.

May we foster an awareness of living every moment in His intimate, personal presence.

Personal Reflection

How does God's omnipresence influence your daily life? Your choices, your decisions? Your attitudes? Relationships? Hobbies, activities, and habits? The places you go? What you watch? Events you attend? Is it comforting to know you're always in His presence? Why or why not?

Chapter Seven

Omniscience: Perfect Knowledge of Everything

We don't know what we don't know.

I've heard this strange quote several times in my career.

On its surface, it seems nonsensical. But when we think about it, we soon realize there's much we don't and can't know. We aren't even *aware* of what we don't know. Only when presented with new facts or new experiences can we expand our knowledge.

With that in mind, here's the new fact.

It's important to know who to follow.

In today's society, people follow all sorts of superficial characters who have little credibility. Others sound knowledgeable, yet their lives resemble a train wreck. These hardly seem like smart choices to follow.

But what if you could follow someone with perfect knowledge about every subject—including yourself. And His life is an example of perfection. Would you consider that Person worth following?

The journey toward Christlikeness requires open hearts and minds to new and refreshing knowledge of Jesus Christ. He already knows what we don't know. May we embrace the evidence of His omniscience.

We've already examined the meaning of *omni*. Now we add science to that. *Science* is "knowledge or a system of knowledge covering general truths, as distinguished from ignorance or misunderstanding."[27] Combining both words results in *omniscience*, the all-knowing attribute of God.

Again, unless identifying specific roles or functions, references to God include God the Father, God the Son (Jesus), and God the Holy Spirit. All of God does all that God does. All Three are equally omniscient.

As omniscient, God perfectly knows everything and all possible outcomes. He knows the best courses of action to achieve His purposes for His glory and our good. Absolutely nothing is beyond His knowledge and understanding.

A similar word adds to the meaning of omniscience. *Omnisapience* means the perfect wisdom of God.

- God alone is "all wise" (Romans 16:27; 1 Timothy 1:17; Jude 1:25).
- God's perfect wisdom "works all things according to the counsel of His will" (Ephesians 1:11).
- God's wisdom is multifaceted or multidimensional (Ephesians 3:10).

While we operate in 3-D, God operates in Infinity-D. He sees things from all angles simultaneously—missing no details. His knowledge far surpasses ours (Isaiah 55:9)

This is why we open our hearts and minds for Him to reveal Himself to us. He promises to share His perfect wisdom to those who ask (James 1:5). So let's ask as we discover His omniscience.

Human Mental Limitations

We can't understand beyond what we've learned, can learn, or can experience.

What we don't know, we tend to imagine or theorize to fill in the gaps.

When researching something, we tend to lean toward conclusions that make sense to us but in reality, may not be factual. By doing this, we rise no further than what we already know or can see around us. This also restricts our knowledge of God.

It may come as a surprise, but humans use only a fraction of our mental capacity. As a mental measurement, Intelligence Quotient (IQ) is a standard used to determine a person's mental capacity in comparison to a group of peers. According to Psych Central, a Healthline Media Company:

> Most people have an average IQ between 85 and 115. Overall, about 98 percent of people have a score below 130. Only 2 percent of the population score above that and are considered above average.[28]

In comparison to God's omniscience, the majority of people have average to slightly above average intelligence. No wonder so many mysteries remain. Even the most intelligent people have unanswered questions. No human knows or can accurately predict what will happen tomorrow. No human has specifically identified why bad things happen to good people. We know certain laws exist (for example, gravity, aerodynamics, attraction, relativity, cause and effect) but we don't know specifically how or why. In fact, without His disclosure of Himself, how can we wrap our brains around the concept of God?

Along with our limitations, we clutter our minds with fake news, half-truths, denominational nuances, personal biases and prejudices, homegrown myths, hand-me-down religiosity—the list goes on and on. Even the current focus on artificial intelligence (AI) and generative pre-trained transformer (GPT) "large language models" incorporate the biases of the programmers. Those engines draw inferences and make suggestions based on those personal biases (think Google search engine and online fact-checkers).

This is why we clear our minds and have them renewed by God's Word and the Holy Spirit. To know the Christ we follow, we must listen to Him. Allowing His truth to soak our hearts and minds aligns us with Him.

Christlikeness involves a renewed mindset—one that's aligned with His truth.

- Be transformed by the renewing of your mind. (Romans 12:2)
- Be renewed in the spirit of your mind. (Ephesians 4:23-24)
- Put on the new man who is renewed in knowledge according to the image of Him who created him. (Colossians 3:10)

On the journey toward Christlikeness, we need His help to rewire our minds. Ask Him to reset your thoughts, mindsets, imaginations, perceptions, opinions, prejudices, preferences, fantasies, arguments, agendas, narratives, and anything else of a mental capacity. Only God's omniscience and perfect wisdom can accomplish this.

Limitless Wisdom and Foreknowledge

God has never learned, and can't learn, anything.

He maintains an absolute awareness about everything. And He doesn't need Google, Bing, DuckDuckGo, or any other search engine for information. It's impossible for Him to learn anything because there's no other uncreated, self-existent being who can teach Him.

> Who has directed the Spirit of the LORD, or as His counselor has taught Him? With whom did He take counsel, and who instructed Him, and taught Him in the path of justice? Who taught Him knowledge and showed Him the way of understanding?
> (Isaiah 40:13-14)

God knows everything from beginning to end—even things that haven't happened yet. "Declaring the end from the beginning, and from ancient times the things that are not yet done, saying, 'My counsel shall stand'" (Isaiah 46:10). Having perfect wisdom, God maintains the ability to devise perfect ends and achieve them by perfect means.

Let's apply that to what Jesus knew and when He knew it.

As part of Triune, Omniscient God, Jesus is all-knowing. Nothing catches Him by surprise. The apostle Peter should know. He spent over three years in daily contact with Him. Peter wrote, "The Spirit of Christ … testified beforehand the sufferings of Christ" (1 Peter 1:11).

"Testified beforehand" is another reference to *foreknowledge*. The Greek word for foreknowledge is *prognósis* (πρόγνωσις) from which we get our English word prognosis—knowing something beforehand. But before what?

This is where things really bend the human mind.

Calvary wasn't a spontaneous, murderous act by spiteful, resentful men. God the Father didn't look down on earth and stammer, *Uh-oh, there's trouble brewing down in Jerusalem. What're We going to do now?* Not even close.

Calvary was foreordained by God. The entire plan of bringing sinful humans back to God was pre-planned before time or Creation ever happened (2 Timothy 1:9). It was purposed "before the foundation of the world" (1 Peter 1:18-20).

God foresaw man's rebellion and rejection. Yet He coordinated the specific thing we need by incorporating our rejection of it.

Pause for a moment and think about that.

If we ever needed evidence of God's sovereign orchestration, it would be Calvary. During a cosmic meeting far back in eternity past God foreknew His *creative* act would require a *redemptive* act.

Imagine that possible conversation.

Cosmic Conference in the Halls of Eternity

"Let's make man."

"Okay, how shall We do that?"

"Let's make him with two eyes to see clearly, two arms to embrace dearly, two legs to follow Us closely. Let's give Him an eternal soul so he can live with Us forever. Oh, let's make him in Our image. And let's give him a mind so he's aware of Our existence.

"What else shall We give Him?"

"Let's give Him free will to make choices for himself."

"Um, that's a problem since We know he will choose to reject Us and rebel against Us. We'll need a plan for that eventuality."

A momentary silence deafened eternity past. God's everlasting heart overflowed with pure love for His future creation. Yet His pure holiness would never tolerate anything that challenged Him or His absolute authority.

Then a raised hand broke the silence.

With tears in His eyes and Calvary on His mind, the eternal Word, Jesus, the second Person in the Triune Godhead said, "I'll take care of that."

The Christ we follow knew ahead of time what He would suffer. Yet He loves us so much He did it anyway (Romans 5:8).

Foreknowledge of the Crucifixion

Jesus foreknew the price, the pain, the shame, and the outcome of Calvary.

Just before His glorious transfiguration, Jesus told His disciples He must "go to Jerusalem and suffer many things from the elders and chief priests and scribes, be killed, and be raised the third day" (Matthew 16:21).

On the way to Jerusalem, Jesus didn't disguise Himself or hide among the disciples. He led them, out front, as He always did. He knew full well "the things that would happen to Him" (Mark 10:32).

Shortly after His triumphal entry into Jerusalem, Jesus said, "Now My soul is troubled, and what shall I say? 'Father, save Me from this hour'? But for this purpose I came to this hour" (John 12:27).

At the Last Supper, He told His disciples, "Truly the Son of Man goes as it has been determined [appointed; foreordained]" (Luke 22:22).

In the Garden of Gethsemane, as the authorities and mob came to arrest

Him, He didn't try to escape. "Knowing all things that should come upon him" (John 18:4), He met them face-to-face.

After the Holy Spirit came at Pentecost, Peter declared Jesus's crucifixion was no random act of murder. On the contrary, Jesus was crucified by the "determined purpose and foreknowledge of God" (Acts 2:23).

Shortly thereafter, Jewish religious leaders arrested Peter and John and warned them against preaching in the name of Jesus. Peter responded by acknowledging Christ's sufferings and crucifixion happened by God's hand and purpose that were determined beforehand (Acts 4:27-28).

Sure, those murderers had the freewill choice to let Jesus go or demand His crucifixion. Yet God in His before-time-began foreknowledge already knew the outcome of their choice and orchestrated His plan of salvation accordingly.

Before time began. Foreknowledge. Eternal purpose. Pre-determination.

Only omniscience explains this. As God the Son, Jesus was at that pre-time cosmic planning session when everything was foreknown and foreordained.

In this divine, infinite foreknowledge, true followers of Christ find their ultimate purpose—Christlikeness.

> Whom He foreknew, He also predestined [purposed] *to be* conformed to the image of His Son. (Romans 8:29)

God created man in His image. Sin distorted that image. Jesus died and rose again to restore that image. Christlikeness is what transforms that image.

Predestination Versus Foreknowledge

Yeah but, Nate, doesn't the word predestined mean that God mandates, coerces, or orchestrates Christlikeness only on His chosen few?

First, let's consider predestination. Scripture plainly states God doesn't show favoritism or partiality (Romans 2:11). In addition, God doesn't want anyone to perish (2 Peter 3:9). He repeatedly calls "whoever" to believe on Him.

Whoever means anyone. The action verbs associated with *whoever* indicate personal choice. Faith, belief, and placing trust in Jesus aren't forced decisions. They express human choice and personal willingness.

Second, let's revisit the concept of foreknowledge. To do so, let's step outside of time. Consider time as a small capsule God holds in His hand. As infinite, eternal God, He isn't confined to time as we are.

Outside time, being everywhere simultaneously, and having perfect omniscience, God already foreknows who will genuinely place their trust in Him. But just because He foreknows something doesn't remove each person's free will to determine, express, and act upon personal choice.

We'll dive deeper into this topic when reviewing God's omnipotence and sovereignty. For now, we understand that His foreknowledge already sees genuine followers of Christ and reveals their ultimate purpose of becoming like Christ.

Foreknowing Us and Calling Us to Himself

God knows all things in perfection—instantly, effortlessly, and without recall.

He knew everything about each of us before He ever created anything. He knows what we think (Ezekiel 11:5) and the secrets of our hearts (Psalm 44:21). Nothing is hidden from Him.

Let that thought sink in.

The infinite, eternal, uncreated, self-existing, self-dependent, self-sufficient, self-sustaining, omnipresent, omniscient, omnipotent, Almighty Creator knows *you*. And He knows you better than you know yourself. He sees the real person behind all the discounts, facades, false impressions, and untruths you hide behind. Hallelujah!

When I was born, God didn't say, *Uh-oh, Nate was born today. We need to increase our love, mercy, grace, patience, and forgiveness because We're going to need it!* Nope, He already knew all about me long before.

God knows everything about us—our past history, our present struggles, and our future choices. This enables our intimate honesty with Him. We can't hide anything because He already knows about it. We may hide things from other people, but it's impossible with God.

To forgive us, to cleanse us from sin, God must know every detail. If He doesn't know everything about us—every failure, every sin—He can't be our Savior. If He isn't omniscient, He might overlook something. Then when we stand before Him, He could say, *Oops, My bad. There's something here you didn't disclose and I didn't forgive. But now it's too late. I'm so sorry.* And if He isn't omniscient, we could con Him into thinking we're better than we truly are. Thank God He is all-knowing.

In addition to knowing us fully, He calls us to Himself. Even with all our faults, failures, and fears, He wants to have a personal relationship with us. He chose us before the foundation of the world (Ephesians 1:4). He "saved us and called us with a holy calling ... according to His own purpose [intention beforehand] and grace which was given to us in Christ Jesus before time began" (2 Timothy 1:9). Wow!

There's so much to unpack in those two verses. First, He called and chose us. Second, He calls us to holiness. Third, we can't add anything to His salvation and grace because we weren't at that pre-time cosmic meeting when He planned those details. Fourth, we have salvation and God's redeeming grace only through Jesus. Lastly, all of it was determined before this thing called *time* ever began.

Jesus said, "You did not choose Me, but I chose you out of the world" (John 15:16, 19). We come to Him because He first came to us and revealed Himself to us. He created, called, chose, and commissioned His followers to be separate from the world. He calls us to a holy life and blameless lifestyle.

He designed us for Christlikeness.

Omniscient God Won't Change His Mind

Some may wonder if God still loves them when they fall into sin.

How can God love me when I am who I am and do what I do? He must hate me.

That's another amazing thing about omniscience. God doesn't change His mind.

In addition to being all-knowing, God is also immutable. That means He is changeless (Malachi 3:6). He's ever the same. Faithful to who He is. That includes His Word, nature, characteristics, and attributes.

Contrary to current-day sentiment, no part of God is progressive. His moral standard isn't flexible. He doesn't tolerate our preferred perversions. Society's devolving moral standard doesn't influence Him. As Holy God, He remains who He is. He can't and won't change. There's not even any gray area with Him (James 1:17).

The good news about God's immutability is that He never stops loving us.

Walk with me quickly through the process. First, God doesn't change. Second, God is love (1 John 4:8). That doesn't mean God is merely loving. He *is* love. Love is one of His eternal attributes. Next, because of this infinite love, Jesus sacrificed His life for us (John 3:16). And He did so fully aware of our sinful state.

> God demonstrates His own love toward us, in that while we were still sinners, Christ died for us. (Romans 5:8)

This means we can't be good enough for Him to love us more or so bad that He loves us less. God already knows our freewill choices and decisions. From outside of time, dwelling in the eternal present tense, He already sees what we will do from this moment forward. He has no mood swings, personality changes, or abrupt alterations. Omniscient God has no "aha" moments, discoveries, surprises, or regrets.

Oh, He doesn't condone or overlook our sin. He still disciplines. But His attitude toward us remains the same in eternity future as it has been in eternity past and the present. Any change in our relationship and fellowship with Him depends on us. He remains eternally the same.

We can trust God's omniscience toward us.

- He understands everything about us. (Psalm 139:3)
- He knows each individual's journey. (Job 23:10)
- He orchestrates circumstances for His glory and our good. (Romans 8:28)
- He knows the plans and purposes He has for us. (Jeremiah 29:11)

He even knows what goes on in the dark—in those secret, dangerous, hostile, adverse corners of life (Psalm 139:11-12). Isaiah recorded God as saying, "I will give you the treasures of darkness and hidden riches of secret places" (Isaiah 45:3). If He can give them, He already knows about them. The prophet Daniel confirmed this by saying God "knows what *is* in the darkness" (Daniel 2:22).

There's still much that remains beyond human discovery. There are depths of God's wisdom and knowledge that remain unfathomable (Romans 11:33). The apostle Paul referred to this as "unsearchable" (Ephesians 3:8).

Though God reveals what we *need* to know about Him, much remains locked away in the storehouse of His omniscience. For now, we have everything we need to know.

An awareness of His perfect knowledge awakens the faith to trust Him completely and follow Him wholeheartedly.

We can do this!

Personal Reflection

Since God is omniscient, why struggle with believing what He says or with being completely honest with Him at all times, in every circumstance, with every topic? How comforting is it knowing He already knows everything about you? How grateful to know we can trust Him completely—especially for what we don't know.

Chapter Eight

Omniscience: What God Reveals to Us

*If only he would tell you the secrets of wisdom,
for true wisdom is not a simple matter. (Job 11:6, NLT)*

All we know about God, we know from God. By disclosing His omniscience, God reveals in human terms His wisdom and understanding. Yet even with this knowledge, it's still difficult to understand Him fully. Conceptually, we understand the *Who* and *why*. But we struggle with the intricacies of the *how* of omniscience and sovereign orchestration.

Paul had the anointing of divine inspiration to write a majority of the New Testament. But even he struggled to understand. "Oh, the depth of the riches both of the wisdom and knowledge of God! How unsearchable are His judgments and His ways past finding out!" (Romans 11:33).

Thankfully, we develop an understanding about God as we read, study, and meditate on His Word.

- With Him are wisdom and strength, He has counsel and understanding. (Job 12:13)
- Counsel is mine, and sound wisdom; I am understanding. (Proverbs 8:14)
- There is no wisdom, understanding, or counsel against the LORD. (Proverbs 21:30)
- The counsel and plans of the LORD stand forever. (Psalm 33:11)

With the Living and written Word, and the Holy Spirit to enlighten us, God reveals all we need to become Christlike.

Mysteries Revealed—To Help Us

Genuine Christ followers study His Word, seek His illumination, and apply His truth to their lives.

God reveals these *mysteries* or hidden truths to those willing to find them. "To you it has been given to know the mysteries of the kingdom of God" (Luke 8:10).

Yeah but Nate, why would God speak in mysteries? Why not just speak clearly?

Paul explains that God spoke in mysteries to hide things from Satan. Ever since God's promise in Genesis 3:15 to provide a Savior Who would finally and forever crush Satan, this devious Being has been trying to thwart God's plan (1 Corinthians 2:7-8).

In the Old Testament, before Jesus came to earth, and before we had the written Word of God, many things remained hidden. Prophets like Isaiah, Jeremiah, and Daniel looked to future events with eyes of faith. Yet events like Christ's arrival, the dispensation of grace, and the regathering of the Jews to their own nation were far-off mysteries.

From today's perspective, we look back with certainty on those events. But even with these prophetic fulfillments, we still look with eyes of faith to expected future events. The Rapture. The seven-year Tribulation. The glorious return of Jesus as King of kings and Lord of lords.

We may have a clearer vision than the Old Testament saints, but there's still much to learn. Still much to anticipate. Still much faith to exercise as we await these future mysteries to unfold.

One such revealed mystery is the "mystery of godliness." This is basically the gospel story. Paul summarized it in one verse.

> Great is the mystery [hidden truth] of godliness: God was manifested in the flesh [Immanuel], justified [recognized as righteous] in the Spirit, seen by angels [at Christ's birth and His resurrection], preached among the Gentiles [by both Peter and Paul], believed on [salvation] in the world, received up in glory [ascension]. (1 Timothy 3:16)

Of all the verses to memorize and study, this is an awesome candidate. God's Word gives us enough information to know Him, come to Him, have faith in Him, and cultivate a relationship with Him. But He hasn't revealed everything (John 21:25). Some mysteries remain.

Christ followers can rest assured knowing omniscient God has revealed all we need to know.

Jesus Revealed—To Save Us

Genuine Christ followers claim Him as Lord and Savior. But they also recognize Him as God with us (Matthew 1:23).

God the Son, Jesus, the Living Word, came to earth in the form of human flesh (John 1:14). How better to reveal Himself to us in a form, language, and existence we could understand? Through Jesus, we begin to understand God the Father.

- No one knows the Father except the Son, and the one to whom the Son reveals Him. (Matthew 11:27)
- No one has seen God at any time. The only begotten Son has declared Him. (John 1:18)

Jesus is divine, part of the Holy Trinity. He is the mirror image of God the Father. He's the Creator of all things. He's the Savior of the world by His death on Calvary's cross and subsequent resurrection. He's on His throne in heaven awaiting His Father's signal to return to earth and claim His true followers.

Scripture reveals much information about the Christ we follow.

God ... has spoken to us through his Son [Jesus] to whom he has given everything and through whom he made the world and everything there is. God's Son shines out with God's glory, and all that God's Son is and does marks him as God. He regulates the universe by the mighty power of his command. He is the one who died to cleanse us and clear our record of all sin, and then sat down in highest honor beside the great God of heaven. (Hebrews 1:1-3, TLB)

Christ Jesus ... being in the form of God, did not consider it robbery to be equal with God, but made Himself of no reputation, taking the form of a bondservant, and coming in the likeness of men. And being found in appearance as a man, He humbled Himself and became obedient to the point of death, even the death of the cross. (Philippians 2:5-8)

Jesus is referred to as "the wisdom of God" (1 Corinthians 1:24) and "the Word" or intelligence of God (John 1:1-3). He knows all things. "Jesus ... knew all men and had no need that anyone should testify of man, for He knew what was in man" (John 2:24-25). "Jesus knew from the beginning who they were who did not believe and who would betray Him" (John 6:64).

His disciples eventually came to understand Jesus' omniscience. "Now we are sure that You know all things ... By this we believe that You came forth from God" (John 16:30).

All these confirm Jesus' omniscience as well as His deity.

The Holy Spirit Revealed—To Transform Us

Genuine Christ followers are regenerated, indwelt, and influenced by the Holy Spirit.

It was the Holy Spirit who produced the miraculous virgin birth of Christ (Luke 1:35). He visibly descended upon Jesus at the beginning of Christ's earthly ministry (Luke 3:22). He came in dramatic fashion at Pentecost (Acts 2:1-4). He lives inside each genuine child of God (1 Corinthians 3:16). He conducts the transforming work of Christ in us (Galatians 4:19).

Genuine followers of Christ are to be "filled with the Spirit" (Ephesians 5:18). This is an anointing over and above His indwelling. We are to "walk in the Spirit" (Galatians 5:16). This is a lifestyle wholly influenced by and surrendered to Him. We are not to "grieve" the Holy Spirit (Ephesians 4:30) or "quench the Spirit" (1 Thessalonians 5:19). *Grieving* is doing what the Holy Spirit doesn't want us to do. *Quenching* is resisting what the Holy Spirit wants us to do.

To better understand this, picture a freshwater river rushing from a snow-covered mountain into a lake. To maintain a flow of fresh water, both the inlet and outlet must be clear. If something dams up the incoming flow (grieving), fresh water doesn't arrive. Should something dam up the outflow (quenching), the water stagnates.

The Sea of Galilee and the Dead Sea are great examples. The Sea of Galilee remains fresh and teeming with life since it has a clear inlet and outlet. The Dead Sea, however, has no outlet. Even though the Jordan River brings fresh water into it from the Sea of Galilee, the Dead Sea maintains no life.

In the same way, we maintain a fresh-flowing fellowship with the Spirit of God as we listen, obey, and surrender to Him as He conforms us into Christlikeness. What the Holy Spirit restricts, we stop. What He removes, we yield. What He reveals, we apply to our lives. Where He leads, we follow.

Any revelation by the Holy Spirit through God's Word is absolute truth. When Jesus promised the arrival of the Holy Spirit, He said,

> When He, the Spirit of truth, has come, He will guide you into all truth … He will tell you things to come. (John 16:13)

The ability to reveal "things to come" points to omniscience. Again, all of God does all that God does.

All three persons of the Triune Godhead are omniscient and in agreement (1 John 5:7). As the Living Word of God, Jesus knows the "thoughts and intents" of our hearts (Hebrews 4:12). The Holy Spirit of God illuminates our minds as we read God's written Word. The Holy Spirit confirms everything Jesus said and did (John 16:14). As all are part of the Triune God, there's no conflict between them. All three eternally agree.

This also confirms that God doesn't lead anyone to do, think, or believe anything that conflicts with His Word or Spirit. God's purpose always aligns with His holiness.

Christ's Return Revealed—To Motivate Us

Genuine followers of Christ eagerly await His return.

Another omniscient revelation is the advance warning of Christ's return. He even promised a crown of righteousness to all who live with an urgent expectancy that we could meet Him any day (2 Timothy 4:8).

God specifically outlined the *what* and *how* of this mystery. Only the *when* remains.

> Behold, I tell you a mystery: We shall not all sleep [die], but we shall all be changed—in a moment, in the twinkling of an eye, at the last

trumpet. For the trumpet will sound, and the dead will be raised incorruptible, and we shall be changed. For this corruptible must put on incorruption, and this mortal must put on immortality.
(1 Corinthians 15:51-53)

The Lord Himself will descend from heaven with a shout, with the voice of an archangel, and with the trumpet of God. And the dead in Christ will rise first. Then we who are alive and remain shall be caught up [raptured] together with them in the clouds to meet the Lord in the air. And thus we shall always be with the Lord. (1 Thessalonians 4:16-17)

God has done everything possible to reveal His omniscience.

He created us. He placed His fingerprints throughout the world and universe. Jesus came to live a sinless life among us, teach us, and die an agonizing death for us. We have His eternal, written Word. The Holy Spirit convicts us, draws us to Christ, guides us into all truth, and transforms us into Christlikeness.

It's up to each person to accept Christ. We each must read, study, and meditate on God's Word as His infinite intelligence, foreknowledge, and wisdom. We each must choose to apply God's Word to our lives so we live in a way that pleases, honors, and glorifies Him. Each person faces the choice of surrendering to the Holy Spirit for spiritual illumination and supernatural transformation.

This is how we access and appropriate God's revealed omniscience on our journey to Christlikeness.

Why is Understanding God's Omniscience Important?

It's important to understand God's omniscience because we need to know we can trust Him fully. We can and need to be completely honesty with Him. After all, whatever we tell Him, He already knows.

That's the definition of *confession*: telling and agreeing with God on what He already knows (Amos 5:12). He patiently waits at the heart of each person, asking us to open it and invite Him into every aspect of our lives (Revelation 3:20).

Jesus promised, "If anyone loves Me, he will keep My word; and My Father will love him, and We will come to him and make Our home with him" (John 14:23). When invited in, the Triune God makes the human heart His permanent home. The decision is ours; the inner transformation is His.

Knowing and trusting His omniscience should make the decision easier. When we fully realize He created, called, chose, and commissioned us for Christlikeness, that should prompt us to joyfully embrace the journey.

Becoming like Christ involves accessing God's wisdom and perfect intelligence. We do this by spending undistracted, quality time with His Word and listening to His Spirit. His Word enlightens us (Psalm 119:105). His Spirit guides us into His truth (John 16:13).

As the omnipresent Source of all truth, who sees and knows our tomorrows, we can trust Him implicitly.

Personal Reflection

God has done all He can to reveal Himself to you. He's given you His Son (Jesus), His Word, His Holy Spirit, and the free will to choose for or against Him. How will you respond? Will you trust Him to fully accept all He has revealed? Will you begin the journey to follow Him and become like Him?

Chapter Nine

Omnipotence: Absolute and Unbounded Power

Fear not ... I am your God. I will strengthen you [omnipotence], yes, I will help you, I will uphold you with My righteous right hand. (Isaiah 41:10)

Building on what we've discovered from omnipresence and omniscience, we now focus on omnipotence.

We know *omni* means all—absolute and universal. *Potent* is "having or wielding force, authority, or influence; being powerful; achieving or bringing about a particular result."[29] Omnipotence, therefore, means absolute, sovereign power—unmatched, inexhaustible, reliable strength. It comes from the Greek word *Pantokratōr* (Παντοκράτωρ) that means All Powerful, Almighty, or Omnipotent.

Here are some Scripture references containing this word.

- "I will be a Father to you, and you shall be My sons and daughters," says the LORD Almighty [*Pantokratōr*]. (2 Corinthians 6:18)
- And I heard, as it were, the voice of a great multitude, as the sound of many waters and as the sound of mighty thunderings, saying, "Alleluia! For the Lord God Omnipotent [*Pantokratōr*] reigns!" (Revelation 19:6)
- "I am the Alpha and the Omega, the Beginning and the End," says the Lord, "who is and who was and who is to come, the Almighty [*Pantokratōr*]." (Revelation 1:8)
- Holy, holy, holy, Lord God Almighty [*Pantokratōr*], who was and is and is to come! (Revelation 4:8)

Other verses in Revelation also translate *Pantokratōr* as Almighty. Heaven resounds with worship and praise for Almighty, Omnipotent God. They recognize Him for who He is—absolutely all-powerful and sovereign—and worship Him in adoration.

Imagine the spiritual strength we'd have by keeping this majestic view of Jesus in mind. Let's follow Him in the power of that strength.

Human Weakness and Dependence

In 1957, Paul Anderson—dubbed the "world's strongest man" by the Guinness Book of Records—lifted 6,270 pounds in a back lift. It was touted as the "Greatest Lift."[30] That's the equivalent of eleven average car engines. From a human standpoint, if we needed a champion to represent us, that superhuman feat qualified him for the task.

In comparison, using math and the laws of gravity, scientists estimate the weight of the Earth to be 13 thousand, 170 trillion billion pounds.[31] Stated another way, it's one trillion elephants plus one billion pounds. If that isn't phenomenal enough, the sun weighs 333,000 times more than the Earth.[32]

As enormous, brilliant, and fiery as the sun is, it pales in comparison to Arcturus. That distant star is twenty-five times bigger than the sun and is just under thirty-seven light years from Earth.[33] Putting that in perspective, a light year is the time it takes light to travel in one year. That places Arcturus approximately 222 trillion miles from earth. Yet that colossal star only ranks as the fourth brightest star in the night sky, behind Sirius, Canopus and Alpha Centauri.[34] Even those are but a fraction of the universe as we know it.

Now for the truly amazing, mind-boggling fact.

Jesus spoke it all into existence.

That's the powerful Christ we follow!

To fully grasp omnipotence, we must admit our own weakness and dependence.

Some of us are stronger than others, but we all wear down eventually. Some people go to great lengths to exercise, do aerobics, spinning classes, gymnastics, whatever we can to strengthen our bodies and maintain overall health. But even at our peak, we eventually fade. We become exhausted and need to rest.

We try to stay healthy and energized. But we still grow old. Joints begin to ache. Ultimately, we slow down. At our biggest, baddest, and boldest, a stark reality still faces us all—physical death is inevitable (Hebrews 9:27).

Even Paul Anderson, "the world's strongest man," died on August 15, 1994.

Our Source of Strength

Our strength, resolve, and life itself all come from God.

Jesus said, "Without Me you can do nothing" (John 15:5). As Omniscient God, He knows our frailty (Psalm 103:14). And as our High Priest in heaven, He sympathizes with our weaknesses. In His humanity, He was "in all points tempted as we are, yet without sin" (Hebrews 4:15).

The Holy Spirit also helps in our weakness (Romans 8:26). We have an amazing power source. "The Lord is my strength" (Psalm 28:7). We have all the power we need through Christ (Colossians 1:29) by the energizing of the Holy Spirit (Ephesians 3:16). How marvelous to know that the infinite, eternal, omnipresent, omniscient, omnipotent Creator of everything makes Himself available to strengthen us!

But the counterintuitive secret of His strength lies in the recognition of our weakness and complete dependence on Him. The apostle Paul learned that only when he was weak, then he was strong (2 Corinthians 12:10).

How does this work? If we are strong in our own efforts, we tend to ignore or overlook God's strength.

When a parent offers to help a struggling child, a natural response is, "I do it!" The parent patiently watches the child's futility, knowing full well the need for greater strength and assistance. We tend to do the same. We tell God, "I do it" as He patiently waits for us to ask for His help.

Sadly, it's usually when we experience unbearable health issues, overwhelming difficulties, or harsh adversity that we turn our eyes to Jesus. How comforting to know that when we depend on God, He gives us His strength.

God told Paul, "My strength is made perfect in [your] weakness." To which Paul responded, "Therefore most gladly I will rather boast in my infirmities, that the power of Christ may rest upon me" (2 Corinthians 12:9).

The pursuit of Christlikeness involves allowing His strength, through the work of the Holy Spirit, to overcome our weaknesses. We surrender to God's will with the same submissive, obedient, humble disposition that Jesus had. In Gethsemane, He asked three times, if at all possible, His bitter cup might pass from Him. Yet He "learned obedience" by the things He suffered (Hebrews 5:7-8). He "humbled Himself and became obedient to the point of death, even the death of the cross" (Philippians 2:8). May we pray as He did, "Not my will but Yours be done."

In our journey toward Christlikeness, let's keep our eyes on Jesus. He endured the cross, despised the shame, and sat down at the right hand of the throne of God (Hebrews 12:2). Let's stay focused on the eternal while living through the temporary (2 Corinthians 4:17).

Unbounded, Measureless, Supreme Power

There cannot be two infinite, sovereign, omnipotent sources in the universe. One must be above all other powers and authorities to claim supreme rule.

Heaven already recognizes God's supreme rule. It's only a matter of time before the earth recognizes it too. Jesus taught us to pray for His absolute rule here on earth. "Your kingdom come. Your will be done on earth as it is in heaven" (Matthew 6:10).

Supreme rule means there's only one supreme Ruler—the "I AM WHO I AM" (Exodus 3:14). As already seen, Jesus used many "I am" statements. But one in particular directly connects to this verse. "Jesus said to them, 'Most assuredly, I say to you, before Abraham was, I AM'" (John 8:58). This clearly confirms "Jesus was the Jehovah of the Old Testament."[35]

Jesus will one day rule the universe with unquestioned power and unchallenged authority (Revelation 19:15-16). He will be King of kings and Lord of lords.

I AM. LORD. Jehovah. Almighty. Supreme Ruler. Immanuel. All identify Jesus as God.

Those on the journey toward Christlikeness follow such a supreme Ruler. May we live each day knowing we follow universal, infinite royalty.

Supreme Creator

Creation itself reveals Christ's omniscience and omnipotence.

Paul said the creation of the world clearly reveals His "eternal power and Godhead" (Romans 1:20). This removes all excuses for any doubters, unbelievers, or scoffers. All they have to do is look around at the wonders of creation.

To get a clear vision of Jesus, imagine the genius and power necessary to speak everything into existence.

In His omniscience, His creative *genius* invented all the varied animals, plants, insects, birds, and sea creatures. He originated expansive starry galaxies as well as miniscule laminin, the glycoprotein that holds our molecular cells together. He also made the tree from which the Cross was formed as well as Mount Moriah (Calvary) on which He would die.

Then in His omnipotence, His creative *power* made it all happen. He did it all effortlessly, without diminishing His strength, without fatigue, or any need to eat, rest, or sleep (Psalm 121:4). He simply spoke everything into existence, and all was obedient to His authoritative, omnipotent command.

> He has made the earth by His power; He has established the world
> by His wisdom, and stretched out the heaven by His understanding.
> (Jeremiah 51:15)

Everything comes from His omnipotent hand. Every person, angel, and creature in heaven understands this and erupts in praise for His unbounded, measureless power.

> You are worthy, O Lord, to receive glory and honor and power; for
> You created all things, and by Your will they exist and were created.
> (Revelation 4:11)

Through the prophet Isaiah, God said, "Is there a God besides Me? Indeed there is no other ... I know not one" (Isaiah 44:8). The theme of only one supreme Ruler continues into the New Testament. The apostle Paul confirmed, "There is no other God but one" (1 Corinthians 8:4). There's no other source of omnipotent power. Jesus said, "With God all things are possible" (Matthew 19:26).

Such is supreme power with no impossibility.

Supreme Sacrifice

Consider the magnitude of Jesus' sacrifice.

He laid aside all this glory and power and came to earth as a humble servant. He is referred to as both the power [omnipotence] and the wisdom [omniscience] of God (1 Corinthians 1:24). He displayed a veiled level of these while here on earth.

He displayed *omniscience* in His kingdom teaching, in His authoritative manner, and unchallenged wisdom. "No man ever spoke like this Man!" (John 7:46). "He taught them as one having authority" (Matthew 7:29).

He exhibited *omnipotence* in a variety of ways. Healing countless people. Walking on water. Turning water into wine. Feeding thousands with minimal food. Raising the dead. Casting out demons. But here's the primary evidence of His omnipotence. His ability to lay down His life and take it back up again.

> I lay down My life that I may take it again. No one takes it from Me, but I lay it down of Myself. I have power to lay it down, and I have power to take it again. (John 10:17-18)

Ready for another mind-blowing reality?

Abundant, Eternal Life

The same power that raised Christ from the dead dwells in every true follower of Christ (Ephesians 1:19-20).

This power gives us abundant and eternal life. Jesus said, "I have come that they may have life, and that they may have it more abundantly" (John 10:10). Some have mistaken this to mean the accumulation of possessions or wealth. But the Greek word translated *abundantly* refers to quality of life, not quantity of things accumulated.

Paul confirmed this indwelling power and overflowing, living, eternal life.

> But if the Spirit of Him who raised Jesus from the dead dwells in you, He who raised Christ from the dead will also give life to your mortal bodies through His Spirit who dwells in you. (Romans 8:11)

Notice, it isn't just eternal life in the hereafter. It's abundant life here, now, in our mortal bodies. Let this incredible truth sink deep into your soul.

This all-powerful, creative, life-giving, life-enabling, life-sustaining, ongoing, perpetuating, transforming power resides within every regenerated person. We have all the power necessary to live a Christlike life (2 Peter 1:3). We can do this! But we must surrender to that power to release its full authority.

This is why we must not grieve or quench the Holy Spirit. We embrace Him and authorize Him to take full control of our hearts, minds, and lives. We die to self daily and surrender fully to His work as He transforms us into the likeness of Jesus.

The pursuit of Christlikeness admits His supreme authority and surrenders fully to it.

Power with Loving Restraint

A superior power can compel or expect obedience. But only a loving, sacrificing, interceding, and energizing Power compels love and willing surrender.

A clear vision of God's omnipotence involves understanding His loving self-restraint. Just as Christ veiled His divine glory while on earth, His infinite love restricts His omnipotence in one way. Though He has all power, He coerces no one regarding salvation, self-denial, or surrender.

When God made man in His image, He sovereignly decreed man free to exercise moral choice. He didn't want robots who respond to Him without desire or choice. He wants us to willingly acknowledge Him, come to Him, and love Him of our own free will.

He puts it in our hearts to seek Him (John 6:44) and makes it possible to know Him (Romans 1:20). He loves us. He wants a personal relationship and intimate fellowship with each person. To accomplish this, He prompts His Spirit to draw us to himself. But He forces no one.

Yeah but, Nate, doesn't God's predestination override our free will?

That argument persists because it removes a person's accountability before God. Hiding behind a belief that God will do whatever He wants and we're just along for the ride presumes (quite falsely) that we are cleared from any personal responsibility.

Another view of this argument is from those who believe they are the *elect* who hold some greater privilege than the poor lost souls who aren't God's chosen few.

But there are too many invitations of "whoever will" in Scripture. The same God who wants all to come to repentance (2 Peter 3:9) and doesn't reject anyone who comes to Him (John 6:37) would contradict Himself if He already made up His mind regarding who He predestined.

On the contrary, He's the perfect gentleman who restricts His omnipotence to our personal choice. Numerous verses in God's Word reveal the individual freewill choice of "whoever" for salvation, self-denial, and surrender.

- Whoever believes in Him should not perish but have everlasting life. (John 3:16)
- Whoever believes in Me should not abide in darkness. (John 12:46)
- Whoever calls on the name of the Lord shall be saved. (Acts 2:21; Romans 10:13)
- Whoever desires to come after Me, let him deny himself, and take up his cross, and follow Me. (Mark 8:34)

Whoever, whoever, whoever drums out the cadence of free will.

To resolve the challenge of predestination between God's foreknowledge and man's free will, let's revisit God's foreknowledge. Foreknowledge is much different than predestination. To understand foreknowledge, we must step outside of time and dwell in eternity as God does. From that vantage point, and with omniscience, we then see all and know all.

Omnipresence allows us to move between the past, present, and future. Omniscience, or foreknowledge, knows who will do what, when, and where (Isaiah 46:10). But just because we foreknow an outcome doesn't mean we influence or coerce any actions or choices toward that outcome.

Presume, if you will, I have a friend living in the Amazon jungle. He has no contact with the outside world—no internet, news outlets, social media venues, nothing. After five years in that isolated environment, I invite him to come visit me. He says he'd love to watch last year's Super Bowl game.

Knowing I watched it and knew the final score, he asks me not to tell him anything about it. He wants to enjoy it from his unaware standpoint. If I tell him, "Don't bet against ..." and name the team who won the game, that's foreknowledge, not predestination. My comment in no way removed or restricted the coaches' play-calling or the players' action. They had free will as the game was played.

In the same way, God foreknows and foresees our freewill actions. He's fully aware of our choices and outcomes. He allows us to choose for or against Him. He foreknows who His *elect* will be. Yet forces or predestines no one.

This leads into our next topic of God's sovereignty. A less sovereign God—non-omnipresent, non-omniscient, non-omnipotent—wouldn't grant such moral freedom. He'd be afraid to do so. What if all His creation rebelled against Him? What if everyone He loved rejected Him? Yet All-Sovereign, Omni-Everything, I AM is large enough to grant and respect such moral freedom to choose.

Along with this freedom comes personal responsibility and consequences. Our free will invites a divine response, whether correction for our good (Hebrews 12:6) or eternal judgment for those who reject Him (Revelation 20:11-15). On this individual, freewill choice hangs our eternal destination and many aspects of this life. Forgiveness. Power over sin. Spiritual victory. Abundant life. Fulfilling life purpose. Inner peace. Unspeakable joy. Contentment.

No one can afford to get this choice wrong. Yet God still grants us the ability to choose. He reveals Himself and offers everything to those who choose Him. But He restricts His omnipotence by leaving that ultimate choice to us.

Christlikeness isn't forced. Those who choose to follow Him find the power to "walk worthy of the Lord ... strengthened with all might, according to His glorious power" (Colossians 1:10-11). In Him alone do we have the power to become like Him.

Why is Understanding God's Omnipotence Important?

By wrapping our minds around God's omnipotence, we come to realize we can rely on Him fully and find our strength in Him.

He alone empowers us to become Christlike. He can handle our struggles. When we stumble, He can lift us up. He welcomes our burdens, worries, and anxieties (1 Peter 5:7). His shoulders are big enough. We can give every burden to Him, fully trusting that He will sustain us (Psalm 55:22).

Blessed *is* the man whose strength *is* in You [God] (Psalm 84:5)

Christlikeness involves relying fully on His omnipotence instead of our own strength. We can't model Him in our own efforts. Instead of trying to show how strong we are, may we exhibit His humility, obedience, and surrender. May we shoulder our crosses and walk beside Him. Leaning when we must. Trusting all the way. Praying, "Not my will but Thine be done" in complete surrender.

Becoming like Christ involves accessing His supreme power. We do this by applying to our lives what we find in His Word. It's our instruction manual in what's right, what's wrong, how to get right, and how to stay right (2 Timothy 3:16).

Additionally, Christlikeness involves appropriating the power inherent in His infinite, eternal, energizing, life-giving blood. We accomplish this only through salvation in His name, forgiveness and cleansing by His blood (1 John 1:9), and sanctification through His Word (John 17:17). We also listen and surrender as His Spirit instructs, convicts, and guides in His ongoing transformation.

When we are weak, His omnipotent power makes us strong.

Personal Reflection

Are you struggling with burdens instead of releasing them to Jesus? Are you trying to follow Him your own way, in your own strength? Why not acknowledge that you're no match for His omnipotence? Are you willing to surrender to what He wants to do in your heart and life?

Chapter Ten

Sovereignty: Absolute Authority

The LORD does whatever pleases Him. (Psalm 135:6, NLT)

God is everywhere, knows everything, and has supreme power. But how can we be sure He's involved in the everyday details of life? To follow Someone we declare as sovereign Lord, we must be able to trust His control.

How do we know He's in control and sovereignly orchestrating all things, not just allowing random things to happen? Bad things happen to good, unsuspecting, even innocent people. Why does He allow this? If He's in control, why does it seem like He's absent?

We define sovereignty as supreme power, freedom from external control, and being autonomous.[36] It's the supreme authority of a self-governing entity. To be Sovereign God, He must be *omnipresent*. He cannot be absent from any place. He must be *omniscient*. There can be no secrets or anything of which He is unaware. He must be *omnipotent*. There can be no threats or competition against His authority. He must also be absolutely free with no boundaries. He can have no dependence on any other source or any interference with His ultimate purpose.

Since the Great I AM is all this and more, He is absolutely sovereign with absolute authority.

There cannot be two absolutely free beings in the universe, for sooner or later two completely free wills must collide.[37]

Christlikeness involves recognizing Jesus' absolute authority. This is the reason why we surrender fully and freely to Christ's Lordship.

Human Limitations and Lack of Control

Clearing our vision of God's sovereignty involves admitting our limited power and overall lack of control.

Contrary to popular belief, we aren't masters of our own destinies. Sure, we try to create our own fate and control our plans. But circumstances often affect and override our best attempts.

To a limited extent, we can control or manipulate some things. For example, I can have a ham and cheese sandwich for lunch. That's well within my control if I have, or can get, bread, ham, and cheese.

But life isn't that simple. Many things remain outside our control. To cope, we either accept or modify them as best we can. Uncontrollable variables affect us. Varying decisions. Different events. Changing circumstances. The free will of others.

At some point, we realize God orchestrates events and circumstances to fulfill His ultimate purpose. "A man's heart plans his way, but the LORD directs his steps" (Proverbs 16:9). We can plan everything down to the smallest detail, but God is still in control. Wise King Solomon discovered, "All things come alike to all: one event happens to the righteous and the wicked" (Ecclesiastes 9:2). He also said, "In the day of prosperity be joyful, but in the day of adversity consider: surely God has appointed the one as well as the other" (Ecclesiastes 7:14).

To encourage us against despairing at the seeming futility and randomness of life, God gives His assurance.

> All things work together for good to those who love God, to those who are the called according to His purpose. (Romans 8:28)

God has a purpose and He will fulfill it.

But how do we reconcile between pointless randomness and God's authoritative involvement? Let's look at a great example.

Joseph was around seventeen years old when we first read about him in Genesis 37. He endured horrible and undeserved treatment. His youth was stolen from him. Any career plans were shattered. He went from favored son to imprisoned convict in a matter of months. Both family and foreigners rejected, abused, and abandoned him. If this happened to any of us, how angry and resentful would we be? But not Joseph. He relied steadfastly on God and His sovereign control.

> Even though other people caused horrific and undeserved storms in his life, he forgave them. Instead of blaming others, he acknowledged God's sovereign hand working behind the scenes. With eyes of faith, he looked at the painful, humiliating, unjust, life-changing experiences and acknowledged, "You intended to harm me, but God intended it for good." What incredible trust![38]

Only an Omni-Everything God could move sovereignly and supernaturally through all those horrible events and immoral choices. He sovereignly wove all those threads into the fabric of His ultimate purpose. His presence never left Joseph. His foreknowledge and wisdom understood all the circumstances. He restrained His power to respect human moral choice. In spite of man's horrible use of free will, God coordinated everything to fulfill His ultimate will and plan. He saved His people from possible extinction and continued fulfilling His covenant promise to Abraham.

Without God's sovereign interaction, we'd be lost. Hopeless. Left to bounce around in an existence of randomness. Though we may not always understand it, thank God for His sovereign orchestration. He may not coerce our freewill choices, but He's always in control.

Sovereign Attributes

Let's look at God's attributes from the lens of infinity.

Both He and His attributes have no beginning (self-existent), end (eternal), or limits (infinite). He didn't start loving at John 3:16. He didn't start extending grace at the Cross. He didn't change between the Old and New Testaments. His attributes are infinite and eternal. They're also of spotless purity (holiness). All are incomprehensibly vast and immeasurably intense. All are uncaused and unchanging.

We can't expend, deplete, or fatigue who God is. He never contradicts Himself, His holy standard, His Word, or His character. We sometimes take moral shortcuts. But a holy outcome isn't achieved by unholy means. Holy God always acts in agreement with His holy nature and sovereign purpose.

He isn't *progressive* nor will He ever be. He is who He is and always will be. His attributes are inseparable, independent, incomparable, and immutable.

Inseparable

No attribute of God can be isolated from any other.

His mercy is as infinitely constant as His justice. His goodness is eternally the same as His holiness. His everlasting compassion and truth walk hand-in-hand. His love is inseparable from His discipline. His omnipresence and omniscience are forever linked (Psalm 139:1-18).

By isolating one attribute over the others, we cloud our vision. Oh, we relish His love, grace, mercy, and forgiveness, but we often overlook His holiness and justice. Yet His love for us doesn't negate His call for our obedience. His infinite, abundant grace doesn't grant us license to sin.

Paul said, "I do not frustrate [neutralize; nullify] the grace of God" (Galatians 2:21, KJV). And he said this right after saying, "I have been crucified with Christ; it is no longer I who live, but Christ lives in me" (Galatians 2:20).

Crucified, surrendered Christ followers don't presume against one of His attributes when it suits them. We accept Him in totality.

Independent

God is self-existent, self-sufficient, and absolutely autonomous.

He needs nothing. He has life in Himself (John 5:26). He can't and doesn't receive anything from us He hasn't first given us. For example, let's look at His attribute of love. We love Him because He first loved us (1 John 4:19). God pours His love into our hearts by the Holy Spirit who was given to us (Romans 5:5). Then we have the capacity to love others (John 13:35).

He first gives us His love. Only then can we love Him as well as others. This isn't a comfortable feeling of loving those we like. It's the all-encompassing demonstration of loving as Jesus does. Genuine followers of Christ have this as a distinguishing characteristic. Love is in our spiritual DNA because God is our Father.

It's the same with the praise we offer Him. King David, the Psalmist, said, "I will bless the LORD at all times; His praise *shall* continually *be* in my mouth" (Psalm 34:1). He didn't say, *my* praise but *His* praise. We praise Him, not from our graciousness or wealth of wisdom, but in response to His righteousness, salvation, holiness, grace, mercy, and all other attributes.

How humbling to know all we have, all we offer Him, comes from Him.

Our loving Him, praising Him, believing or doubting Him, neither adds nor takes away anything from Him. He is who He is. We respond to what He has given and done for us.

Incomparable

As Almighty, Omni-Everything, Sovereign God, He doesn't *need* us.

That might shock those who selfishly think their spiritual contribution is irreplaceable. *I have to serve God because things wouldn't get done if I didn't. I have to teach a Bible study class because it's expected of someone with my spiritual knowledge. I have to tithe because God needs my money.* That mindset doesn't understand the infinity of God. He doesn't *need* any of us—but He *wants* us.

In His infinite, sovereign love, He invites us to participate with Him in His plans and purposes. Being part of His eternal kingdom is our highest calling and utmost privilege. Everything He gives us—time, finances, and talents—is for this purpose.

Since He is holy, all His attributes are holy. Holy love. Holy grace. Holy mercy. Holy justice. Everything that is His is holy.

This includes His genuine followers. This is why He says, "As He who called you is holy, you also be holy in all your conduct, because it is written, 'Be holy, for I am holy'" (1 Peter 1:15-16). *All conduct* means God's holiness floods every aspect of the lives of true followers of Jesus. Holiness is a trait of genuine children of God. It isn't legalistic or forced holiness in our best efforts. Nor is it an unrealistic, unreachable, utopian concept. God wouldn't expect it of us if it wasn't possible.

As already seen, "He chose us in Him ... that *we should be holy* and without blame before Him" (Ephesians 1:4, italics added). "God did not call us to uncleanness, *but in holiness*" (1 Thessalonians 4:7, italics added). "Pursue ... holiness, without which no one will see the Lord" (Hebrews 12:14).

This last verse alone is compelling enough for us to pursue a life marked by Christlikeness.

Immutable

God is immutable. He is unchanging and faithful. All of God does all that God does. All He does aligns with all He is.

For example, since He is love and since He is infinite, His love is infinite. Nothing we do reduces His infinite love. Sure, we break His heart when we reject or disobey Him. But we simply cannot decrease or deplete His love.

Nothing in the universe prevents Him from loving us (Romans 8:38-39). Zephaniah said God will "quiet you with His love" (Zephaniah 3:17). King Solomon said, "His banner over me is love" (Song of Solomon 2:4). Picture a plane flying overhead with a huge banner that declares: I LOVE YOU! God's infinite love won't ever leave us. And this is just one of His many attributes.

Oh, what peace we have trusting who and what He declares Himself to be and do. "You will keep him in perfect peace, whose mind is stayed on You, because he trusts in You" (Isaiah 26:3). From this verse alone we see how God's infinite love and infinite peace interact.

Now apply that infinity and immutability to all God's other attributes. Wow!

Sovereign Deity

Absolute sovereignty means there can be only one ruler in authority.

There can be only one God.

The Infinite, Omni-Everything, Sovereign God we're discovering repeatedly revealed this about Himself. Moses declared, "The LORD our God, the LORD is one!" (Deuteronomy 6:4). Jesus, God with us (Immanuel), reiterated that declaration (Mark 12:29). The prophet Isaiah echoed that theme. "I *am* the LORD, that *is* My name; and My glory I will not give to another" (Isaiah 42:8). In His high priestly prayer, Jesus referenced the singularity of "the only true God" (John 17:3).

Regardless of other religions or opinions, there is only one true I AM.

- Before Me there was no God formed, nor shall there be after Me. I, *even* I, *am* the LORD, and besides Me *there* is no savior. (Isaiah 43:10-11)

- The LORD *is* the true God; He *is* the living God and the everlasting King. (Jeremiah 10:10)

Paul spelled things out quite clearly. "For us there is one God, the Father … and one Lord Jesus Christ" (1 Corinthians 8:6). This links the sovereignty of God the Father with the sovereignty of God the Son, Jesus.

We've already seen evidence of Jesus' deity in how He laid down His life and had power to take it up again (John 10:17-18). He surrendered His Spirit into His Father's hands at Calvary (Luke 23:46). He foretold His resurrection (Matthew 16:21) then He walked out of the grave (Matthew 28:6). He does what He does because He is who He is—Sovereign God.

Linking Saviorship to Lordship

Many people readily admit the *Saviorship* of Jesus. But they often resist or reject His *Lordship*.

We understand and accept several things about Him as Savior. He came to earth as the Savior of mankind (1 John 4:14). He died for the sins of the whole world (1 John 2:2). But then we start seeing the word *Lord* in reference to Jesus. There is one Father, one Lord, and one Spirit (Ephesians 4:4-6). "The … gift of God is eternal life in Christ Jesus our Lord" (Romans 6:23). We don't get the gift without the Giver. Notice how Scripture highlights the Lordship of Christ.

- If we confess with our mouths "the Lord Jesus" and believe in our hearts that God raised Him from the dead, we will be saved. (Romans 10:9)
- Whoever calls on the name of "the LORD" will be saved. (Romans 10:13)
- Believe on "the Lord Jesus Christ," and you will be saved. (Acts 16:31)
- Grow in the grace and knowledge of our "Lord and Savior Jesus Christ." (2 Peter 3:18)

If Jesus isn't Lord, He cannot be Savior.

Yeah but, Nate, I've accepted Jesus as my Savior. Why is His Lordship important?

There's no disconnect between His redeeming Saviorship and His sovereign Lordship. He's the same Person with inseparable titles. He is "the Lamb slain from the foundation of the world" (Revelation 13:8). By Him all things were created (John 1:3). As the Creator of everything, He is Lord over everything.

Imagine telling Him, *Thank You for dying a horrible death for me and saving me from eternity in hell. Now, just let me live my life, and I'll try to keep You happy. You rule things in heaven; let me rule my time on earth.* This will never be acceptable.

But it seems many people want the relationship that way. They fear going to hell for eternity and readily accept Jesus as personal Savior. However, the Lordship thing—that's where the struggle for authority begins. But if Jesus isn't Lord *of* all, He's not Lord *at* all.

There's no partial Lordship.

Either we surrender everything to Him or He isn't our Lord. The benefit of heaven comes with the surrender to the One who makes heaven possible. As Sovereign Lord, our free will must bow before Him. Sooner or later, it will—either voluntarily while still alive here on earth or involuntarily when we stand before Him (Philippians 2:9-11).

For those who wait until the hereafter to declare His Lordship, it'll be too late. As eternal Judge, He will then sentence them to eternal damnation.

As His creation, made in His image, we're His by *creative* right. As the sacrificial, crucified, and risen Lord, we're His by *redemptive* right. Either way, we're His and He is absolute Lord.

Jesus said, "A disciple is not above his teacher, but everyone who is perfectly trained will be like his teacher" (Luke 6:40). The master-servant, teacher-student, Jesus-follower relationship is plainly evident. The subordinate isn't above his superior. A Christ follower takes up his cross, dies to self, and follows [obeys; becomes like] Christ.

The word *perfectly* in this verse implies becoming complete or putting something in its appropriate position. The grammatical tense behind "everyone who is perfectly trained" is a completed action with continuing results. As we follow, surrender to, and obey Jesus, we become more like Him. Obedience and love are eternally connected. In fact, obeying God is the truest and fullest test of our love for Him.

A son honors *his* father and a servant *his* master. If then I am the Father, where *is* My honor? And if I *am* a Master, where *is* My reverence?" says the LORD of hosts. (Malachi 1:6)

Why is Understanding God's Absolute Authority Important?

In a Lordship relationship, "a servant is not greater than his master" (John 15:20). If we claim to be in a personal relationship with Jesus as Savior, the only way that happens is by first claiming Him as Lord.

Lordship requires individual surrender. Surrender means the war of wills is over. The resistance, the struggling, the negotiation—all done. Once we choose Him, we're all in. We surrender to His absolute authority and obey what He says in His Word. If there's a Lord, there's a servant. If there isn't a servant, there isn't a Lord (Romans 6:16-18).

God's ultimate purpose for genuine Christ followers is Christlikeness (Romans 8:29). Let's surrender to that purpose and embrace the pursuit of being transformed into His likeness. May we renew our minds (Romans 12:2). May we yield to what the Holy Spirit wants to do in us (2 Corinthians 3:18). Jesus has absolute authority since He created everything—even us—and it all belongs to Him.

The journey of Christlikeness comes full circle. We surrender to Jesus as Lord. We embrace Him as Savior. We yield to the Spirit as He transforms us. And we do this all because "we are His workmanship, created in Christ Jesus for good works, which God prepared beforehand that we should walk in them" (Ephesians 2:10).

His workmanship.
Created for good works.
Called to Christlikeness before time began.
Wow!

Personal Reflection

How does knowing God has absolute authority over everything affect you? Is there any trace of resisting His authority? Remember, God forces no one. Do you willingly and gladly embrace Him as both Lord and Savior? How can viewing all His holy attributes combined help on the journey to becoming more Christlike?

Chapter Eleven

Sovereignty: Divine Orchestration

Behold, I am the LORD ... Is there anything too hard for Me?
(Jeremiah 32:27)

Nothing happens without first passing through the sieve of God's allowance.

This doesn't mean God approves or causes bad things. He's still on the throne and sovereignly in control. But we naturally question why disturbing and disgusting things happen. Babies born with deformities. Church and school shootings. Genocide in various parts of the globe. Racist attacks. Abortion on demand. Anti-Semitism. Perverse preferences protected by legislature. Tornadoes ripping through towns.

This crazy, upside-down world seems out of control. People call evil good and good evil (Isaiah 5:20). In exercising our God-given free will, humans do some horrifying things.

Through it all, God faithfully works behind the scenes. Although He foresees and knows all, He doesn't override anyone's free will. Should He do so, it would no longer be *free* but mandated. Yes, He sometimes orchestrates circumstances and disciplines to prompt certain behavior (think Balaam's donkey). But He strong-arms no one.

Here's the sobering reality. Along with free will comes the associated consequences of how we exercise it. King Nebuchadnezzar learned this the hard way. After God disciplined him for his pride, he said, "[God] does according to His will ... No one can restrain His hand or say to Him, 'What have You done?'" (Daniel 4:35).

A psalmist echoed this reality: "Our God ... does whatever He pleases" (Psalm 115:3). Even Job, after suffering the loss of everything, confirmed God's unexplained yet sovereign ways. "The LORD gave, and the LORD has taken away; blessed be the name of the LORD" (Job 1:21).

Christ followers recognize God's sovereign orchestration. We trust Him to fulfill all things, according to His plan and purpose, for His glory and our good.

Impressive Coordination

In His sovereign omniscience and omnipotence, God coordinates events and circumstances in different ways.

As an example, when the Israelites finally left the bondage of Egypt, Pharaoh had second thoughts. He gathered his army and chased after them. The Israelites were no match for Pharaoh's speed because they had children, animals, and household belongings. When Moses saw the approaching army, he cried out to God for help.

Instead of raining fire down from heaven on the Egyptians, God sent a cloud between the two groups.

> So it came between the camp of the Egyptians and the camp of Israel. Thus it was a cloud and darkness to the one, and it gave light by night to the other, so that the one did not come near the other all that night. (Exodus 14:20)

One cloud, yet different effects and results for each group. That's sovereign orchestration. God sees all and coordinates all to His ultimate plan and purpose.

In our limited mental capacity, we don't always understand God's sovereign orchestration. A seeming downturn for one may be a blessing for another. As hard as it may be to understand, a sudden, unexplained heart attack may be a blessing in disguise. That person's clogged arteries may have created a blood clot that would've disabled him for life. God in His mercy took him home to avoid such a stroked-out existence.

We simply won't know all answers until we meet the Great I AM face-to-face. We can't figure it out now because His thoughts are not our thoughts nor does He do things like we would do them (Isaiah 55:8-9).

Genuine Christ followers accept His wisdom and rest in His presence. In doing so, we learn to rely on His power and trust His faithful precision.

Absolute Precision

God's faithful precision and sovereign orchestration give science and faith their foundations.

God established inviolable laws through which He coordinates everything. As long as we respect these laws, we're safe. When we don't, we suffer the foreordained consequences. There are creative laws, physical laws, and moral laws.

Creative Laws

Among other things, creative laws include seasons and reproduction.

God established the four seasons with a progressive order. We anticipate Spring to follow Winter and begin planting accordingly. To expect a harvest in the cold of Winter is foolish.

In Genesis we find reproduction "after its kind." We don't expect to get kittens out of chicken eggs or peaches from grape vines. God's law of harvesting is precise: we reap what we sow (Galatians 6:7). This applies in nature as well as in our lives.

Sometimes in His sovereign justice, God allows what we sow to yield an exponential harvest. "They sow the wind and reap the whirlwind" (Hosea 8:7). After all, a planted kernel of corn yields a cornstalk full of ears of corn. This explains why some negative consequences may seem extreme compared to the crime. "There is a way that seems right to a man, but its end is the way of death" (Proverbs 14:12).

But the opposite also holds true. God blesses our good seed too. "He who sows to the Spirit will of the Spirit reap everlasting life" (Galatians 6:8).

Physical Laws

Some of the more well-known physical laws involve gravity and electricity.

Gravity is a great thing. Imagine the chaos and danger if it didn't exist and things just floated around or off into space. But gravity is also harmful when disrespected. Should I believe I can fly and jump off a cliff, gravity reminds me of the foolishness of my choice.

Electricity is another great example. In its proper use, it is highly beneficial. Flip a switch and a room lights up. Turn on an electric stove and you can cook a meal. An electric blanket will keep you warm. But disrespect the law of electricity and you'll get the shock of your life. Possibly worse. The power is always there, but the results depend on how we respond to that power.

Actions have consequences. Even though modern, progressive thought leans toward removing personal accountability for choices, God doesn't recognize such nonsense. His laws are fixed and without excuse. We disrespect them at our own peril.

Moral Laws

God's moral laws are no different than His other precise laws.

We reap what we sow. God isn't mean. He's a holy God who created us in an environment of certain moral laws. Only two genders: male and female (Mark 10:6). Only a man and woman in marriage (Genesis 2:24). Run away from youthful lusts (2 Timothy 2:22). Lay aside your preferred sin or it will ensnare you (Hebrews 12:1).

Such moral laws aren't insensitive, intolerant, or any other word we wish to attach to them. God is who He is. As Infinite, Omni-Everything, Sovereign Creator, and absolute Lord, He sets the rules. We can reject, rebel against, or ignore them if we choose to do so. But that won't change them—or the consequences of our choices.

It isn't hateful or bigoted to speak God's truth as long as I do it in love (Ephesians 4:15) and not legalistic, self-righteous condemnation. Because I speak loving truth about His moral laws doesn't make me any more hateful than if I warned someone against touching an ungrounded, uninsulated wire. Should someone say, *Just let me (fill in the blank)*, that's as foolish as saying, *Just let me shove this electrified wire in my eye.*

God's laws, especially His moral laws, exist for our protection. They also guarantee against surprises. Imagine the anxiety of planting a crop not knowing what would grow. A strawberry farmer would be ruined if he found his fields covered in cucumbers or thorns. Trying to manipulate God's moral laws to suit our immoral preferences directly opposes sovereign God. And we suffer the associated consequences.

We don't have to apologize for or defend what God has said. His Word is what it is. It stands on its own merit and has stood the test of time. God does what He does and says what He says because He is who He is. As Absolute Ruler, He makes the rules.

Sovereign Majesty and Throne Room

To get a clearer vision of God's absolute and majestic sovereignty, let's peek inside heaven's throne room.

Until we actually reach that place, our eyes of faith look through the eyes of those who had such a glorious vision. After reading through the following scenarios, close your eyes and imagine being there. Let your heart leave the runway of the temporal and soar to those celestial, majestic heights.

Here's what the prophet Isaiah saw.

> I saw the Lord sitting on a throne, high and lifted up … Above it stood seraphim … one cried to another and said: "Holy, holy, holy *is* the LORD of hosts; the whole earth is full of His glory! (Isaiah 6:1-3)

After seeing this, Isaiah cried out, "Woe *is* me, for I am undone! Because I *am* a man of unclean lips … my eyes have seen the King, the LORD of hosts" (Isaiah 6:5). Can you picture it? The sight brought him to his knees. He acknowledged God's majesty and his own unworthiness.

The prophet Daniel, referred to as a "man greatly beloved" by God, also had a heavenly vision.

> The Ancient of Days [Father God] was seated; His garment *was* white as snow, and the hair of His head *was* like pure wool. His throne *was* a fiery flame, its wheels a burning fire; a fiery stream issued and came forth from before Him. A thousand thousands [1 million] ministered to Him; ten thousand times ten thousand [100 million] stood before Him. And behold, *One* like the Son of Man [Jesus], coming with the clouds of heaven! He came to the Ancient of Days, and … to Him was given dominion and glory and a kingdom, that all peoples, nations, and languages should serve Him. His dominion is an everlasting dominion, which shall not pass away, and His kingdom *the one* which shall not be destroyed. (Daniel 7:9-10, 13-14)

The majestic view of Sovereign God on His throne made Daniel "grieved" and "troubled" (Daniel 7:15). He said, "my thoughts greatly troubled me, and my countenance changed" (Daniel 7:28). After subsequent visions, he "fainted and was sick for days" (Daniel 8:27). This heavenly, powerful sight distressed him mentally, emotionally, and physically.

Let's move forward approximately seven hundred years to a small island called Patmos, off the coast of modern-day Turkey. The apostle John was exiled there due to severe anti-Christian persecution under Roman Emperor Domitian. While there, John also saw incredible heavenly visions.

> Behold, a throne set in heaven, and *One* sat on the throne. Around the throne *were* twenty-four thrones, and on the thrones I saw twenty-four elders sitting, clothed in white robes; and they had crowns of gold on their heads. And from the throne proceeded lightnings, thunderings, and voices. And in the midst of the throne, and around the throne, *were* four living creatures ... *The* four living creatures ... do not rest day or night, saying: "Holy, holy, holy, Lord God Almighty, Who was and is and is to come!" Whenever the living creatures give glory and honor and thanks to Him who sits on the throne, who lives forever and ever, the twenty-four elders fall down before Him who sits on the throne and worship Him who lives forever and ever, and cast their crowns before the throne, saying: "You are worthy, O Lord, to receive glory and honor and power; for You created all things, and by Your will they exist and were created." (Revelation 4:2-11)

Can you picture it? Imagine the majesty, splendor, and raw power emanating from the throne of Almighty, Triune God. Hear the thunderous praise and reverent worship from all who are in His presence.

John, who leaned against Jesus during the Last Supper and who was also called, "beloved," fell prostrate several times during his vision. He vividly described his Friend, the Lamb of God, Jesus.

> The four living creatures and the twenty-four elders fell down before the Lamb ... And they sang a new song, saying: "You are worthy ... for You were slain, and have redeemed us to God by Your blood." Then ...

I heard the voice of many angels around the throne, the living creatures, and the elders; and the number of them was ten thousand times ten thousand [100 million], and thousands of thousands [innumerable], saying with a loud voice: "Worthy is the Lamb who was slain to receive power and riches and wisdom, and strength and honor and glory and blessing!" And every creature which is in heaven and on the earth and under the earth and such as are in the sea, and all that are in them, I heard saying: "Blessing and honor and glory and power be to Him who sits on the throne, and to the Lamb, forever and ever!" (Revelation 5:8-13)

Oh, the splendid glory and thunderous praise to Almighty God, the Lamb, Jesus Christ, and to the Holy Spirit for who They are and what They have done! Millions of voices ring out as all genuine followers of Christ gather around that sovereign throne.

The voices of true Christ followers will join them one day soon.

Behold, a great multitude which no one could number, of all nations, tribes, peoples, and tongues, standing before the throne and before the Lamb … crying out with a loud voice, saying, "Salvation *belongs* to our God who sits on the throne, and to the Lamb!" All the angels stood around the throne and the elders and the four living creatures, and fell on their faces before the throne and worshiped God, saying: "Amen! Blessing and glory and wisdom, thanksgiving and honor and power and might, be to our God forever and ever. Amen." (Revelation 7:9-12)

All who encountered such close contact with God, or even a vision of Him, fell in weakness, unworthiness, worship, reverence, and godly fear. The awesomeness of His sovereignty, His unapproachable light, far exceeds the presence of any earthly ruler.

Abraham. Joshua. Isaiah. Jeremiah. Ezekiel. Daniel. Peter. Paul. John. All these righteous, godly saints fell in worship when they encountered His presence. All surrendered to His sovereign authority.

This is the Christ we follow and represent!

May we, like righteous Job, acknowledge His majesty and sovereign rule over everything. Job confessed, "Now my eye sees You. Therefore I abhor *myself* and repent in dust and ashes" (Job 42:5-6).

Christlikeness involves a humble, reverent understanding of who Jesus is. It involves seeing Him high and lifted up, no longer the obedient, suffering Lamb, but the victorious Lion of Judah seated upon His throne in glory. He is worthy of our praise and surrender.

How mind-boggling to know the privilege of following and serving the mighty, sovereign God. Even more so, what an incomprehensible opportunity to surrender to His transformation as He conforms us into His likeness.

Why is Understanding God's Sovereignty Important?

It's important to understand, respect, trust, and surrender to God's sovereignty because it motivates authentic Christlikeness.

God is worthy of our trust, obedience, service, and worship. In Him alone do we find our true identity and worth. "In Him we live and move and have our being" (Acts 17:28). We've been bought and paid for by the precious [costly] blood of Jesus (1 Peter 1:18-19). In Him alone do we find significance and purpose. Through Him alone are possible eternal kingdom roles and rewards.

God's rewards are as faithful as His law of sowing and reaping. He rewards faithful, loving service with His favor in this life and rewards in the life to follow. If we pursue God's righteousness, He rewards with mercy (Hosea 10:12). Our ultimate reward is to see a smile on His face and hear Him say, "I see My Son in you. Well done, good and faithful servant."

Christlikeness involves trusting His mindset, His Word, and His divine orchestration even when we don't understand it. It's placing our faith, allegiance, and well-being in Jesus Christ alone. It's fully surrendering to Him as Lord and not allowing our self-life to usurp the throne of our lives.

Being Christlike is living each day in complete surrender to His perfect will. This isn't a begrudging surrender—it's delighting in, having strong affection for and attraction to, God's perfect will (Psalm 40:8).[39] May we pray daily, "God, help me live a life that pleases You. Purify my heart and remove from me all those things, situations, and people who diminish my intimacy with You. As Lord of my life, may I honor You in my behavior, thoughts, motives, lifestyle, and reputation. Help me trust you in all events and circumstances."

Personal Reflection

Since God is sovereign, how does that affect your freewill choices and outlook on life's circumstances? How does it affect your view of setting yourself apart (being holy) for Him? How does it affect your identity, self-worth, and purpose? How does it affect your participation in God's kingdom? What troubling or challenging event are you facing? Do you trust Him in it?

SECTION 3

Embracing the Christ of Calvary

Chapter Twelve

Calvary: Why Did Jesus Die?

*Without Jesus, the Bible makes no sense;
without His atoning death on the cross, the Bible makes no difference.*[40]

Bullying makes my blood boil. Out of pure meanness and rottenness of soul, bullies torment others who they believe are weaker than themselves. Having been bullied in junior high school, I'm familiar with its humiliation and pain. But my current height and size discourage such nonsense now.

I try to protect and defend those who experience it. But I struggle between encouraging the bullied to stand up for themselves and me knocking some sense into the bullies. Domestic violence is a particularly disgusting form of bullying. I can't watch scenes with this type of violence on television or in movies. I find it repulsive.

When I realize the incredible torment Jesus suffered at the hands of His bullies, I want to lash out. "Leave Him alone!" Yet my accusing finger is covered in blood. My clenched fists hold the hammer and nails. Knowing it was my sin (and yours) that nailed Jesus to the cross sickens me.

Because of our spiritual bullying, Jesus suffered the agony of Calvary. Yet this time we cannot, we dare not, look away.

> King of my life I crown Thee now—Thine shall the glory be;
> Lest I forget Thy thorn-crowned brow, lead me to Calvary.
> Lest I forget Gethsemane, lest I forget Thine agony,
> Lest I forget Thy love for me, lead me to Calvary.[41]

Reality of Calvary

Becoming Christlike is impossible without Calvary.

A clear view of Calvary helps us understand Jesus better and why He did what He did there. True Christ followers appreciate Calvary's significance and cherish it with deepest reverence.

Yet most people hesitate to linger there. It's a horrible place of horrific consequence.

Infinite innocence, purity, and sinlessness was murdered. Hell raged in fury against the great I AM. Demons slithered and hissed. Satan gloated in apparent victory. Human nature revealed its ugliness as free will rebelled against its Grantor. Creation held its collective breath as the Creator climbed that hill to die.

Though foreordained before time began, the crucifixion ordeal was nonetheless excruciatingly real. Bible expositor, John Phillips, captured its grotesque details.

> It would be hard to imagine a more cruel death than crucifixion. There was the fearful pain as the iron nails were driven through hands and feet. There was the sickening thud as the cross was dropped into its socket, the agonizing continuous pain as the weight of the body was thrown onto the nail wounds, and the torture of the unnatural position and of disjointed bones. In many cases, as with that of Christ, the whole terrible business came after the victim had been scourged to the bone. Every movement sent fresh stabs of pain through the nervous system. The sufferer had to cope with the lacerated veins, crushed tendons, inflammation, terrible cramps from tortured muscles and swelling arteries, especially those of the stomach. Added to all this were the swarming flies, the burning heat, the raging thirst.[42]

Keep in mind this was Jesus. The Son of God. The eternal, uncreated, self-existent second person of the Godhead. God with us. Our loving Creator. Sovereign Lord. The One adored and praised by seraphim, cherubim, and countless angels for eternity—all who watched in horror as mankind murdered Him. Surely, they must have "strained against the battlements of heaven"[43] waiting for one small sign to come to Jesus' aid.

Jesus said He could have twelve legions of angels at His immediate disposal (Matthew 26:53). A Roman legion was approximately five to six thousand soldiers. This means there were potentially seventy-two thousand angels on standby. This is an astonishing number considering one angel killed one-hundred eighty-five thousand people in one night (2 Kings 19:35). One word from Jesus would have annihilated the planet's entire population.

And yet that signal for assistance never came.

Instead, Jesus prayed, "Father, forgive them."

Scripture doesn't go into the gory details of the crucifixion. That's left for historians, researchers, authors, and movie producers. The most vivid portrayal I've seen of Christ's sufferings is Mel Gibson's 2004 movie, *The Passion of The Christ*.[44]

I recall sitting in a packed movie theater, stunned, tears streaming. I couldn't move or process what I'd just seen. I've studied Scripture and the crucifixion story for decades. Yet the movie's visual effects burned a lasting imprint on my mind.

Scripture sums it up in four short words. "There they crucified Him" (Luke 23:33).

Most everyone has heard the crucifixion story. They've seen movies, read books, or heard sermons on it. Yet as time weaves its dulling cobwebs across our minds, we forget. Familiarity truly does breed contempt. We know the story so well we become familiarized, complacent, and almost flippant about it. Even worse, we develop a sense of entitlement to the sacrificial love that purposed Jesus to that cross.

Yet as we discover Infinite, Eternal, Omni-Everything, Sovereign I AM, we face a new realization. This same Jesus gave His life in this unimaginably horrific manner for me. For you. Infinity for the finite. Sinlessness for the sinner. Holiness for the utterly impure. Love for pure hatred. He who spoke everything into existence and holds it in the palms of His hands, surrendered to Almighty wrath and man's worst treatment.

We can barely wrap our minds around the *Who* of Calvary. Now to try and grasp the significance of *why* ...

Sin and Our Sin Nature

To get a clear vision of Calvary, we need to understand sin and our sin nature.

The cross of Calvary knows no compromise. It exposes us for who and what we truly are. It reveals the evil core of human nature—and provides the remedy. The *what* of human sinfulness explains the *why* of Calvary.

No one enjoys confronting the reality of sin. Some people argue against its reality. Others downplay it, pointing to moral people or momentary heroics. But the reality remains.

- There is none righteous, no, not one; there is none who understands; there is none who seeks after God. (Romans 3:10-11)
- All have sinned and fall short of the glory of God. (Romans 3:23)

Sure, there are morally good people. Yet God's Word clearly explains the impassable gulf between His holy standard and our best efforts. Breaking even the smallest part of God's moral law renders a person guilty of it all (James 2:10). In comparison to God's holy standard, our moral best is like a pile of disgusting, rotting rags (Isaiah 64:6).

Sin is all-inclusive. Since the Fall in the Garden of Eden, it runs rampant in every human soul from birth.

Yeah but Nate ...

Now is not the time to defend or excuse whatever mindset we may have. Sin is real. Just look at young children. As precious as they are, we don't have to teach them to get angry. They don't need to learn to pout, yank toys away from other children, or scream in defiance. That is evidence of the inbred sin nature exposing itself without outside influence.

And we don't get to define what is or isn't sin. God has already defined it. We don't have the authority to excuse or justify our sinful habits and preferences because we want to maintain them. Nor can we change God's mind about sin or its ultimate judgment. The only option we have is to accept God's authoritative view and remedy for sin.

Origin of Sin

Many people believe "original sin" began in the Garden of Eden.

Here again, simply believing something doesn't make it true. Surprisingly, sin originated in heaven. It was Lucifer, son of the morning, chief among cherubs, who introduced sin (Isaiah 14:12-17).

God created Lucifer as a beautiful worship leader in charge of heaven's music. But he became proud. "I will ascend into heaven; I will exalt my throne above the stars of God; I will also sit on the mount ... I will ascend above the heights of the clouds, I will be like the Most High."

Can you see it? "I ... I ... I ..." What's the middle letter in the words *sin and pride?*

In his pride, Lucifer exalted himself. He rejected God's sovereign authority. And his rebellion against God became his downfall. Expelled from heaven, he made earth his new realm.

Enraged, he turned his attention and poisonous whispers to Eve. He refused God's authority and didn't want mankind under God's authority either. He "opposes and exalts himself above all that is called God or that is worshiped" (2 Thessalonians 2:4). The thought of humans worshiping, praising, and serving the God he loathes only stokes his hatred. So he strategically assaults the human race with his infectious disease.

Definition of Sin

In a nutshell, sin is contempt for the authority of God as Sovereign Lord.

It is puny creatures shaking their collective fists in God Almighty's face and shouting, "We won't recognize Your rightful authority and rule over us!" At its core, it is pride and self-sufficiency. An arrogant independence from God. It's the childish "I do it" mentality.

Various words in Scripture describe sin as moral crookedness or distortion. It is perversity at its worst. Restless lawlessness. Revolt and defiance against God. "Missing the mark" of God's moral standard. Imagine all mankind trying to jump over the Grand Canyon. Some might make it farther than others, but all inevitably fail and fall to their deaths.

Sin is a moral pollution that clings to our souls. It's a determined, hellbent opposition to God that blinds our spirits to its ugliness. There's no favorable outcome with sin.

The apostle Paul acknowledged, "I know that in me ... nothing good dwells" (Romans 7:18). He wrote most of the New Testament and evangelized a large portion of the world. If he admitted the sinfulness of his heart, the rest of us are equally in trouble.

Sin is so putrid, so rancid that when Jesus took on our sins at Calvary, God the Father turned away. In His holiness, He couldn't look upon such a sight. He darkened the sun for three hours to cover the scene (Luke 23:44-45). In this separation, Jesus cried out, "Why have You forsaken Me?" (Mark 15:34). Never before and never since did such divine separation exist.

But that's the nature of sin—it separates us from God.

> Your iniquities have separated you from your God; and your sins have hidden His face from you, so that He will not hear. (Isaiah 59:2)

There are no minor or *pet* sins. No excusable white lies or divine winks at minor indiscretions. God doesn't grade on the curve. He doesn't chuckle and say, *Oh gosh, Nate fibbed again. He's such a character*. As holy God, no sin is excused. His moral standard isn't progressive. His Word tell us, "All unrighteousness is sin" (1 John 5:17). *All* includes every sin, by every person.

To underscore sin's severity, Jesus said, "Whoever commits sin is a slave of sin" (John 8:34). Contrary to man's belief, sin isn't the freedom to do as we please. It's sheer bondage. Just ask any addict. What seemed pleasurable became unbearable—an unbreakable chain. What seems appealing in the moment eventually becomes appalling.

To get a better picture of sin's enslavement, let's revisit the Garden of Eden. God created Adam and Eve perfectly. Once they chose to disobey God, they abandoned His authority and accepted the authority of Satan. They sold themselves into the slave market of sin.

Every descendant since then, including you and me, remains under that sentence. We're not sinners because we sin. We sin because we are sinners. We all operate under the stinking, disgusting, degrading conditions of sin's slave market.

Even worse, the penalty or price tag of sin is death.

- The wages of sin *is* death. (Romans 6:23)
- Just as through one man sin entered the world, and death through sin, and thus death spread to all men, because all sinned. (Romans 5:12)
- The soul who sins shall die. (Ezekiel 18:4)

Yes, we all die physically. But we weren't originally created to die. Eternal, Infinite God created us in His image. We were intended to live in constant, eternal fellowship in His presence. But sin distorted that image and introduced death to the human race.

Sin's price tag involves far more than physical death. Without divine intervention, sin's penalty is eternal separation from God. Without Calvary, without Jesus' shed blood, we are doomed.

Personal Reflection

Understanding the enormity and all-pervasive nature of sin, how does Jesus' sacrificial death on Calvary for you become more personal? Beyond the excuses and justifications for preferred sinful behavior, can you see how sin separates you from God? How does His infinite, eternal love motivate you to forsake your sin and run into His embrace?

Chapter Thirteen

Calvary: Why Blood?

What is the value of Christ's blood?

A clear vision of Calvary comes with a better understanding of Christ's blood.

This blood makes Christlikeness possible. To determine its amazing value, let's discover what God says about blood.

Throughout Scripture, from the closed gate of Eden to the opened gate of heavenly Mount Zion, we find blood. Its repetition reveals its importance.

In the Garden of Eden after Adam and Eve sinned, they tried hiding from God. For the first time ever, they found themselves naked, exposed in shame. So off they ran to hide. Then God confronted them and introduced the shedding of innocent blood. To cover their nakedness, innocent animals died so God could make clothing from their skins (Genesis 3:21).

Adam and Eve must have shared the knowledge of sacrificial blood to their sons. We find Abel, Adam and Eve's second son, shedding lamb's blood in his sacrifice to God. It's interesting to read how God "respected Abel and his offering" (Genesis 4:4).

Fast forward about sixteen-hundred years to the Flood. Man's sinfulness increased exponentially and every intent of his heart was "only evil continually" (Genesis 6:5). As a result, God decided to destroy everyone except Noah and his family. The Ark protected them from God's judgment. After the flood waters receded, Noah and his family came out of the Ark. Again, innocent blood was shed as he sacrificed animals on an altar before God (Genesis 8:20).

Down through the ages we arrive at Mount Moriah. It was there God tested Abraham's faith. God told him to sacrifice what was most precious to him—his promised, long-awaited son, Isaac. Abraham passed the test, and God spared Isaac's life. As a substitute, God provided a ram that Abraham sacrificed (Genesis 22:13). Incidentally, Mount Moriah is synonymous with

Mount Calvary. The shedding of blood in Abraham's story pointed to the blood of the Lamb of God years later.

We move next to Mount Sinai where Moses led the Israelites after their exodus from Egypt. There God introduced His Law and countless animal sacrifices. Blood spilled every day in accordance with God's atoning requirements. Countless people performed God's required offerings during the age of the Law that lasted fifteen hundred years. Imagine the volume of blood that was shed. Man's innumerable sins required vast gallons of innocent blood.

Blood, blood, and more blood.

All the way to Calvary where sinless blood was shed for sinful man.

But the question remains: Why blood? What's so significant about this metallic, sticky, reddish liquid that flows through humans and animals?

Value of Blood

No blood, no life.

According to Leviticus 17:11, life is in the blood. God created it to carry life-sustaining oxygen throughout the body while also disposing of impurities.

> Blood transports oxygen from the lungs to the cells of the body, where it is needed for metabolism. The carbon dioxide produced during metabolism is carried back to the lungs by the blood, where it is then exhaled.[45]

Blood also helps regulate body temperature and prevents major blood loss through clotting. This medical information helps clarify the criticality of blood to sustain life.

But why is it necessary to shed it as a sacrifice for sin? What is it about blood that makes it the steady drumbeat throughout Scripture? What characteristic makes blood the central theme of redemption in both Old and New Testaments?

Blood has a voice. When Cain murdered Abel, God told him, "The voice of your brother's blood cries out to Me from the ground" (Genesis 4:10). Blood also speaks in heaven. Referring to Christ's shed blood, Hebrews 12:24 reveals it "speaks better things than that of Abel."

Blood will be avenged. In heaven, martyrs cry out, "How long, O Lord, holy and true, until You judge and avenge our blood?" (Revelation 6:9-10). Countless millions have died horrible deaths for their faith in Jesus Christ. God comforts these martyrs by promising to avenge them in due time.

Jesus associated guilt and judgment for shedding righteous blood (Matthew 23:35). Imagine God's judgment for the millions of innocent babies aborted for human convenience.

All this confirms the special value God places on blood. He created it. He sustains it. And He ultimately avenges it.

To better understand the value of blood, let's peek inside two holy places. The earthly Holy of Holies and the heavenly Holiest of Holies.

For the Old Testament tabernacle, God gave Moses specific instructions about the Holy of Holies. It was to be protected behind a thick veil (Exodus 26:33). This place was so holy that no one but the high priest could enter—and only once each year. Inside sat the Ark of the Covenant, beneath the Mercy Seat. God told Moses, "Put the Mercy Seat on top of the Ark … there I will meet with you, and I will speak with you from above the Mercy Seat" (Exodus 25:21-22). It was the place designated where blood was sprinkled before God's presence (Leviticus 16:14).

We find something similar in the heavenly Holiest of Holies. After His death on Calvary, Jesus entered this holy place and sprinkled His blood on the altar in God's presence (Hebrews 9:12; 24-26). God places such immeasurable and incomprehensible value on blood that where it is sprinkled, that's where we find His throne, His presence, and His intimate fellowship.

To summarize, life is in the blood. Blood has a voice before God. God avenges the shedding of righteous blood. God places incredible value on blood.

Now let's combine that with what we've discovered about Jesus. He is eternal. He is uncreated and self-existent—the second person of the Godhead. He's the great I AM. Immanuel, God with us. He spoke everything into existence. He is Infinite, Omni-Everything, and Sovereign Lord of all.

Keep this in mind as we now look at Christ's blood.

Blood of Jesus Christ

No nobler blood flowed through nobler veins.

Since life is in the blood, and since Jesus has eternal life within Himself (John 5:26), His blood is life-giving, infinite, and eternal. Peter described it as precious or costly (1 Peter 1:19). Since Jesus was divinely-conceived (Luke 1:31-35), the eternal life of the infinite Godhead is in His blood (Colossians 2:9). His blood is divine, sinless, and incorruptible—referred to as God's own blood (Acts 20:28).

This is the blood Jesus shed on Calvary for you and me. Amazing.

If you're squeamish or don't like talking about the blood of Jesus, you won't be comfortable in heaven. No grander theme is mentioned and worshiped there. The book of Revelation declares various anthems of praise for the blood of Jesus.

- To Him who loved us and washed us from our sins in His own blood. (Revelation 1:5)
- You are worthy ... for You were slain, and have redeemed us to God by Your blood. (Revelation 5:9)
- Worthy is the Lamb who was slain to receive power and riches and wisdom, and strength and honor and glory and blessing! (Revelation 5:12)
- These are the ones who come out of the great tribulation, and washed their robes and made them white in the blood of the Lamb. (Revelation 7:14)
- They overcame him by the blood of the Lamb and by the word of their testimony. (Revelation 12:11)

Even Jesus, at His glorious appearing (Titus 2:13) will be "clothed with a robe dipped in blood" (Revelation 19:13).

Yeah but Nate, how does knowing about Jesus' blood help make me more Christlike?

It's important to understand the specific meaning of "the blood of the Lamb." Usually, we understand it to mean the shed blood of Christ as the sacrificial Lamb of God who "takes away the sin of the world" (John 1:29). But there's also significant meaning in the *disposition* of the Lamb.

Keep in mind true Christ followers reflect His disposition.

Lambs are usually gentle. They are soft and innocent. Such characteristics mirror Jesus' disposition. His gentleness made the brutality of His death all the more gruesome. That the most gentle, sinless Lamb suffered what He did at the hands of a rebellious race adds significantly more value to that blood.

As the opposite of Lucifer's harsh pride and arrogant boasting, Jesus came as the humble Lamb of God. He said, "learn from Me, for I am gentle [meek] and lowly in heart [humble], and you will find rest for your souls" (Matthew 11:29). It was through His gentleness and meekness that He subjected Himself to the Father's will.

> He humbled Himself and became obedient to the point of death, even the death of the cross. (Philippians 2:8)

Sin is arrogant. But humility surrenders to God's rightful authority. Through gentleness and humility, Christ willingly shed His infinite, eternal blood on Calvary. This same disposition, bestowed upon us through His blood, is what drives out selfishness and pride. Dying to self and humbly surrendering to Jesus gives victory over the terminal venom of Lucifer.

By this precious, costly, infinite blood, Jesus opened and cleared out Paradise (Ephesians 4:8-10). Between His death and resurrection, Jesus marched into the lower parts of the earth, up to the gates of Paradise. He snatched the keys of Death from the Devil's icy grip (Revelation 1:18). Then He led the Old Testament saints to the celestial city where He returned as Conqueror over sin, death, and Satan (Hebrews 2:14). He then entered the throne room, into the presence of God. There in the Most Holy Place (Hebrews 9:12), with nail-scarred hands, He sprinkled His blood on the altar on our behalf (Hebrews 9:24-26). There Jesus remains, at God the Father's right hand, with all authority and power (1 Peter 3:22).

Christ's eternal, infinite, all-powerful blood:

- Grants us access to God. (Hebrews 4:14-16)
- Offers us reconciliation with God. (Colossians 1:20)
- Cleanses us from all sin. (1 John 1:7)
- Saves and sanctifies us. (Colossians 1:13-14)
- Washes us whiter than snow. (Psalm 51:7)

Talk about amazing.
But there's more.

Result of Christ's Blood

Without Christ's shed blood, there is no salvation (Acts 4:12). There's no forgiveness of sin (Hebrews 9:22). And there's no indwelling Holy Spirit (John 16:7).

After His resurrection, Jesus repeated His promise to send the Holy Spirit. This promised Spirit would grant His genuine followers "power from on high" (Luke 24:49).

After completing His atoning work in heaven, I imagine Jesus turned to His Father and said, "Father, I finished the work we foreordained. I paid the price for mankind's sins. Now I have a request. I promised to send My followers another Comforter (John 15:26). Let's now send the Holy Spirit, not to dwell *upon* them, but to dwell *in* them" (John 14:17).

This blood—in which is the eternal life of Jesus, that is always on the altar in heaven before God the Father—accomplishes several things.

- It assures us of a full redemption. Nothing is overlooked or missed.
- It's a sign of Christ's rightful possession of His true followers (Ephesians 1:14). He created us. He redeemed us. We are twice His own.
- It grants full, immediate, and intimate access to God (Ephesians 2:18). Only by Christ's blood may we "come boldly to the throne" to obtain mercy and find grace (Hebrews 4:16).

The power of the blood is in the worth of the life.
Read that again slowly. Based on Who Jesus is, His blood is eternal, infinite, and powerful enough to "save to the uttermost" (Hebrews 7:25).
Thank God for the blood of the Lamb!

The blood that is powerful in heaven, is powerful in my heart. The blood that works wonders in heaven, works wonders in my heart. The blood of the Lamb is my life, my song, my joy, my power, my perfect salvation.[46]

Paul emphasized the power source of salvation. He said, "We preach Christ crucified, to the Jews a stumbling block and to the Greeks foolishness, but to those who are called ... Christ the power of God and the wisdom of God" (1 Corinthians 1:23-24).

The cross of Calvary is offensive to the Jews, and they reject Him because of it. They want a militant messiah, not a crucified criminal. The cross of Calvary is foolishness to the Greeks (Gentiles), and they dismiss Him because of it. They look for a philosophical professor, not a murdered madman. The cross of Calvary means nothing to many others. They deny its supernatural aspects and ignore its sovereign Savior.

How wrong they all are. But they will know soon enough.

The cross of Calvary is everything to those who personally claim and appropriate what Jesus accomplished there. They have access to God's presence, wisdom, power, and eternal life.

Christlikeness involves a heart full of gratitude and a mind full of praise for all Jesus has done for us. We follow a powerful, risen Savior whose infinite, eternal, all-sufficient blood opens everything for us.

May we remain faithful to that invaluable blood—never apologizing for it, never softening its impact. May we revel in it and appropriate its infinite power. Not merely for forgiveness and cleansing but for its full and victorious sufficiency.

What is the value of Christ's blood to you?

Personal Reflection

Some people consider a blood relationship the strongest human bond. Family members are usually drawn closer and band together against all else. With this in mind, how much stronger is a relational bond made by infinite, eternal blood? How should that strengthen your faith and intimately affect your life?

Chapter Fourteen

Calvary: God's Holiness

God doesn't take caterpillars where only butterflies can go.

We find the essence of Christlikeness in God's holiness. Jesus lived a holy earthly life. God created and calls us to live in holiness. Our purpose is to become like Christ. Deductive reasoning brings us to the discovery and pursuit of holiness.

God defines holiness in both the Old and New Testaments. In Hebrew, the base words for "holy" are *qāḏōsh* and *qāḏash* (שָׁדַק; שָׁדוֹשׁ). Their basic meanings involve being sacred, pure, consecrated, separated, and free from moral imperfections and failures. It identifies holy things and people as completely set apart for God and His service.[47]

In Greek, the base words for "holy" are *hagios* and *hagnos* (ἅγιός; ἁγνός). Their basic meanings are: hallowed, sanctified, purified, separated from defilement, impurities, and anything unholy. They imply a withdrawing from fellowship with the world by first gaining fellowship with God.[48] A related word, *hagiasmos* (ἁγιασμῷ) identifies the activity of the Holy Spirit to set us apart to salvation as well as enable us to be holy even as God is holy.[49]

God's holiness is His infinite, unchanging lack of, and intolerance for, anything impure, immoral, and unholy. "God is light and in Him is no darkness at all" (1 John 1:5). He dwells in "unapproachable light" (1 Timothy 6:16). Jesus said, "I am the light of the world. He who follows Me shall not walk in darkness, but have the light of life" (John 8:12). This light is pure holiness without even a tint of gray (James 1:17).

God's infinite purity and righteous perfection won't ever tolerate or accept sin. He isn't progressive and doesn't change His standard based on our devolving societal morals or personal preferences. He never says, *Nate messed up again, but he's better than sixty-five percent of the population so I'll give him a break.*

God does not condemn sin in the sinner and then condone it in the saint."[50]

As Holy God, He loves and bestows what is good. He also hates and condemns what is evil. It's as simple as that. There's no confusion or guesswork.

Calvary's Focal Point

Sin separates us from God.

But remember, all of God does all that God does.

His holy love and holy wrath unite at Calvary. His love wouldn't let man go (1 John 4:8). Yet His wrath couldn't be surrendered (Romans 1:18).

This created a seemingly divine paradox. How would God reconcile His love and His wrath? He loves His creation too much to destroy us or condemn us to eternal damnation. Yet He cannot yield His holy wrath against sin.

Blood must be shed. Without it, there's no forgiveness of sin (Hebrews 9:22).

An atoning, sacrificial substitute was necessary. Someone powerful enough to not only cover sin but to cancel and remove it forever. Someone qualified to restore the relationship and fellowship between God and man.

As already discovered, "God has sent His only begotten Son into the world, that we might live through Him" (1 John 4:9). The *love* of God, through Christ's sacrifice on Calvary, delivers from the *wrath* of God. Jesus faced and endured God's wrath for us. Those who accept Christ as Lord and Savior will never face this wrath. Those who reject Christ face God's fierce wrath and punishment on their own (John 3:36).

Atonement

Atonement is the satisfactory reparation for an offense or injury.[51]

Sin is the offense or injury. Its sentence is death (Romans 6:23).

But if each person died for his own sin, reconciliation with God is impossible. Sinful mankind needed help from outside ourselves. Any ordinary human wasn't good enough to self-atone, so that process wouldn't work. A qualified substitute was necessary. We needed an extraordinary, supernatural human to pay the penalty for our sin, once and for all.

To better understand all that's involved in atonement, let's review the process the high priest went through to atone for the Israelites' sins (Leviticus 16). First, he removed his priestly garments. These were considered holy, anointed, "glorified" garments that represented his role. He then put on linen garments which were specific for performing the atoning sacrifice.

Yeah but Nate, that's the Old Testament. It no longer applies.

I disagree. Even within the description of Ezekiel's future Millennial Temple, the priests have a separate place to change into and out of their holy garments (Ezekiel 42:13-14). God reserves the right to separate the holy from the unholy.

In the atonement process, the high priest first offered a sacrifice for himself before offering one for the people. Once each year, on a designated day, he went in alone, behind the protective veil, into the Holy of Holies. There he offered incense in a censor filled with hot coals. The resulting smoke clouded the Mercy Seat and shielded him from face-to-face interaction with God's glory. Such proximity would result in immediate death.

Then the high priest sprinkled blood on the Mercy Seat, the place where the golden cherubim bowed forward and inward, forever occupied with the blood sprinkled there. After this, while still inside the tabernacle, he removed the linen garments. Undoubtedly, they were spotted with blood so he left them there. Before leaving, he put on the priestly garments of glory he had previously laid aside. Thus, he resumed their positional "glory."

Are you ready to have your mind blown?

Jesus replicated this process as our High Priest (Hebrews 4:14-15). But He didn't have to atone for Himself because He was sinless.

He laid aside His glory (not His deity) when He came to earth. He took on the garment of sacrifice coming in the likeness of man (Philippians 2:5-8). He presented Himself as the Sacrificial Lamb by dying on Calvary. Then, ascending to heaven, He sprinkled His blood in the Holiest Place where God is enthroned.

This didn't just cover sin. It canceled sin once and for all—for *all* time for those who appropriate it (Hebrews 9:11-15). Jesus presented His infinite blood as the eternal ransom for sin. This opened the way to God for all who believe on Jesus.

> If you ... set your heart on something surpassing all that you have hitherto experienced, and if you fix your attention on the Holy of Holies now opened, and on the unchangeable priesthood of your Lord Jesus, then you will see that the divine provision for your unbroken enjoyment of His fellowship is perfect.[52]

Infinite Blood—Infinite Effect

When Jesus returned to heaven, He reclaimed His previous glory.

To this day, He sits enthroned in honor at the Father's right hand (Hebrews 8:1-6; Philippians 2:9-11). There He intercedes for us constantly (Romans 8:34) and awaits His Father's signal to come get His Bride, the true Church (Ephesians 5:25-27). Through the "power of an endless life" (Hebrews 7:16), His followers receive continual cleansing for sin and power to walk in His abundant, victorious life. Hallelujah for the blood!

Thankfully, Jesus paid our sin-debt in full. As the Great I AM who forever exists in the present tense, what He does is presently ongoing. This includes His sprinkling, His intercession, and His advocacy on our behalf.

Jesus is God. He acts like God. He will never change who He is or how He acts. How He currently acts in heaven is how He acted while here on earth. His likeness, character, conduct, disposition, mindset, and attitude all remain the same. As a result, we have access to, and the benefit of, His unceasing work, power, and nature.

All of which brings us to justification.

Justification

Justification is the act of being declared righteous by God through the blood of Jesus Christ.

This means when God looks at a true believer, He no longer sees sin. All He sees is the blood of His precious Son, Jesus.

Just like in the story of the Passover in Egypt, as the destroying angel went through the land, when he saw the blood applied to the doorpost and lintels, he "passed over" that house. God said, "When I see the blood, I will pass over you" (Exodus 12:13).

It's been said that *justified* can be described as *just as if I'd not sinned*. Paul explained it:

> God, in his grace, freely makes us right in his sight. He did this through Christ Jesus when he freed us from the penalty for our sins. For God presented Jesus as the sacrifice for sin. People are made right with God when they believe that Jesus sacrificed his life, shedding his blood. God did this to demonstrate his righteousness, for he himself is fair and just, and he makes sinners right in his sight when they believe in Jesus. (Romans 3:24-26, NLT)

In the Old Testament, God required a spotless Passover lamb, innocent and gentle. Once sacrificed, its blood made temporary atonement for sin. The destroying angel came through with one directive. Either there was a dead lamb or there would be a dead firstborn son. He didn't pause before each home and consider the identity, social status, or net worth of its inhabitants. He simply looked for the blood.

In the New Testament, Jesus became the sinless, loving Lamb of God (John 1:29). But His blood permanently canceled sin. It didn't just cover it as the Old Testament sacrifices did. They needed continual sacrificing to cover sin. Jesus suffered once (1 Peter 3:18) and completed atonement's work for all who believe it and receive it. Calvary required either a crucified Lamb or eternally dead, doomed sinners.

Thank God for His omniscience to foresee our need and His infinite love to provide Himself a spotless Lamb.

> There is therefore now no condemnation to those who are in Christ Jesus, who do not walk according to the flesh, but according to the Spirit. (Romans 8:1)

Hallelujah! God's wrath is satisfied. His love delivers from His wrath. With the blood of Jesus personally accepted and applied, God:

- Blots out our sins like a thick cloud. (Isaiah 44:22)
- Casts all our sins behind His back. (Isaiah 38:17)

- Throws all our sin into the deepest sea. (Micah 7:19)
- Rearranges earthly coordinates to remove our sin "as far as the east is from the west." (Psalm 103:12)
- Forgets our "sins and lawless deeds." (Hebrews 10:17)

Once we're under Christ's atoning blood, God the Father casts our sin into the depths of His forgetfulness.

Doesn't that make you jump for joy? "Sing unto the LORD, O ye saints of His, and give thanks at the remembrance of His holiness" (Psalm 30:4, KJV). May we ever remember and rejoice for God's holiness.

Because of Jesus, God's love is restored and will never be removed (Romans 8:35-39). He is eternal. He is love. He is Omnipresent. Upon being reconciled to Him, with sin forever removed, we are reconciled to His love. Nothing can ever separate us from His love or His presence. God's love and wrath are reconciled in Jesus' finished work. God's glory and holiness are maintained. Fellowship between God and man is restored.

Talk about sovereign orchestration.

Maintaining this clear view of Christ and His finished, atoning work is great comfort to His true followers. It keeps our eyes focused on Him (Hebrews 12:2). It fills our hearts with intense love, gratitude, and praise (1 Corinthians 15:57). It motivates us to live daily under the complete influence and control of the Holy Spirit (Galatians 5:16). It helps us celebrate God's holiness. Finally, it helps us understand that we *can* and *should* walk in spiritual victory.

We do this by daily surrendering to Him. Applying His Word to our lives. And allowing the transforming work of His Spirit within. Walking in spiritual victory—pursuing God's holiness—is the journey toward Christlikeness.

Personal Reflection

Since God is eternally holy, and He calls His true followers to be holy, how should that affect your life, lifestyle, mindset, and habits? As a genuine child of God, you should resemble Him more and more. What unholiness stunts your growth from becoming more Christlike each day? What expressions of gratitude fill your heart knowing He completely removes confessed and forsaken sin?

Chapter Fifteen

Calvary's Enormous Cost

You want to be like Christ? Become a person characterized by the discipline of sacrifice—the ultimate expression of Christlikeness.[53]

Christ's sufferings involved far more than His beatings and crucifixion. With Jesus being Who He is, doing and experiencing what He did, Calvary's cost is staggering.

Infinity took on the likeness of man in full humanity.

Omnipresence agreed to the confines of time and space.

Eternity became obedient to the sufferings and death on the cross.

Omniscience yielded to every vile thing man could conceive.

Omnipotence allowed man's vicious cruelty.

He who knew no sin was made sin for us.

The Altogether Lovely was "so disfigured he seemed hardly human … one would scarcely know he was a man" (Isaiah 52:14, NLT). Before sovereignly dismissing His Spirit, Jesus was "cut off [wrenched; torn] from the land of the living" (Isaiah 53:8). The prophet Daniel also mentioned Jesus being "cut off" (Daniel 9:26).

The meaning of *cut off* is "death directly inflicted by God, or violent death at the hands of man. It is never used of mere death, nor to express sudden death by natural [causes]."[54]

Followers of Christ are ever mindful of the extreme, violent sacrifice He made so we could have a relationship with Him and become like Him. No greater cost was ever paid.

May this penetrate our minds and pierce our souls. May we never take this lightly or for granted. May we stagger at the enormity. When we remember it often, may our hearts bow in humble gratitude and reverent praise.

When faced with the reality of what Jesus suffered for us individually, how can we remain unchanged? Isaac Watts vividly portrayed the cost and personal effect of Calvary in his song, "When I Survey the Wondrous Cross."

> When I survey the wondrous cross on which the Prince of glory died,
> My richest gain I count but loss, and pour contempt on all my pride.
> See, from his head, his hands, his feet, sorrow and love flow mingled down.
> Did e'er such love and sorrow meet, or thorns compose so rich a crown?
> Were the whole realm of nature mine, that were a present far too small.
> Love so amazing, so divine, demands my soul, my life, my all.[55]

To gain a better understanding of Calvary's cost, let's discover the lessons and parallels of Mount Moriah. We find the story in Genesis 22. It shows Calvary's human pain in a relatable way.

Test of Obedience

Fittingly, Moriah means "foreseen or chosen of Jehovah."
   Mount Moriah is synonymous for Calvary as its location is near the current Temple Mount area in Jerusalem. It's also the place where Abraham faced his toughest test of faith.

> By faith Abraham, when he was tested, offered up Isaac … his only begotten son … concluding that God was able to raise him up, even from the dead. (Hebrews 11:17-19)

God promised Abraham he would have a son. He was seventy-five years old when God promised to make him into a "great nation" (Genesis 12:2). God later told Abraham he would be the "father of many nations" (Genesis 17:4-8). Yet he remained childless for twenty-five more years.
   When Abraham was one hundred years old, Isaac was finally born (Genesis 21:5). Imagine this father's joy and satisfaction. Not only for his son but that his waiting was over. God's promise had finally been fulfilled.
   Then came that fateful morning.
   God told Abraham, "Take now your son, your only *son* Isaac, whom you love, and go to the land of Moriah, and offer him there as a burnt offering on one of the mountains of which I shall tell you" (Genesis 22:2).

I'm sure if it were me, I'd have many doubts and questions. I'd be angry. *Did I hear You correctly? I don't think You meant that. Why are You asking this of me after what You promised? What did I do wrong?*

Once the realization set in that God meant what He said, imagine the pain. The grief. The anguish. The shattered dreams.

And he had to tell his wife, Sarah. Talk about a tough conversation.

Going through pregnancy and childbirth, this meant something deeper to Sarah. Usually dads tell their hurting kids, "C'mon, now. You're okay. Suck it up. Play through the pain. Walk it off." But moms usually don't deal well with their children's pain.

Physical pain is one thing. But this? Heartbreak doesn't seem to describe it well enough. Not to mention confusion and betrayal.

Then there is Issac. Though still a young child, he was old enough to understand what was involved in sacrifice. Imagine the dagger through Abraham's heart when young Issac asked him, "Look, the fire and the wood, but where *is* the lamb for a burnt offering?" (Genesis 22:7). Oh, the heartbreak to look in the face of innocence—the one who had done nothing deserving of death. Picture the look of horror when Issac realized he was to be the sacrifice.

But God's command was clear. "Take now your son, your only *son* Isaac, whom you love …"

Now. Immediately. No delays. No negotiation or begging for more time.

Your son. Specific identification. No confusion about who. No possibility of replacement.

Take your only son. As God the Father's only Son, Jesus relished the intimacy of their relationship. He also knew the heartbreak of this demand. The anguish of the sacrifice. The necessary trust for surrender.

Whom you love. God recognized Abraham's feelings. Yet He expected obedience and surrender regardless of personal heartbreak or loss. In God's eyes, obedience always supersedes our feelings. God won't bless beyond our obedience.

Ultimate Surrender

I wonder what Jesus thought or felt when He created Mount Moriah (Calvary).

I'm sure its shadow rested on His soul from the halls of eternity. Did He visit it often? He frequently went to the Mount of Olives across the Kidron Valley from Jerusalem. Could He see Mount Moriah (Calvary) from there? Did He walk along its rugged pathways praying for human strength to be obedient to His eternal purpose? In Gethsemane He prayed three times, with "vehement cries and tears" (Hebrews 5:7), that the bitter cup of sin might pass from Him. Yet through it all He surrendered. "Not My will but Thine be done."

> Then they came to the place of which God had told him. (Genesis 22:9)

There was no denying it. Not for Abraham or for Jesus. God foreordained the place and purpose. For Abraham, it was a *test* of faith. For Jesus, it was the *price* of faith. Calvary's price was the "precious [costly; of inestimable worth] blood of Christ" (1 Peter 1:19). Jesus paid the enormous price because without the shedding of blood, there is no forgiveness of sin (Hebrews 9:22).

To solve the paradox between sin and holy God, He who was blameless, spotless, without blemish, "holy, harmless, undefiled, separate from sinners," (Hebrews 7:26) was made sin for us (2 Corinthians 5:21). He helped us when we couldn't help ourselves. He "who committed no sin … bore our sins in His own body on the tree [cross], that we, having died to sins, might live for righteousness" (1 Peter 2:22-24).

The righteous One took our sins to exchange our sin with His righteousness. How can anyone resist or reject the offer of a personal relationship with such a loving, self-sacrificing Lord and Savior? How can true followers resist surrendering willingly and gladly to Him?

Knowing who Jesus is, it's difficult to fathom the enormous cost of Calvary. Jesus approached Calvary far more painfully than Abraham approached Mt. Moriah. Even though Jesus foreknew what lay ahead, He still shuddered at the reality (Hebrews 12:2).

He endured the ordeal, looked beyond the horror, and saw the joy of reconciled mankind. He paid the awful cost in full.

In heaven there stands a Man, with nail-prints in His hands,
The scars evidence His love, sacrifice, identity, and authority.
Interceding for you and me, forever removing our sin.
"These are Mine," He cries as Advocate, Redeemer, and Friend;
"Bought and paid for by My blood!"[56]

Personal Reflection

Salvation is God's free gift to mankind. But it wasn't free to Him. It came at an enormous cost. In view of its inestimable worth, how will you approach such precious salvation? Even if you've accepted it, how precious is it to you? Do you hold it in highest esteem and live accordingly? Or do you treat it as an entitlement and live after your own selfish desires and aspirations? Is it precious enough to actively share it with others?

Chapter Sixteen

Calvary's Unimaginable Horror

*How often did Jesus handle a hammer
knowing what a hammer would do to Him one day?*

Only God fully understands the horrific sufferings of Calvary. Human intellect struggles to adequately describe or understand what happened there. In trying to do so, Isaiah exclaimed, "Who believes what we've heard and seen? Who would have thought God's saving power would look like this?" (Isaiah 53:1, MSG). In other words, "You won't believe or understand this!"

Excruciating.

This word describes something extremely painful or causing intense agony. Not just physical pain, but also emotional and psychological pain. When we say something is excruciating, it means hurts—intensely.

Surprisingly, this word originates from the Latin word *excruciare*, which means to torture or crucify. In breaking down the word, *ex* means intensity or "out of," and *cruciare* means "to torment" or "to torture." *Cruciare* comes from the Latin word *crux*, which means "cross." This suggests that the word *excruciating* specifically referred to the intense pain experienced during crucifixion.[57] How ironic that such an intensely painful word originated from the horrific manner of Jesus' death.

Beyond the physical, emotional, and psychological pain Christ endured were countless torments. We find glimpses in God's Word and from Jesus' cries from the cross. Yet we seldom look deeply into that bitter cup.

But the apostle Paul did. He surrendered everything to become intimately acquainted with the fellowship of Christ's sufferings. He wrote, "That I may know [relationally experience] Him and the power of His resurrection, and the fellowship [partnership or communion with] of His sufferings, being conformed to His death" (Philippians 3:10).

Christlikeness—Conformed to His Death

Everyone wants to live in Christ's resurrection power. But few are willing to share the depth of His sufferings.

Conformity to Christlikeness involves knowing Him. Gaining Him. Being found in Him. Being conformed or assimilated to His death. With these thoughts in mind, we now uncover Calvary's unimaginable horror.

With Jesus being Who He is, one would think the horror of bearing the sins of the entire world would affect how He treated people. Yet not once do we find any sarcasm or contempt from Him as He walked among us.

Yes, He boldly challenged the religious elite who thought they had a corner on religiosity. But He anointed even those harsh interactions with compassion for their souls. He lovingly prayed for and restored Peter who denied Him. He would have forgiven Judas had he repented. Even from the cross, He cried, "Father, forgive them."

Nowhere do we find any trace of belligerence or blame. We don't hear, "I had to leave a pristine environment in heaven and come down here to this sin-sick place. You have messed things up so badly, I have to save you lost sinners. Y'all just can't seem to get out of your own bumbling, stumbling way. Now leave Me alone and let me fulfill My destiny."

From a humanistic standpoint, such sentiments would be justified. Yet what do we see from Him? Unconditional love. Compassion when interacting with lost, hurting people. Humility when washing His disciples' feet. Service by giving His life a ransom. Self-sacrifice by surrendering His glory to live among us and die for us.

Remember, Jesus is all God, all man. The God-man. As divine, He *foreknew* all things. As human, He *suffered* all things. As the all-knowing God, Jesus knew the cost and necessity of Calvary.

Agony and Horror

From brief descriptions in Scripture, we see the toll of Calvary.

It started long before Gethsemane, but that's our first glimpse. "Being in agony, He prayed more earnestly. Then His sweat became like great drops of blood falling down to the ground" (Luke 22:44). He prayed "with vehement cries and tears to Him who was able to save Him from death" (Hebrews 5:7).

Calvary's Unimaginable Horror

Three times He prayed earnestly, fervently—and God the Father heard Him. Yet heaven remained silent.

Excerpts from Messianic Psalm 22 describe Calvary's horror in more detail. I inserted words identifying the painful attacks on His humanity.

> My God, My God, why have You forsaken Me [abandonment]? Why are You so far from helping Me [isolation], and from the words of My groaning [silence]? I am ... despised by the people. All those who see Me ridicule [taunt; snarl at] Me. There is none to help [loneliness]. Many ... strong bulls of Bashan have encircled Me [the bestial, raving, maniacal mob of humanity and demons]. They gape at Me with their mouths, like a raging and roaring lion [screaming, hurling insults]. I am poured out like water [dehydration], and all My bones are out of joint [screaming mass of pain]; My heart is like wax [crushing; burning; fading]; it has melted within Me. My strength is dried up ... My tongue clings to My jaws [raging thirst] ... They pierced My hands and My feet [nerves inflamed; arteries bleeding]; I can count all My bones. They look and stare [gawk] at Me. They divide My garments among them [nakedness; shame; theft], and for My clothing they cast lots.

When Jesus cried, "My God, My God, why have you forsaken Me?" He addressed God as *Elohim*, meaning Supreme One. Mighty One. Creator of the universe. And yet Jesus' first and last sayings from the cross began with, "Father."

For the first time in eternity, the Father and Son were separated. Not their relationship, but their fellowship. That's what sin does—it separates. As our sin-bearer, Jesus was alone and abandoned. Holy God the Father couldn't look at sin, even when borne by His Son.

I believe this sin-caused separation from God will be one of the horrors of eternal damnation in the lake of fire. Separated from all God is—His love, His peace, His comfort. Mostly, it's eternal separation from His presence. This crushing loneliness and divine abandonment should motivate any unbeliever to rush to Calvary and accept God's loving sacrifice there.

Excerpts from Messianic Psalm 69 further describe Christ's anguish. Again, I inserted words to further describe His suffering.

Save me, O God! For the waters have come up to my neck [sinking in distress]. I sink in deep mire, where there is no standing [falling]; I have come into deep waters, where the floods overflow me [overwhelming anguish]. I am weary with my crying; My throat is dry [parched]; My eyes fail [weeping] while I wait for my God. Though I have stolen nothing, I still must restore it [the innocent paying instead of the guilty]. You know my reproach, my shame [humiliation], and my dishonor [disgrace] … Reproach [accusation] has broken my heart, and I am full of heaviness [sickness; nausea]; I looked for someone to take pity, but there was none [loneliness]; and for comforters, but I found none [abandonment]. They also gave me gall [bitterness] for my food, and for my thirst they gave me vinegar [sourness] to drink.

Brutality of His Beating

Jesus was beaten beyond recognition.

His visage [appearance] was marred more than any man, and His form more than the sons of men. (Isaiah 52:14)

The prophet Isaiah explains the brutality and savagery of Christ's beating. His face disfigured, ruined. The entire ordeal was excruciatingly painful. It was shameful and humiliating for any common man, much less the Great I AM.

Prior to His crucifixion, Pilate ordered Jesus whipped by soldiers from his elite Praetorian Guard (John 18:28-19:1). This unit consisted of the strongest, most effective soldiers of the Roman army. Its main purpose was protecting the emperor or assigned governors. This special force excelled at death and torture. One of their favored instruments was the *flagrum* or *flagellum*.

> The Romans would … scourge a condemned criminal before he was put to death. The Roman scourge … was a short whip made of two or three leather (ox-hide) thongs or ropes connected to a handle. The leather thongs were knotted with a number of small pieces of metal … attached at various intervals. Scourging would quickly remove the skin.[58]

Whipped mercilessly. Beaten. Bullied. Crushed. Mocked. Humiliated. Shamed. His beard ripped from His face. Face slapped. Unclothed. Standing, then hanging naked. Fevered. Thirsty. Dehydrated. Rejected. Betrayed. Abandoned. He didn't look human.

Are you ready to scream, "Leave Him alone!"?

Suffering on the Cross

Crucifixion was usually a slow, agonizing death by asphyxiation and blood loss.

While hanging from the cross, the unnatural position caused cramped muscles and burning pain. Jesus' chest constricted, and He couldn't breathe.

To catch a breath, a victim mustered his strength to push and pull against pierced hands and feet to lift himself to where his chest could expand. Then he'd drop down, exhausted until the next effort to breathe caused a repeated, painful effort. With each gasp for air, Christ's lacerated back scraped up and down against the rough, splintered wood.

Is His agony becoming clear?

It's difficult to read or imagine, much less to endure.

Creative hands that formed and healed were nailed to the cross. Jesus couldn't wipe tears or blood from His eyes. He couldn't brush away flies from His nose or mouth. He couldn't stretch or massage cramped muscles for momentary relief. Everlasting, beautiful feet that crossed heaven's galaxies and dusty roads to "preach the gospel of peace" and "bring glad tidings of good things" (Romans 10:15) were brutally nailed to a criminal's cross.

Infinity's heart broke under the weight of sin.

And He suffered all this for me.

For you.

For every person who has ever lived.

But we see Jesus, who ... might taste death for everyone. (Hebrews 2:9)

Why Crucifixion?

Why would Jesus subject Himself to such torture, agony, and shame?

He said He was the Good Shepherd who gave His life for the sheep (John

10:11) but why die in such a horrible, shameful, excruciating manner?

Because the horror helps us better understand the depth and putridness of our sin.

The radical nature of sin demanded a radical cure.

Only such an excruciating sacrifice could forever eradicate the disease of sin.

The pursuit of Christlikeness demands an ever-increasing nearness to Him. To know Him intimately is to embrace His salvation along with the "fellowship of His sufferings" (Philippians 3:10).

Intimately knowing and following Jesus involves gladly embracing His brand. We own it, live it, and proclaim it. Furthermore, we promote it as commissioned ambassadors of His coming kingdom. As a wife proudly takes her husband's name, so Christ's followers bravely and humbly bear the association of following Him.

The increase in knowledge and personal experience makes love possible. We can't love the unknown. There must first be a knowing—a personal experience. Then love begins to blossom. To know and experience Jesus is to love Him. To know Him more intimately is to love Him more intensely.

No one can live a holy life without utter dedication to the life-purpose of knowing Christ.[59]

Yes, we rejoice in His love, grace, mercy, redemption and all His other wonderful attributes. Yet, like Paul, genuine, loving Christ followers bear "the marks of the Lord Jesus" (Galatians 6:17). It is the birthmark of our new spiritual birth.

Taking up the cross daily leaves a noticeable mark. It's the distinctive mark of a Christ follower. We forgive instead of holding grudges. We sacrifice "me time" for quiet time with Jesus. We do what God says instead of what we want to do. We forsake all (Luke 14:33) to follow Jesus and become like Him.

Cross bearing is the process whereby genuine Christ followers die to self and align our allegiance with Him. It's the humility of mind to never forget what great love He demonstrated for us. It's the commitment to become like Him no matter the cost.

Personal Reflection

How does the excruciating horror of Calvary affect your daily life? In view of what Christ did for you, what's your response to Him? Do you take up your cross, die to self daily, and follow Him? If not, why not? If so, what are the resulting blessings?

Chapter Seventeen

Calvary's Unmatched Love

Many are acquainted with the Cross; some draw near, few carry it.

Nails didn't hold Jesus to Calvary's cross. It was eternal, infinite love. A clear view of Calvary calls for an uncompromised understanding of love. Since Triune God is love, then the essence and effect of love, along with its motivation and capacity, originate with Him. It's one of His infinite, holy attributes.

- God so loved the world that He gave His only begotten Son, that whoever believes in Him should not perish but have everlasting life. (John 3:16)
- Real love isn't our love for God, but his love for us. God sent his Son to be the sacrifice by which our sins are forgiven. (1 John 4:10, CEV)

Unfortunately, Satan is the great deceiver. He manipulates. He counterfeits. He has taken such a sacred gift from God and twisted its meaning, abused its motivation, and cheapened its effect.

It's no surprise that the venues of this sinful, immoral world—Hollywood movies, romance novels, and perverse websites (to name just a few)—try to describe and demonstrate "love." But they do so from Satan's delusional perspective. As a result, love has been assaulted, stained by the sin-sick world's pigpen.

Even the dictionary definition of love falls short:

Strong affection for another arising out of kinship or personal ties. Attraction based on sexual desire. Affection and tenderness felt by lovers. Affection based on admiration, benevolence, or common interests. Warm attachment, enthusiasm, admiration, or devotion. Unselfish loyal and benevolent concern for the good of another.[60]

Since God is the origin of love, only He accurately defines and demonstrates true love.

- Jesus modeled the greatest love by sacrificing His life for us. (John 15:13)
- We can become His children because of His love. (1 John 3:1)
- Jesus expects love as a characteristic of His genuine followers. (John 13:35)
- We love Him because He first loved us. (1 John 4:19)
- The Holy Spirit pours God's love into our hearts. (Romans 5:5)

When considering the topic of love, the only reliable source is God. He gave us an incredible definition of love.

> Love is patient and kind, never jealous, boastful, proud, or rude. Love isn't selfish or quick tempered. It doesn't keep a record of wrongs that others do. Love rejoices in the truth, but not in evil. Love is always supportive, loyal, hopeful, and trusting. Love never fails!
> (1 Corinthians 13:4-8, CEV)

If we were to sum up love in one word it would be *out-serving*.

Just as our loving God foreknew and met our need for salvation, love is anticipating the needs of others and exceeding them. By humbly washing the disciples' feet, Jesus demonstrated the serving aspect of love. Since love isn't about serving with the expectation of getting something in return, then love is out-serving.

This sets the stage to think about the love Jesus displayed on the cross.

Unmatched Love

To follow Christ fully, we need a clear view of Calvary's unmatched love.

May we never forget or take for granted God's love expressed there. Such love is the basis for and motive behind why we die to self and follow Christ.

As Paul said, "I have been crucified with Christ; it is no longer I who live, but Christ lives in me; and the life which I now live in the flesh I live by faith in the Son of God, who loved me and gave Himself for me" (Galatians 2:20).

F. B. Meyer described such death to self and life in Christ:

> In Him we died on the cross and so met the righteous demands of the holy law. In Him we lay in the grave and so passed out of the region ruled by [Satan]. In Him we rose and ascended far above all might and dominion, principality, and power.[61]

Calvary is the evidence and expression of God's amazing, immeasurable, and everlasting love. "By this we know love, because He laid down His life for us" (1 John 3:16).

Christ's blood is infinite and inexhaustible, just as His love. His blood covers any and all sin, for all time, for anyone who accepts and claims His sacrifice. It conquers all sin's guilt, penalty, and power. It removes sin's guilt through forgiveness. It removes sin's penalty, or price tag, through redemption. It removes sin's power by nailing it to the cross (Colossians 2:13-14).

Such is the power and purpose of Calvary's unmatched love.

Personal Love

Love always suggests or expresses a personal, mutual attachment.

There can be no love without personal experience. I love majestic mountains having seen and walked in them. Parents love their children. There's a relational bonding there. Spouses love each other. There's a relational attachment there. Even loving a sentimental ideal arises from an internal experience, whether fulfilled or not.

In such an intimate relationship, true Christ followers draw near to Him "by the blood of Christ" (Ephesians 2:13). Because of this nearness, we may "come boldly to the throne of grace" to obtain mercy and find grace in our time of need (Hebrews 4:16).

There is liberty and freedom of access in this personal relationship. The loving effect of Christ's blood reconciles us to God (2 Corinthians 5:18) and grants us fellowship with Him (1 John 1:7). We can draw near to God at all times, in any place.

Paul explained that the love of Christ "compels us" (2 Corinthians 5:14). This compelling means to hold completely or hold with constraint.[62] In other words, Christ's immense, infinite love never stops or lets us go. These are all benefits of a personal, loving, intimate relationship with Him.

Those who are in such a relationship with Jesus exhibit this love. A genuine encounter with Calvary infuses Christ followers with His eternal, infinite love. It's part of our spiritual DNA. Calvary's love flows through our veins.

As the distinguishing characteristic of Christlikeness, we look and act like our heavenly Father. As His children, we lovingly embrace our Father's kingdom business (Luke 2:49). We speak the truth in love (Ephesians 4:15). Love dominates our lives as it dominates Christ's heart.

> And can it be that I should gain
> An int'rest in the Savior's blood?
> Died He for me, who caused His pain?
> For me, who Him to death pursued?
> Amazing love! how can it be
> That Thou, my God, should die for me?[63]

Delivering Love

The love of God delivers from the wrath of God.

Jesus endured and satisfied divine wrath for sin on Calvary. Those who accept and appropriate what Christ did there will never face God's wrath. This includes His "end time" wrath.

The "day of the Lord's wrath" describes His final judgment on mankind (Zephaniah 1:14-16). Repeatedly in the book of Revelation, we find God's wrath poured out on this earth in the final days. This is during a seven-year period known as the Tribulation.

However, before this happens, true Christ followers will be "caught up … to meet the Lord in the air" (1 Thessalonians 4:17). This long-awaited event is called the Rapture of the true Church, the Bride of Christ. Until then, we await Jesus, the Bridegroom who "delivers us from the wrath to come" (1 Thessalonians 1:10). Paul further confirmed that "the wrath of God is coming upon the sons of disobedience" (Colossians 3:6), not His Bride.

Thank God for Calvary. Thank God for His love expressed there. Thank God for a love so infinite, so eternal, so powerful that it removes God's wrath forever. God's love never lets us go. It never runs out. It delivers and protects us until we meet Jesus.

Obedient Love

Since Calvary was foreseen and pre-purposed before time, we can't add anything to it. Nor can we do anything to earn it. God clarifies this so we fully understand.

- Man is not justified by the works of the law but by faith in Jesus Christ. (Galatians 2:16)
- Not by works of righteousness which we have done, but according to His mercy He saved us … (Titus 3:5)

We don't do good deeds *for* salvation; we do them *because of* salvation (James 2:17). We serve Him in response to what He's done for and in us. Our service for Him is love-based, not forced or coerced.

Jesus became obedient to Calvary *before* He could sprinkle His blood in heaven on our behalf. Obedience and surrender always precede service—at least they should for those who would follow Christ. They are inseparable.

Accepting Him as Savior includes surrendering to Him as Lord. When we appropriate His blood, obedience to God is our demand. It's the natural, loving response to His loving sacrifice.

We love Him in return for His great, sacrificial love for us (1 John 4:19). Jesus said our obedience is the evidence of our love (John 14:15). "By this we know love because He laid down His life for us. And we also ought to lay down our lives" (1 John 3:16). Obedience to Him is evidence of a genuine, surrendered relationship with Him. Jesus asked, "Why do you call Me 'Lord, Lord,' and not do the things which I say?" (Luke 6:46). As He was obedient, may we likewise be obedient to Him.

The pursuit of Christlikeness doesn't involve the religionized, gold-overlaid cross of today. Christ's cross was brutal and rugged, an agonizing instrument of death. He calls His followers to take up our own crosses as we follow Him (Mark 8:34).

May we always embrace the cross. Oh, may we be ever grateful for His foreknowledge of and obedience to Calvary. May we fully trust His love for us in knowing that cross-bearing develops Christlikeness. May we never become too familiar with or indifferent toward Calvary.

> When my heart is full of Jesus, His blood bleeds over all I do.
> When my eyes are full of Jesus, things of this life fade from view.
> When my ears are full of Jesus, all other calls grow dim.
> When my life is full of Jesus, there is less of me and more of Him.[64]

Personal Reflection

We struggle to understand the immensity of God's infinite, eternal love. Though we may never fully understand it, we can still accept and claim it by faith. Knowing salvation was pre-planned before time began, there's nothing you can add or detract from it. It is God's free gift. Have you accepted it? Since you can't work *for* this free gift, does it make sense to serve God *because* of such a wonderful gift? How does Calvary's love compel you to love others in the spirit of Christlikeness?

Chapter Eighteen

Calvary's Blessings and Victory

There must be full surrender before there can be full blessedness.[65]

Christlikeness is possible because of Christ's finished work at Calvary and His subsequent resurrection.

Calvary makes *salvation* available. The resurrection provides the *power* to become like Jesus. True followers of Christ constantly thank and praise God for the multiplied blessings and victories He gives.

The life Jesus lived and the sacrifice He made are examples for His true followers. Although self-denial, sacrifice, and surrender may sound all doom and gloom, there's a marvelous upside. Surrendering to the transformation into His likeness brings blessings and victories in this life as well as the next.

God wants us to walk in blessing and victory. The apostles Paul and John confirmed this. "Blessed be the God and Father of our Lord Jesus Christ, who has blessed us with every spiritual blessing in the heavenly places in Christ" (Ephesians 1:3). "Thanks be to God, who gives us the victory through our Lord Jesus Christ" (1 Corinthians 15:57). "This is the victory that has overcome the world—our faith" (1 John 5:4).

The blessings and victory from Calvary are countless and eternal. Instead of rushing through the following list, take the time to meditate on each one:

- Pardon and forgiveness for sin (Colossians 1:14)
- Reconciliation with God (2 Corinthians 5:18)
- God's divine nature and power (2 Peter 1:2-4)
- Ongoing cleansing from sin (1 John 1:7)
- Justification (1 Corinthians 6:11)
- Sanctification (1 Thessalonians 4:3)
- Ability to live and walk in holiness (1 Peter 1:15-16; Romans 6:22)
- Access to and union with God (Ephesians 2:18)

- Continual transformation (2 Corinthians 3:18)
- The Holy Spirit's indwelling, filling, and anointing (1 Corinthians 3:16)
- New, abundant, and eternal life (John 10:10)
- Victory over sin (Romans 6:22)
- Victory over death (1 Corinthians 15:54-55, 57)
- Victory over the world, its things, and its temptations (1 John 5:4-5)
- Victory over Satan and his evil dominion (Romans 16:20)
- Ruling and reigning in Christ's eternal kingdom (Daniel 7:18, 22, 27)
- Performing God's will in a way that pleases Him (Hebrews 13:20-21)
- Spending eternity with our Triune God (1 Thessalonians 4:17)

It almost sounds too good to be true. Yet God's Word is sure, steadfast, and enduring (1 Peter 1:25). We can trust our lives and stake our eternal destination on the blessings and victories Scripture reveals.

Resurrection

The biggest blessing from Calvary is Christ's resurrection.

His resurrection makes all other blessings and victories possible. The cross points to what comes next—the resurrection. In essence, Calvary isn't about death; it's about new life. Powerful life. Victorious life. Resurrection life.

> But now Christ is risen from the dead ... For since by man *came* death, by Man also *came* the resurrection of the dead. For as in Adam all die, even so in Christ all shall be made alive.
> (1 Corinthians 15:20-22)

Jesus coming back to life is all the evidence necessary of His deity. He said no one would take His life but that He would lay it down and take it back up of His own will. Three days after sovereignly dismissing His Spirit, He sovereignly burst from death's chains. He later declared, "I am He who lives, and was dead, and behold, I am alive forevermore" (Revelation 1:18).

In addition to many disciples and close followers seeing Him, over five hundred people in one place saw Him physically (1 Corinthians 15:6). Paul also saw the risen Lord (1 Corinthians 15:8), presumably while looking up from the dust of the Damascus Road (Acts 9:1-8).

Those who literally and physically saw Jesus after His resurrection subsequently turned the world upside down. Who can dispute the countless number of eyewitnesses who staked their lives on the resurrected Savior.

As Christ followers, may we constantly remind ourselves of this eternal blessing. May we walk each day in this victorious, resurrection life.

Blessings and Victories

The Holy Spirit, through the power of Calvary's finished work, bestows on every true believer a share in the blessings and victories Jesus achieved on the cross.

We'll have to wait for some of these in our future existence in glory. Yet others He intended for our daily, earthly life.

Some blessings and victories may seem like old news as we've heard them many times and may even take them for granted. Unfortunately, we tend to take precious people and valuable things for granted over time. Only when faced with loss do we remember something's or someone's value.

Though we never lose spiritual blessings and victories, we can diminish their power. Just as a car battery loses its charge through non-use, spiritual blessings and victories can diminish in functional power if we don't incorporate them into our daily lives. May we never become so familiarized or desensitized as to take such miraculous, eternal gifts for granted.

Let's explore a few of these more deeply.

Forgiveness

Three of the most precious words ever heard are, "You are forgiven."

Jesus bought us from the slave market of sin at a steep price (1 Corinthians 6:20). This purchase switches our ownership from Satan to Jesus (Acts 26:18). In Jesus alone do we have "redemption through His blood, the forgiveness of sins, according to the riches of His grace" (Ephesians 1:7). God alone maintains the power and right to forgive sin (Psalm 130:4).

With God's forgiveness comes the removal of sin along with its fear and guilt. As humans, we can *forgive,* yet it's sometimes difficult to *forget.* Thankfully, when God forgives, He removes and also forgets our sin (Hebrews 10:17).

One of the biblical principles about forgiveness is that the person who's been forgiven much, loves much (Luke 7:47). In view of the costly price of our enormous sin debt, may we dearly love our Lord and Savior. May we demonstrate it through obedience and surrender to Him. Let's also forgive others as He's forgiven us (Matthew 6:14).

What a blessing to have God's forgiveness.

Cleansing

Genuine believers are given a divine nature through spiritual rebirth and the indwelling of the Holy Spirit.

But we live in an immoral world. Impurities surround us in every aspect of life. Invariably, sin's filth attaches to us unintentionally and sometimes intentionally. No one reaches sinless perfection until reaching the bliss of heaven. So we need ongoing cleansing.

There's the initial, immediate cleansing from our sin stain—the defilement of our inherent sin nature. Then there's the ongoing cleansing from our daily sins. "If we confess our sins, He is faithful and just to forgive us *our* sins and to cleanse us from all unrighteousness" (1 John 1:9).

Thank God, He not only forgets forgiven sins, He sometimes helps us forget them too. He cleanses minds as well as hearts. This comes "through the washing of regeneration and renewing of the Holy Spirit" (Titus 3:5). It's important to remember this aspect of cleansing.

Sometimes we carry burdens of guilt or memories of past sins. But it isn't God who highlights them. If they've been confessed and forsaken, they are under Calvary's blood and God has already forgotten about them. But a subtle adversary (1 Peter 5:8), a loudmouthed accuser (Revelation 12:10) still hurls insults about past sins. Satan knows they are forgiven, but he wants to discourage us.

To resist his assaults, recognize their source and rejoice in God's gifts of forgiveness and cleansing. Let's allow God to renew our minds with the truth of His Word. We are cleansed by reading and obeying God's Word (Psalm

119:9). Additionally, "the blood of Jesus Christ His Son cleanses us from all sin" (1 John 1:7).

Jesus made this cleansing available so He can "purify for Himself His own special people, zealous for good works" (Titus 2:14). He desires and deserves a clean, spotless Bride. "Christ also loved the church and gave Himself for her, that He might sanctify and cleanse her … that He might present her to Himself a glorious church … holy and without blemish" (Ephesians 5:25-27).

As part of that Bride, may we often return to His cleansing fountain. But just because forgiveness is available, may we never consider it a license to sin (Romans 6). May we fervently protect our sphere of holiness.

Don't Stop Here!

Unfortunately, this is where many believers stop.

We rejoice in God's forgiveness and cleansing. We praise Him for dying for us and granting His salvation. We're forgiven and have a never-ending, always-flowing, cleansing fountain for our sins. But we forget there's more.

> If there were not so many Christians being rocked in the cradle of the infancy of the faith, content with their own personal salvation, cooing to the sweet lullabys of spiritual babyhood, the world would not be reeling like a drunkard toward another international deluge.[66]

May we never be satisfied to stop here. Let's never settle for the entry level of our Christlike journey. May we press on to the full growth of spiritual maturity (Hebrews 6:1). May we draw nearer and walk more intimately with the One who loves us infinitely and eternally. Let's lean in closer to His embrace as part of a worthy Bride.

Sanctification

Sanctifcation is an incredible blessing with absolute, initial, and progressive benefits.

The basic Greek word for sanctification is *hagiazó* (ἁγιάζω). It means to set apart, separate, or hallow.[67] It implies a separation to God which leads to the responsibility to live for Him. It involves the ongoing process of God's transformation and our intentional commitment to a closer walk with God. It never means the removal of our old, sinful nature prior to our glorified state in heaven.

Some people falsely presume sanctification only happens after salvation.

[Sanctification] "is the beginning of the work of the Spirit in the soul, and goes on throughout the believer's life, reaching its consummation at the coming of the Lord, when the saved one, in his glorified, sinless body, will be presented faultless in the presence of God."[68]

This process is threefold, yet not necessarily in chronological order as listed.

First, there is the internal, progressive sanctification by the Holy Spirit (2 Thessalonians 2:13). This involves the initial wooing to salvation and the subsequent ongoing transformation after salvation.

Then there is the sanctification by the blood of Christ. True believers are set apart in Christ and "perfected forever" (Hebrews 10:10). This is the eternal security of being reconciled to God by Jesus' once-for-all atoning sacrifice on Calvary. Amazingly, the Spirit and the blood work together in the process of sanctifying genuine believers (1 Peter 1:2).

Finally, there is sanctification by God's Word (John 17:17). This is a daily cleansing that only God's Word brings (Ephesians 5:25-26). Christ followers read, learn, apply, and obey God's Word as evidence of the new, divine nature and fruit of the Holy Spirit.

Remember, all of God does all that God does. The combined benefit and effort of sanctification results in being "washed … sanctified … [and] justified in the name of the Lord Jesus and by the Spirit of our God" (1 Corinthians 6:11).

The Holy Spirit transforms the inside while we work on the outside. The Holy Spirit's work continues unhindered so long as we don't grieve or quench His efforts. But there's also work for us to do. "Let us cleanse ourselves from all filthiness of the flesh and spirit, perfecting holiness in the fear of God" (2 Corinthians 7:1).

Yeah but, Nate, salvation is free. We don't have to work for it.

Salvation is freely extended as a gift, but it's quite costly. May we never devalue it simply because it's freely given. Secondly, it's true we don't work *for* salvation (Ephesians 2:8-9). We work as a *result of* salvation (Ephesians 2:10).

Consecration

Consecration is the recognition that God has undisputed right of occupancy and possession.

We consecrate ourselves by recognizing God's rightful authority by creative and redemptive rights. He has *creative* right as He made us from nothing. He has *redemptive* right by purchase as He redeemed us with His blood (Revelation 5:9). May we never forget that He rightfully owns us.

We grant Him full occupancy and possession by allowing Him to influence and transform our lives. This happens when we obey and incorporate what He says in His Word. We allow the Holy Spirit free reign by giving Him the keys to our hearts and minds and flinging open every door to every room. We hide nothing—He already knows about it anyway. Whatever He brings to mind, we immediately yield to His authority and direction.

Spiritual Maturity

Christlikeness involves spiritual growth. A new birth is followed by growth and development (Philippians 3:12-15).

When my children were born, I knew my life had changed. The hospital made us take them home! There was feeding, changing, bathing, and rocking to do. As they grew, so did our interaction. There was also an expectation for increasing maturity. Infants are cute. But those same cutesy characteristics are weird for an adult.

The apostle Paul scolded believers who remain in an infant stage (1 Corinthians 3:1-3). He called them *carnal*. They continually needed milk instead of solid food. Think of it this way. A baby can't digest solid food on his own. As breastfed, he can only tolerate nutrition that's been digested by his mother.

Sadly, far too many believers rely on someone else for their spiritual nutrition. But genuine, maturing, Christ followers learn to feed themselves from God's Word through reading, studying, meditating, prayer, and divine illumination by the Holy Spirit (Hebrews 5:14).

As recipients of Christ's new nature, our character, conduct, mindsets, and attitudes are supposed to increasingly resemble His likeness. While the Holy Spirit works on the inside, we *put off* the old life and *put on* the new life characteristics.

Yes, the *old* sinful nature struggles daily to overwhelm and defeat the *new*, divine nature. But as we willingly die to self and gladly yield to the Holy Spirit's work inside, we claim Christ's victory over the *old* nature, including its desires and disposition (Titus 2:12).

> While Christ dwells in the believer's new nature, He has strong competition from the believer's old nature. The warfare between the old and the new goes on continually in most believers. This is accepted as inevitable, but the New Testament does not so teach. A prayerful study of Romans 6 to 8 points the way to victory. If Christ is allowed complete sway, He will live in us as He lived in Galilee. Unless He is hindered by our resistance, He will act in us precisely as He acts in heaven.[69]

Paul related the *putting on* of our new life in Christ to a change of clothing. We remove dirty clothes and change into fresh, clean clothes. The emphasis is that we *can* and *should* look, talk, think, and behave like Christ. Authentic Christ followers are wise to memorize and follow the specific instructions of Colossians 3:10, 12-17 (NLT).

> Put on your new nature, and be renewed as you learn to know your Creator and become like him. Since God chose you to be the holy people he loves, you must clothe yourselves with … [prayerfully incorporate the listed Christlike qualities and actions]. And whatever you do or say, do it as a representative of the Lord Jesus.

There's a more in-depth description in Ephesians 4:17-5:33. Yes, there's much work for each Christ follower to do. But it *is* possible. Each day as we die to self, take up our crosses, follow Jesus, and yield to the Holy Spirit, we put into practice what His Word says.

It's all there within our grasp. We can do this!

Power

We've already discovered that life is in the blood.

Since Jesus is infinite, eternal, and omnipotent, there's infinite, eternal power in His blood. That same power grants us ongoing spiritual victory. As Lewis E. Jones wrote in the hymn, "Power in the Blood,"

> Would you be free from the burden of sin?
> Would you o'er evil a victory win?
> Would you do service for Jesus, your King?
> Would you live daily His praises to sing?
> There's wonderful pow'r in the blood.[70]

As regenerated, renewed, and indwelt Christ followers, with resurrection life available to us, we have the power to:

- Overcome the influence and temptation of sin. (1 John 4:4)
- Overcome sinful habits and addictions. (Philippians 4:13)
- Have an effective prayer life. (James 5:16)
- Bear spiritual fruit. (John 15:1-5)
- Let our light shine before others. (Matthew 5:16)
- Actively pursue holiness. (Hebrews 12:14)
- Serve God joyfully. (Psalm 100:2)
- Remain faithful until Christ returns. (Luke 18:8)
- Live like Christ. (Romans 8:29)

Oh, may we never be satisfied to stop at the blessings of forgiveness and cleansing. May we press on to claim and live in all the spiritual victory available to us.

Priceless Value of Calvary

The value of something is usually derived by the price paid for it.

If I buy something expensive, I value it more than something of little cost. Imagine the value Calvary's blood places on each person who appropriates it. The price paid is the precious, eternal blood of Jesus. Understanding the infinite price and power behind this reality is staggering.

When Jesus cried from the cross, "It is finished" (John 19:30), it was more than an acknowledgment of death. It was His declaration of freedom, giving us the ability and victorious power to "walk in newness of life" (Romans 6:4). Jesus now sits enthroned in heaven, lifting nail-scarred hands and interceding on our behalf (Romans 8:34). His doing so isn't a one-time or occasional occurrence. It's ongoing (Hebrews 7:25).

The infinite, eternal *power* behind His blood, His resurrected life, His prayers for us is astounding. May we continually grow and live in the strength of this power.

Calvary stands between me and my past. This is forgiveness and deliverance. Calvary stands between me and the world. This involves separation and sanctification. Calvary stands between me and myself. This is my self-denial and the pursuit of Christlikeness. Calvary stands between heaven and eternal damnation. This involves a person's freewill choice.

Calvary is the pivotal point that makes all the difference in this world and the next.

Take Me to the Cross

I recently read a moving story about a cross standing in the courtyard of London's Charing Cross Railway Station. Located in the heart of the city, it contains much history and many stories. One such story is of a little girl who was there with her mother. In the crowd, she and her mother became separated. Frightened and alone, she began to cry.

A local policeman spotted her and tried to help. He asked, "Are you lost? Where do you live?" The little girl was so confused she couldn't tell him.

He began naming some famous places in the hopes of sparking her recollection. Did she go by Buckingham Palace on her way home? St. Paul's Cathedral? Houses of Parliament? Big Ben? Westminster Abbey? At each name, the little girl sadly shook her head.

But at the mention of Charing Cross, she brightened. "Yes! If you take me to the cross, I can find my way home from there."[71]

Personal Reflection

Have you grown accustomed or desensitized to Calvary's cross? Do you revel in its blessings and victories? Are you maturing spiritually? Do you walk daily in its forgiveness, cleansing, sanctification, consecration, and power? If you do, are you gladly sharing this with others? If not, what holds you back from claiming everything Calvary makes available to you?

Chapter Nineteen

Calvary: A Personal Choice

What will we do with Calvary?

In view of what Jesus suffered, accomplished, and offers from that sacred mount, we face the personal response Calvary demands.

Calvary is personal.

In describing Christ's sufferings and purpose of Calvary, the personal pronouns of Isaiah 53:4-6 practically jump off the page.

> Surely *He* has borne *our* griefs and carried *our* sorrows; yet *we* esteemed *Him* stricken, smitten by God, and afflicted. But *He* was wounded for *our* transgressions, *He* was bruised for *our* iniquities; the chastisement for *our* peace was upon *Him*, and by *His* stripes *we* are healed. All *we* like sheep have gone astray; *we* have turned, every one, to *his* own way; and the LORD has laid on *Him* the iniquity of *us* all.

Notice the *our*, *we*, and *us* words used. To personalize it further, let's substitute *me*, *I*, *my*, and *mine*.

> Surely He has borne *my* grief and carried *my* sorrows; yet *I* esteemed Him stricken, smitten by God, and afflicted. But He was wounded for *my* transgressions, He was bruised for *my* iniquities; the chastisement for *my* peace was upon Him, and by His stripes *I* am healed. Like a lost sheep *I* have gone astray; *I* have turned to *my* own way; and the LORD has laid on Jesus *my* iniquity.

That perspective changes things, doesn't it?

Personalizing the brutality and agony Jesus endured clears our vision and presents us with a personal response.

What will I do about it? What will you do about it?

Calvary demands a personal choice to accept or reject it. Even indifference or ignoring it are choices against Jesus and what He did there.

Making these verses personal allows the truth of Calvary to have its deserving, demanding effect. Christ was bruised or crushed by the weight of our sin. We wove the crown of thorns and shoved it on His head. We hammered the nails that pierced His hands and feet. We thrust the sword that pierced His side. God laid all our sin—our disgusting thoughts, our perverse desires, our filthy fantasies, our self-centeredness, our rebellion against God, all of it—on Jesus.

As our atoning Substitute, Jesus endured God's holy wrath for us (1 Thessalonians 1:10; 5:9). Those who reject what Jesus did will face God's wrath on their own. It's the most important choice of our lives.

So what will we do with Calvary?

If we accept it, we embrace Jesus as personal Lord and Savior. As Lord, He deserves our love and surrender. He deserves our obedience and wholehearted pursuit. As Savior, Jesus shields us from God's wrath and eternal judgment. Our willing surrender to Him is the pathway to fully appropriate the power of Calvary and experience the life of God.

In presenting this eternal choice, God doesn't sugarcoat the cost or benefits of Calvary. He doesn't offer an exotic or glamorous *experience* but an execution. He doesn't offer a charismatic *feeling* but a cross. Yet the benefits far outweigh any personal cost.

God's infinite, holy attributes are all at our disposal. His love, grace, mercy, peace, joy ... His intimate omnipresence. His indwelling Holy Spirit. His foreknowledge and omniscience. His omnipotence that safeguards us eternally. We have His power and promise to overcome sin, the world, the grave, and the Devil. His new and abundant life in this world and eternal life in the world to come are ours.

Acceptance of what Jesus did on Calvary is acceptance of it all. His Lordship and His Saviorship. Membership has its costs and privileges.

In choosing Jesus, we also surrender to His disposition. The life He lived and His obedience to the ordeal of Calvary reveal His determined yet humble surrender. Jesus said, "Learn from Me, for I am gentle and lowly in heart" (Matthew 11:29). As Christ followers, we surrender to His humble, obedient, and surrendered mindset (Philippians 2:5,7-8).

The disposition and mindset of Jesus flow in His blood. By claiming and appropriating His blood, we embrace His disposition and mindset.

> He who desires to have the benefit of the blood must first submit himself to an obedience of faith, which must characterize his whole life. He who truly experiences the power of the blood of Jesus will manifest it by a life of obedience.[72]

Faith without surrender is imagination. A fantasy. A belief without substance.

When Jesus said, "If anyone desires to come after Me, let him deny himself and take up his cross daily and follow Me" (Luke 9:23), He meant it. The new birth of salvation is a one-time occasion. But self-denial and surrender are daily, moment-by-moment, deliberate choices. They are lifetime Calvary manifestations of an inner disposition. We radiate Christ's humility and obedience through the submission of our lives and our wills to God's will, His way, and His Word.

> The will is the kingly power of the heart. It is governed by our love or hatred, and by it ... the whole man is governed. When the will is on ... the Cross, the fellowship of the Cross will soon extend its power over the whole man.[73]

In choosing Jesus, we surrender everything. Jesus said, "Whoever loses his life [self-denial; self-death] for My sake and the gospel's will save it" (Mark 8:35). We submit to the Holy Spirit's insight and influence. We put off the *old*. "Those who are Christ's have crucified the flesh with its passions and desires" (Galatians 5:24). This involves the deliberate rejection of our preferred sin and sinful tendencies (Psalm 18:23). We put on the *new* by gladly embracing the transformation of being conformed—made into the likeness of—the Crucified One.

> No one falls there [death to self] who does not rise to newness of life and service. But remember, it costs the sentence of death in self; the thorough reconstruction of the inner life.[74]

The personal choice of Calvary eternally separates genuine believers from professing believers and unbelievers. Jesus explained this dividing line in His story about the rich man and the beggar named Lazarus.

Jesus described this eternal divide as a "great gulf fixed" (Luke 16:26). The word translated *gulf* is the Greek word *chasma* (χάσμα) from which we get the word chasm. Luke, the author of the book bearing his name, was a physician. He used this medical word that means "an open wound."[75]

Sin is that unhealed, festering wound that separates heaven from eternal damnation. This gaping chasm can only be crossed by Calvary's blood of "the Lamb of God who takes away the sin of the world" (John 1:29).

The world wants no part in spiritual healing and remains forever on one side of the chasm. But those who accept Christ's wounds from Calvary are forever healed. As such, we recognize the enormous cost of His sacrifice.

Calvary's power can be ours. But we must choose.

May we fully choose and gladly embrace the cross. May it become the characteristic and power of our lives.

> He was crucified in weakness, yet He lives by the power of God. For we also are weak in Him, but we shall live with Him by the power of God. (2 Corinthians 13:4)

The cross is our only salvation—the only means of escaping God's eternal wrath and realizing the bliss of heaven forever in His presence. The blood of Calvary covers our sin and empowers our lives. May we fully surrender to its transforming power. May we live in the shadow of the cross while turning our backs on the world.

> Nay world, I turn away, though thou seem fair and good,
> That friendly, outstretched hand of thine is stained by Jesus' blood.[76]

Personal Reflection

What's the value of Calvary's blood to you? Is it of sufficient value to personally accept and appropriate? Is the costly, precious blood of Calvary of sufficient value to surrender everything for it? Is it of sufficient value to sacrifice your desires to obtain its eternal blessings and victories? What will you do with Calvary?

Chapter Twenty

Calvary: What It Expects from Us

Calvary's blood is powerless unless accepted and appropriated.

The impact of Calvary's power is directly connected to each person's response to it.

For unbelievers, this means acceptance of what Christ did on the cross and the appropriation of His blood. To appropriate something is to claim or take it for yourself. Every person who comes to God must come through Jesus (John 14:6). We do this through confession of Who He is and calling out to Him in prayer (Romans 10:9-10, 13).

To reassure us of salvation, the apostle John clarified, "These things I have written to you who believe in the name of the Son of God, that you may *know* that you have eternal life" (1 John 5:13, italics added). It's not a *hope so* salvation, it's a *know so* salvation.

If you haven't accepted Jesus as your personal Lord and Savior, I encourage you to do so now. God has done all He can. The rest is up to you. He lovingly and patiently awaits your response.

> There is a line, by us unseen, that crosses ev'ry path,
> The hidden boundary between God's patience and His wrath.
> And yet the doomed man's path below like Eden may have bloomed,
> He did not, does not, will not know nor feel that he is doomed.[77]

For believers, those who are genuinely reborn spiritually and not just talking the talk, there is much to do. We are the temples of God's Holy Spirit (1 Corinthians 6:19-20). Jesus also confirmed, "The Spirit of truth ... dwells with you and will be in you" (John 14:17). We are His home!

Being the dwelling place of God's Holy Spirit is a sacred privilege and responsibility.

God's Dwelling Place

To discover the significance and application of what this means, let's go back in time to the Old Testament.

Before God's presence came to dwell among His people, He needed a holy environment. To that end, God gave Moses precise measurements and specific materials from which to build a dwelling place for His visible presence.

God also gave Aaron and the priests strict orders about how to dress and act when they entered His holy sanctuary. The smallest infraction resulted in God's immediate judgment. God has specific reasons for everything He does and what He requires of us.

God is and always will be holy. His holy standard is unchanging and never progressive. May we never presume upon His grace or take shortcuts in obeying Him.

> By those who come near Me I must be regarded as holy.
> (Leviticus 10:3)

As we can imagine, the priests zealously performed precise sacrifices and consecration rituals. They guarded against anything or anyone defiling the tabernacle's (and later the temple's) purity. This was done partly out of fear but mostly out of reverence to God. They didn't want His Shekinah glory to leave. This would break communication with Him. It would also bring God's judgment and leave them vulnerable before their enemies.

> Fearing' God is often the motivation which effects godly living. [But] God is interested in much more then outward conformity.[78]

Sadly, years later when idolatry crept into the Israelites' worship, God's glory did, in fact, leave (Ezekiel 10). His holiness doesn't, can't, and won't share the stage with anything unholy or impure. As the dwelling place of God's Holy Spirit, let's protect our sphere of holiness with similar sacred passion.

Protect Your Sphere of Holiness

The condition of a man's home is a reflection on the man.[79]

Is Jesus at home in your heart?

Once His Spirit takes up residence inside, is He there as an invited guest or as the host? Is He comfortable with the living arrangements? Is everything put away and orderly or are boxes cluttering the hallway? Is He allowed to toss out the messy, broken things? Or must He maneuver around all your piles?

With a typical move to a new place, we initially expect some clutter and chaos. But once things settle down, with everything put away, life should move to a clean and orderly routine. The journey toward Christlikeness is more than a move to a new neighborhood. It's a move to a higher and holier spiritual plane.

Just as God expected the tabernacle and temple to be holy and protected, we must be pure and holy dwelling places for God. We must protect our sphere of holiness from even the slightest impurity. As temples of an unchanging, holy God, there can be no tolerance of "pet sins," justifying what we think are insignificant indiscretions, or relaxing of His holy standard. God won't ever share or profane His glory (Isaiah 48:11).

So let's keep our distance from anything even remotely impure. Let's not toy with sin or excuse it. Instead of excusing ("There's nothing wrong with …"), may our moral standard always be God's ("Does … glorify Him?").

> Whoever is born of God does not sin; but he who has been born of God keeps [guards; protects] himself. (1 John 5:18)

This means God empowers and expects us to purify and protect ourselves against sin.

Yeah but, Nate, it seems you're trying to insert works into a free salvation. What happened to "as people sin more, God's grace is even more abundant"?

Abusing God's Grace

God's grace *is* abundant just like His other infinite attributes.

But we are foolish to think true believers can sin as much as they want because they can't out-sin God's grace. Paul refuted this mindset in Romans 6. He also said, "I do not frustrate [nullify; neutralize; make void] the grace of God" (Galatians 2:21, KJV). He couldn't imagine a true Christ follower abusing God's grace with active, habitual sin.

Paul actually instructs genuine, regenerated followers of Christ to "not let sin reign in your mortal body ... do not present your members *as* instruments of unrighteousness to sin, but present yourselves to God as being alive from the dead, and your members *as* instruments of righteousness to God" (Romans 6:12-13). This implies an allowance of *letting* and *presenting* ourselves either to sin or to God. It is because of God's grace "sin shall not have dominion over you" (Romans 6:14). So why would a Christ follower continue to sin and abuse the very grace whereby he is freed from it?

A continuing desire to sin reveals a nature that quite possibly hasn't been regenerated. A new *root* will exhibit new *fruit*. If the old fruit is still rampant, the root becomes suspect.

> Whoever has been born of God does not sin, for His seed remains in him; and he cannot [habitually; intentionally] sin, because he has been born of God. (1 John 3:9)

Those who are truly born of God, with His DNA running through their spiritual veins, "practice righteousness" (1 John 2:29). The *old* sin nature may remain, but there's no allowance to fulfill the *old* passionate desires and longings. The Holy Spirit of God doesn't live in a garbage dump without conviction or consequences.

When God rebirths us spiritually, He transfers us from the kingdom of darkness to His kingdom of light (Colossians 1:13-14). We become Christ's purchased possession (Ephesians 1:13-14). Satan is no longer our slave master. We're set free from sin. Bought out of sin's slave market. We become servants of righteousness (Romans 6:17-18). This world is no longer our home. We become citizens of heaven (Philippians 3:20) with assigned seating in heavenly places (Ephesians 2:6).

While here on our temporary assignment, we shouldn't be distracted by the world and its tempting trinkets (1 John 2:15). We are ambassadors of God's heavenly kingdom (2 Corinthians 5:20). A crown of righteousness awaits those who eagerly await our Lord's return (2 Timothy 4:8).

In this state of expectancy and readiness, let's not abuse God's grace.

Conformed to Christ's Death

That I may know Him ... being conformed to His death. (Philippians 3:10)

Christlikeness involves taking up the cross and conforming to Christ in His death.

Conforming to Christ's death involves being made equivalent to or participating fully in it. It's the intentional dying to self and becoming alive in Him. We willfully surrender personal desires to His perfect will and sovereign orchestration. What He gives, we gladly accept. As He removes, we readily relinquish.

If such a self-death sounds unglamorous and undignified, it is. There's no pretense in crucifixion. It's a gruesome, humiliating, and painful death.

> [The cross] always has its way. It wins by defeating its opponent and imposing its will upon him. It always dominates. It never compromises ... never surrenders a point for the sake of peace. It cares not for peace; it cares only to end its opposition as fast as possible. If we are wise, we will ... submit the whole pattern of our lives to be destroyed and built again in the power of an endless life. The cross will cut into our lives where it hurts worst, sparing neither us nor our carefully cultivated reputations. It will defeat us and bring our selfish lives to an end. Only then can we rise in fulness of life to establish a pattern of living wholly new and free and full of good works.[80]

Being conformed to Christ's death means I relinquish my rights, entitlements, desires, will, strength, expectations, mindset, personality, nature ... everything. I yield to His desires. His heart. His purpose. His will. When I delight myself [soften; become pliable] in Him, He gives me the desires of my heart (Psalm 37:4). A surrendered heart is receptive to Christlikeness.

When I yield completely, God fills me with Himself. His presence. His mind. His power. His disposition. I come to Him emptyhanded in humility and gratitude for all He has done for me. Augustus Toplady said it best in his hymn, "Rock of Ages,"

Nothing in my hand I bring, simply to Thy cross I cling.[81]

Dying to Self

When we come to the end of self, we come to the beginning of Christ.[82]

A crucified man no longer makes demands or fulfills his desires.

What most people fail to understand is this. Upon the new birth of salvation, we are already dead to sin (Colossians 3:3). We died with Christ since He died in our place (1 Peter 2:24). This is why Paul told us to, "Look upon your old sin nature as dead and unresponsive to sin, and instead be alive to God, alert to him, through Jesus Christ our Lord" (Romans 6:11, TLB). Though already dead with Christ, we must still sign our own death warrants.

In the power of Christ's death, I must refuse my old life. On the basis of Calvary and of my oneness with Christ in His death, I must refuse to let self lord it over me. How can I have the benefits of Christ's death while I still want my own way?[83]

Only through the death of *self* do I have the power of God to live the victorious, Christlike life (2 Corinthians 13:4). By considering myself dead to what I want, I open myself to the Holy Spirit's ongoing transformation into Christlikeness.

Dying to self involves a personal identification with Christ's death. As my substitute, Jesus died *for* my sin so I can die *to* sin. My self-life died at salvation and must continue to die daily for my ongoing transformation into His likeness.

Yeah but, Nate, you've mentioned several times this dying to self? How exactly do I do that?

Visualize grabbing your old nature by the arm and dragging it up Calvary's rocky path as the condemned criminal it is. True to its sin nature, *self* will resist. It will scream in anger and beg for mercy. It will whine about unfair and unloving treatment. It will demand its rights. But keep going.

Upon arrival, point to the cross and say, "This is where you belong. I am nailing you here with all your twisted, morally bent, perverse ways. The old me died with Christ. The life I now live is one of Christlikeness."

Then turn and walk away.

But beware. The old self is sneaky and persistent. It may take several trips up Calvary's hill before the heart and mind fully understand what such a self-death means. A crucifixion is a slow, agonizing death. But remember, we are to make everything captive to the obedience of Christ (2 Corinthians 10:5). As He was obedient to death, may we also be obedient in our death to self.

There's no such thing as partial crucifixion.

The man with a cross no longer controls his destiny; he lost control when he picked up his cross. That cross immediately became to him an all-absorbing interest, an overwhelming interference. No matter what he may desire to do, there is but one thing he *can* do; that is, move on to the place of crucifixion. The man who will not tolerate interference is under no compulsion to follow Christ.[84]

To truly die to self, I remove myself from the throne of my life.

Recognizing that Jesus bought me at an infinite price, I'm no longer my own. I belong completely to Him. I can't even scoot over a bit and invite Him to share the throne. Self and Jesus don't and cannot share the same throne. If Jesus is Lord, self must yield. If self is lord, Jesus isn't.

No one can serve two masters; for either he will hate the one and love the other, or else he will be loyal to the one and despise the other. (Matthew 6:24)

Dying to self includes death to worldly affections and forbidden cravings (Colossians 3:5). Our old, sinful nature still craves carnal affections. Sinful influences and worldly desires may still attract us. But we relinquish anything contrary to God's Word and the Spirit's empowering guidance.

What does this look like?

Self-denial [dying to self] is no mere cutting off of an indulgence here and there, but "laying the axe at the root of the tree of self, of which all indulgences are only greater or smaller branches."[85]

This emphasizes the criticality of placing ourselves under the complete authority, influence, and teaching of God's Word and the Holy Spirit. They are the sources of power and victory to live Christlike (Galatians 5:16). Christ's blood and the Holy Spirit's transforming work enable us to live in a way that pleases God the Father (Hebrews 13:20-21). This is another way to become like Christ—Jesus always pleased His Father (John 8:29). This is our reasonable response in consideration of all He has done for us.

Surrender and Obedience

There's no negotiation in surrender.

As followers of Christ, we've been purchased by His precious blood. We either give the keys to the rightful Owner or leave them in the hands of the Enemy.

Yet many people struggle with surrender. They associate it with losing something valuable. Abandoning rights. Giving up control.

These associations make the Lordship of Christ seem burdensome and personally threatening. Yet God's Word plainly states obedience to Him isn't burdensome or grievous (1 John 5:3). Since the loving, omni-everything God has the best interests of His children at heart, surrendering to Him takes on new meaning.

> Surrendering is the opposite of struggling. If we're struggling, the inner war still rages. Self still competes for the throne of life. Selfish desires, preferential passions, even unyielded ambitions are signs of struggling. On the other hand, surrender means the war is over. Self raises the flag of truce and fully yields the throne to God.[86]

Paul gave a relatable example. Jesus is the Head, His genuine followers are the body (Colossians 1:18). In the human body, the head holds the power to command and coordinate the body's function. Yet the body must be healthy, strong, and willing enough to obey the head's commands.

Our surrender and obedience to Jesus are the natural functions of a healthy body. Healthy arms and legs don't move on their own or against what the head instructs them to do. Only disease and atrophy cause the body to respond improperly or resist the head's commands.

As followers of Christ, we voluntarily exchange our lives and destinies for the abundant life and destiny of Christ. The cross becomes a reminder of our daily yielding to the control of Jesus and His Spirit. This is what the apostle Paul meant when he said, "I die daily" (1 Corinthians 15:31) and "I bear in my body the marks of the Lord Jesus" (Galatians 6:17). The cross becomes our possession, our priority, our passion.

Thank God, we have help.

The Holy Spirit (remember His *holy* disposition) helps us along the way. In His transforming work, He helps break the power of sin in our lives. But it still isn't easy. Paul equated the Christlike life with a grueling sporting event for which he disciplined his body to ensure peak performance (1 Corinthians 9:27). Seasoned athletes know there can be no days off from training, no tempting fast food.

There are no shortcuts to Christlikeness.

Dying, Yet Struggling to Live

Something crucified is dying, yet may still struggle to live.

In a dead state, surrender should come naturally. A corpse has no life, no will, no response. The secret to success is in not resuscitating the sinful corpse. Besides, who in their right mind cozies up to a corpse? Leave it dead and buried. Then walk in the newness of life in Christ and in the power of His resurrection.

> No grave, no resurrection: only resuscitation. If a corpse says it is dead, it isn't. You do not need to feel its pulse; it is talking.[87]

Yeah but, Nate, what if surrender is too difficult? What if I choose not to yield my self-will? What if I choose to fully leverage God's love, grace, mercy, and forgiveness after doing my own thing?

An unsurrendered heart reveals one of two possible realities. First, it may reveal the absence of the Holy Spirit, meaning the unsurrendered person hasn't been truly born again. The Holy Spirit only indwells those who've been regenerated spiritually. Secondly, if a person is a true believer, an unsurrendered life reveals spiritual callousness, immaturity, or fear. He either still wants his own way or doesn't trust Omni-Everything God with his life. He resists or quenches the very evidence of being a blood-bought believer (2 Corinthians 1:22).

As Christ followers, let's look to Jesus. He is humble and obedient. My resistance to God's leading usually stems from fear or pride. I fear God will do something I think is foolish. My pride makes me think I know better than all-knowing God. Both traits reveal a lack of trust. Jesus summed it up well.

> It is enough for a disciple that he be like his teacher, and a servant like his master. He who does not take his cross and follow after Me is not worthy of Me. (Matthew 10:25, 38)

God calls His true followers to holiness as He is holy. Calvary makes it possible. Christ's precious, costly blood gives the power to live in holiness (1 Peter 1:15-19). We are called to live supernatural, "set apart," Christlike lives. Yes, this requires a supernatural effort, but it *is* possible. We can do this!

So let's leave our excuses and defenses behind. Let's chase after Christ so passionately, so recklessly abandoned to Him, that we discard all else. May we live surrendered to Christlikeness as a witness to the power of Calvary's blood. May we rearrange our lives so Christ always has the preeminence.

Calvary's expectations seem high. But its privileges, blessings, and victories are well worth it. They position us to walk in Christ's newness of life.

> Have thine own way, Lord! Have thine own way!
> Thou art the potter, I am the clay.
> Mold me and make me after thy will,
> while I am waiting, yielded and still.
> Fill with thy Spirit till all shall see
> Christ only, always, living in me![88]

Personal Reflection

How are you protecting your sphere of holiness? Is the Holy Spirit convicting you about something that is an unholy portal? How often does your *old* nature sneak back onto the throne of your life? What part of surrender do you find yourself resisting? Is it lack of control? Doubting that God knows the best outcome for you? As a result of Calvary, are you willing to surrender to Him?

SECTION 4

Glorifying the Christ of Eternity

Chapter Twenty-One

The Call to Newness of Life

As Christ was raised from the dead by the glory of the Father, even so we also should walk in newness of life. (Romans 6:4)

Jesus Christ brings a newness and vibrancy of life unparalleled by anything this world offers.

With the new spiritual birth comes forgiveness of sin, removal of sin's burden, and freedom from sin's bondage. It's a new beginning. A new life. A clean slate. A do-over of sorts. Yet with such a fresh start, why do so many professing believers cling to the *old* life and the call of the world? Why is spiritual mediocrity so prevalent? Why do so few pursue Christlikeness?

The LORD has set apart for Himself him who is godly. (Psalm 4:3)

Even with such a new start, there are attacks, obstacles, and temptations.

Jesus warned against the subtle creeping of the world into our hearts (Luke 21:34). The inherent danger is being so preoccupied with this world's distractions that Christ's return catches us off guard. As His Bride, the return of our Bridegroom demands our complete attention.

The journey toward Christlikeness is a well-defined, scriptural process. The Holy Spirit performs the majority of this transformational journey. But there's also work for us. Both inner and external transformations depend on personal willingness to surrender to and partner with the Holy Spirit. The entire journey begins with a new, spiritual birth (John 3:3, 7).

New Birth

A new birth is unmistaken.

When both my children were born, I knew their births happened. Life around the house became different. Routines changed. There were new expenses and different needs. Old things passed away; all things became new. There was a new birth on both occasions. They didn't piggyback on one another's birth experience, nor was there any uncertainty as to whether or not they had been born. The new birth was proof of new life.

With salvation, when the spiritual birth takes place, there's a noticeable change. Lifestyles change, along with mindsets and habits. Values align with Scripture. A new family resemblance occurs. The Holy Spirit moves in and takes possession. A spiritual transformation takes place. Once the heart—the inner, hidden core—is changed, everything else changes.

Just as newborns are born on different days and mature at different rates and times, true believers are also on individual journeys. But a new journey it is, and it starts with the new birth. No birth, no baby.

New Creation

Once a person is saved through faith in Christ, he becomes a new creation. Old things fade away; all things become new (2 Corinthians 5:17).

How interesting to see the inclusion of *things* in this verse. The former, sinful *things* are gone and all current *things*—the *things* of our new life in Christ—are brand new. New nature. New mindset. New values. New priorities. New agenda.

Like the transformation of a caterpillar into a beautiful butterfly, the old menu and price tag of sin are exchanged for the new menu and riches of Christ's righteousness (Romans 3:21-22). The butterfly no longer eats worm food. It drinks sweet flower nectar. The *old* no longer satisfies.

True believers have changed lives with Christ dwelling within. A changed nature leads to a changed mindset. A changed mindset leads to changed values. Changed values leads to changed things.

> The Holy Spirit will give to the praying saint the brightness of an immortal hope, the music of a deathless song, in His baptism and

communion with the heart, He will give sweeter and more enlarged visions of heaven until the taste for other things will pall, and other visions will grow dim and distant. He will put notes of other worlds in human hearts until all earth's music is discord and songless.[89]

Yeah but, Nate, we can't be perfect in this life. So why even try now?
It's not a matter of *trying* but in *being*.

Our family status and resemblance have changed. A true believer doesn't look, act, think, or react like the world's children. Children are in their father's gene pool and share his characteristics and nature (John 8:41-44).

Sure, God's true children occasionally misbehave, and He disciplines to correct their behavior. But they grow up reflecting His nature. His characteristics. His disposition. His desires and priorities become theirs. A leopard can't change its spots because that's what identifies it as a leopard (Jeremiah 13:23).

If the world is still attractive to someone, perhaps his nature hasn't been changed.

To say believers can't be holy—can't completely shun attraction to and affection for the world—discounts the nature of the new birth. It slanders God's character and denies His Word because this is the very purpose for which He created, called, and chose us.

He gives us this new nature. He gives us His Spirit and calls us to walk in His newness of life (Romans 6:4). Thankfully, we are enabled to do so by living in alignment with God's Word and surrendering to His Holy Spirit's transforming work (Galatians 5:16, 25).

New Nature

At salvation, God plants a divine seed inside.

This seed germinates and grows as we submit to the Holy Spirit. Its roots run deeper as we experience adversity and trials. Branches and new leaves sprout as we grow in our knowledge and grace of Jesus. As we apply what God says to our lives, fruit appears. Spiritual maturity develops as we become increasingly and steadily more Christlike.

As branches of the True Vine (John 15:1-8), we are to resemble that Vine and bear the fruit of that Vine. All the Vine has, He gives to the branches so we can bear fruit for Him. All the branches have, they give to the Vine as the expression of the sap—the fullness, the filling, the life flowing to and through them. We should so identify with the True Vine—resemble It and surrender to Its life-giving flow—that our lives demonstrate the same nature, power, spirit, and fruit.

True believers resemble Christ.

- Our inner nature has been changed. (1 John 3:9; Galatians 3:26; 6:16)
- Human nature is invaded by divine nature. (2 Peter 1:4; 1 Peter 1:23)
- Our new identity is in Christ. (Philippians 3:7-9)
- We are established, anointed, and sealed by the indwelling Holy Spirit of God. (2 Corinthians 1:21-22)

Our *root* has been changed so our *fruit* is different. "The godly are well-rooted and bear their own fruit" (Proverbs 12:12, NLT). As the fruit follows the root, obedience to God is the evidence of His regeneration (1 John 2:3-6).

We no longer draw sap from the world's root. Our life source has changed. We draw energy from God, His Word, His Son, His Spirit, and His coming kingdom.

> Water obeys the downward pull of this world; steam, or vapor, overcomes the downward pull. Water always seeks the lowest level; steam, or vapor, soars to its highest level. Water gravitates toward the sea; vapor rises to the sky. Water has its place on earth; it belongs eventually in the sea. Vapor has its seat in the heavenlies; it belongs ultimately with the clouds. What is it that seats vapor in the heavenlies? The sun! It draws the water to itself and seats it on high. Not all water responds to the drawing power of the sun, but that which does dwells above.[90]

Even with a redeemed nature, our old nature, with its worldly desires, occasionally trips us up. Our address may have changed, but we still like driving around the old neighborhood.

Some people who never consider walking in darkness sure enjoy a little stroll in the shade.[91]

It reminds me of the Israelites after God brought them out of Egypt. He redeemed and freed them from bondage, torment, discontent, and anguish. What a joy to leave and head toward God's Promised Land. Yet the difficulties of the journey to the Promised Land made them want to return to Egypt.

In the Christlike life, Egypt is symbolic of the world. Upon salvation, God cleansed us from the world's sin stain. He redeemed us from the penalty of sin. He freed us from the bondage of sin and set us on a new path of holiness and righteousness. The former life is past, and we rejoice in our new birth, new life, and freedom in Christ.

And yet ...

Although separated from the world, in weak, carnal moments we tend to reminisce. We remember the fun times and romanticize splashing around in the pigpen. We get as close as we can to the world to catch a sniff of its raunchy pleasures and carnal desires.

Though we have cleansed hearts, they can still desire the pleasures and lusts of the world. Without complete and ongoing surrender to the Holy Spirit, our hearts are "deceitful above all things, and desperately wicked" (Jeremiah 17:9). Who can trust or follow such a heart?

God calls us out of the world and warns against it. He wants us to set our sights and hearts on the Promised Land of Canaan. But sometimes it seems Canaan doesn't hold the same fascination or entertainment of Egypt. We miss the world's pulse, rhythm, taste, smell, habits, attraction, status, and friends. Even though our true home is the Promised Land, it's tempting to straddle the border with Egypt.

This is when the Holy Spirit convicts us to confess and forsake (Proverbs 28:13) whatever sin or *thing* entangles us (Hebrews 12:1). We have God's promise for help and victory.

> Obey only the Holy Spirit's instructions. He will tell you where to go and what to do, and then you won't always be doing the wrong things your evil nature wants you to. (Galatians 5:16, TLB)

New Desires

Christ frees us from the bondage of sin and the pleasures of this world.

Once this happens, we own part of the responsibility to change our desires. Yes, the Holy Spirit performs His supernatural transformation. However, He doesn't force our eyes off the world. We must choose to do so.

> If then you were raised with Christ, seek those things which are above, where Christ is, sitting at the right hand of God. Set your mind [affections] on things above, not on things on the earth. (Colossians 3:1-2)

The more my mind dwells on my eternal home, the less it dwells on this world. If my taste buds long for the feast of heaven, this world's morsels won't tantalize me. But the more I chase the pleasures of this world, the less pleasurable will be the things of God's kingdom. The more I assimilate here, the less I look forward to over there.

Paul encouraged us to, "Stand fast therefore in the liberty by which Christ has made us free," and not reengage with the *old* life (Galatians 5:1). Understandably, he questioned, "How is it that you turn again to the weak and beggarly elements, to which you desire again to be in bondage?" (Galatians 4:9). Jesus pushed it further by saying those who turn back aren't "fit for the kingdom of God" (Luke 9:62).

> When by the grace of God we have been delivered from grosser forms of sin, we are still liable to the subtle working of self in our holiest and liveliest hours.[92]

But we can do this!

Victory comes when we stop struggling and surrender completely to God by crucifying "the flesh with its passions and desires" (Galatians 5:24). We stop negotiating with our favored past times. We stop justifying what we don't view as wrong. Christ becomes our all in all when we turn our backs on Egypt, intentionally cross over the Jordan River (symbolic of self-death), and commit wholly to living in the center (not the peripheral) of God's perfect will.

With each step, we place more distance between us and the world. Once fully surrendered, the world and its *things* no longer hold the same intense fascination or appeal. We have new appetites, the fresh fruit of the new land. We've surrendered the old and received the sweet nectar of the new life in Christ. The old world is behind us; behold, God makes all things new. And He calls us to walk in that newness of life (Romans 6:4).

Yeah but, Nate, I don't love the world—I just enjoy its experience. I know its agenda and strategies are wicked and perverse. But what's wrong with enjoying the things of the world while we're here?

Okay, let's look at those *things* that aren't necessarily sinful, but distracting. The ones that turn our attention to this world and cause us to overlook the world to come. Those we justify or argue to defend our personal preferences. Those we allow to influence us more than the Holy Spirit. The ones to which we give more time than we do the Word of God. We're talking about those *things*, right?

Too often we settle for the measly handouts of the world instead of appropriating the riches and abundance of heaven. As F. B. Meyer said, the Devil "puts some little morsels of worldly pleasure, evil imagination, and lust, and he says, 'Come along, come along, come along.'"[93] All the while he lures us out from under God's protecting shadow (Psalm 91:1-3).

> At times God cannot hear the prayer of your lips because the desires of your heart after the world cry out to Him more strongly and loudly.[94]

A typical response for justifying worldly tendencies is, "There's nothing wrong with it." But that should never be the standard for Christ followers. Instead, of justifying my preferred activity, I should ask some critical questions. "Does it glorify God? Does it meet God's righteous standard? Does it make me more like Jesus? Am I representing Him or the world? Is this (fill in the blank) helping to further the kingdom of God or am I following the world's influences?"

> Whatever keeps me from the Bible is my enemy, however harmless it may appear to be. Whatever engages my attention when I should be meditating on God and things eternal does injury to my soul.[95]

True believers have the everlasting, satisfying fountain of Jesus springing up within (John 4:14). So why carry our pitchers to the shallow, impure wells of the world? Why feast on this world's garbage when God has given us a heavenly appetite? When at war with another country, why blow up our supply lines so we can buy supplies from our enemy? Why continue supporting the *things* of the world when the world hates us?

The more I die to self and surrender to God, the world and all it holds becomes less and less appealing. For me personally, I don't want anything of this present world. Not its entertainment, sporting events, fashion and trends, music and movies, celebrities, values, social statuses, influences, political agendas, false narratives, nothing.

I've aligned myself with Joshua who declared, "Choose for yourselves this day whom you will serve … as for me and my house, we will serve the LORD" (Joshua 24:15). Elijah asked, "How long will you falter between two opinions? If the LORD is God, follow Him" (1 Kings 18:21).

The answer seems clear. But it comes down to personal choice and surrender. Will we choose to follow Jesus or the world? We cannot seek the things of heaven with our eyes and heart set on this world.

New Fruit

Believers owe everything to Christ who gave them His all.

There's no real life apart from Christ. Chasing what the world offers is tantamount to the branches dropping from the Vine to attach themselves to shiny garden tools. The tools give no life but are mere instruments for the Master Gardener (John 15:1).

The things of this world are tools at God's disposal. He gives them as He sees fit for His glory and our good. It's the Vine, not the things of the world, Who gives us life, purpose, and fruit—all to God's glory.

As the Master Vinedresser, God sometimes uses adversity to free the branches from harmful attachments. Jesus said, "Every branch in Me that does not bear fruit He takes away; and every branch that bears fruit He prunes, that it may bear more fruit (John 15:2).

We don't like discipline or any form of corrective adversity. And yet those trials may be God's refining fire that removes unnecessary entanglements that hinder our spiritual growth and fruit-bearing. "No discipline is enjoyable while it is happening—it's painful! But afterward there will be a peaceful harvest of right living for those who are trained in this way" (Hebrews 12:11, NLT).

As our loving Father, God prunes away whatever prevents our full abiding in Him.

> By suffering, the Father would lead us to enter more deeply into the love of Christ. Our hearts are continually prone to wander from Him; prosperity and enjoyment all too easily satisfy us, dull our spiritual perception, and make us unfit for full communion with Himself.[96]

Once a person is spiritually reborn, spiritual fruit and maturity should follow. As we partner with the Holy Spirit, Spring arrives and the fruit of the Spirit blossoms (Galatians 5:22-23). Christlikeness becomes more evident.

In becoming more Christlike, we also do what He tells us to do. Scripture outlines a basic, clearcut mission statement for reborn, renewed, transformed followers of Jesus.

1. Seek first His kingdom and His righteousness (Matthew 6:33). This aligns our *priorities* with His, from earthly to eternal significance.
2. Win the lost and develop other Christ followers (Matthew 28:19-20). This aligns our *hearts* with His, evangelizing and encouraging others along the journey.

We've been created, called, chosen, separated, and appointed to Christlikeness. That's why we're here. Nothing the world offers promotes that goal. Let's walk in His newness by aligning our value systems and heart's desires with Christ's heart, mind, and eternal purpose.

Personal Reflection

What chokes your spiritual branch and restricts the flow of divine sap from the Vine? Is spiritual fruit and maturity evident in your life? How is the Holy Spirit advancing your journey toward Christlikeness?

Chapter Twenty-Two

Called to Holiness

As He who called you is holy, you also be holy in all your conduct, because it is written, "Be holy, for I am holy." (1 Peter 1:15-16)

If something is important to us, we'll prioritize it.

The pursuit of Christlikeness comes down to personal choice and surrender. I must want it. Then I must start the journey. In this sense, we're all as holy as we choose to be.

Please understand, this isn't a self-help journey. Nor do we accomplish it by our own effort. It's an inner passion to apply God's Word to our lives and surrender to the Holy Spirit's transformation. It's the lifelong journey of sanctification. But it starts with an all-compelling inner desire and commitment to the journey.

Scripture has much to say about holiness for true followers of Christ. We're to walk [behave; live; be occupied in heart and mind] just like Jesus (1 John 2:6; Colossians 2:6). We're saved and called "with a holy calling" (2 Timothy 1:9).

Yet few churches preach or teach much about holiness. Even fewer people know about it or can define it. Most don't follow it personally or give much serious attention to it. Or they view it as something mystical or fanatical. Something unattainable in this life. Others consider holiness as something only the Holy Spirit does. Overall, most people complacently accept traditional unholiness as the standard of living.

But God's Word contradicts all such viewpoints. It specifically calls Christ followers to holiness here and now. It's the life we were created, chosen, called, and commissioned to live.

The emphasis God places on holiness should motivate us to discover what He expects and then incorporate it into our lives. God wouldn't require something He didn't expect or we couldn't do. That would be unfair to us and unlike His character.

Holiness isn't what the Holy Spirit secretly and separately does behind the scenes. And there's no instantaneous, "Voila! Now you're holy!" here on earth. It's a steady, developmental journey—in partnership with the Holy Spirit—toward Christlikeness.

Holiness isn't optional. The writer of Hebrews wrote, "Pursue … holiness, without which no one will see the Lord" (Hebrews 12:14). The word *pursue* (*diōkete;* διώκετε) is a present imperative verb indicating continuous, repeated action. It implies an intentional chasing after with intent to catch. We must be in hot pursuit of holiness.

King David said, "My soul follows close behind You" (Psalm 63:8). The Hebrew word for "follows close" is *dāḇəqāh* (דָּבְקָה). It means clings to, pursues hard after, catches by pursuit, or overtakes. Here again, it describes a passionate pursuit after or attachment to God. It's an intentional desire after God's holiness.

Yeah but Nate, how holy do I need to become? I don't want to become a fanatic.

There are no levels of holiness. There's only holy and unholy. God doesn't tolerate varying degrees of holiness any more than we tolerate any degree of mud in our brownies. Since God is righteous and holy, we're foolish to believe He passively tolerates any unholiness in His true children.

Holiness Versus Righteousness

Don't confuse holiness with righteousness. A person may be righteous but not holy. But no one can be holy without first being made righteous.

Righteousness is conformity with the claims of God's higher authority. It's His divine declaration of true believers being made righteous. Jesus imparts *righteousness* to those who accept His gift of salvation (Philippians 3:9).

Holiness is a lifelong process of being set apart for God. It involves withdrawing from fellowship with the world by first gaining fellowship with God. Until we separate from what keeps us *from* God, we will never be fully separated *to* Him.

[Holiness is] the activity of the Holy Spirit to set man apart unto salvation as well as enabling him to be holy even as God is holy."[97]

To explore this separation further, consider some distinctions between unbelievers or those who claim to know Christ and true followers of Christ. Most importantly, genuine Christ followers have the indwelling Holy Spirit. "If anyone does not have the Spirit of Christ, he is not His" (Romans 8:9). We should be able to tell the difference Christ makes in our lives (2 Corinthians 13:5).

The world will hate us because of this difference (John 15:18-19). By choosing to live Christlike lives, we will suffer persecution from the world (2 Timothy 3:12). Those filled with the Holy Spirit understand God's Word—something unbelievers can't do (1 Corinthians 2:14).

True believers discern truth from error—something impossible for unregenerate hearts (1 John 4:4-6). Authentic, righteous believers see through the world's dishonest, perverse, and fake agenda—including its politics. They also recognize the demonic influence behind it.

There is no middle ground, nor can there ever be, between the unrighteous world and a person made righteous through faith in Christ. Light and darkness can't coexist. Genuine followers of Christ, who have chosen the pursuit of holiness, simply cannot coexist with this wicked world. There's no *fitting in*, nor should we want to. We've been called to a higher purpose.

Holiness versus Happiness

When we aren't holy, we aren't happy.

By happy, I'm not referring to temporary giddiness resulting from positive circumstances. I mean the inner contentment only holiness can bring.

To pursue happiness before holiness reverses the divine order—and fails. To pursue holiness is to find God's favor. Jesus said, "Seek first the kingdom of God and His righteousness" (Matthew 6:33), then everything else falls into proper priority. Pursue holiness and you'll find true happiness. Pursue happiness and you'll find neither.

> There can be no real happiness apart from true holiness. God is altogether holy; therefore, He is altogether happy. When we are filled with the [Holy] Spirit, we sing! (Psalm 40:2-3; Ephesians 5:18-19)[98]

The call to holiness is scriptural; a call to happiness isn't. Actually, scriptural holiness often opposes what makes most people happy. We define happiness as a state of well-being and contentment or a pleasurable or satisfying experience.[99] Although happiness sometimes results from serving others, it most often involves self-interests, self-promotion, and self-service. However, holiness involves dying to self, surrendering to God, and faithfully obeying Him.

Too often we mistake the Christian life as one of unbridled happiness instead of holiness. However, I can't find anything in Scripture about personal happiness related to acceptable circumstances, happy events and activities, or even spiritual progress. Although these are all great reasons for joy, human happiness is too fleeting and depends on many changing factors.

Joy, on the other hand, is part of the fruit of the Holy Spirit (Galatians 5:22) and His inner work (1 Thessalonians 1:6). "Let all those rejoice who put their trust in You; let them ever shout for joy ... let those also who love Your name be joyful in You" (Psalm 5:11). We can have joy even when circumstances are harsh (Colossians 1:11), events are adverse (James 1:2), and spiritual progress is painful.

> God is more concerned with the state of people's hearts than with the state of their feelings. Undoubtedly the will of God brings final happiness to those who obey, but the most important matter is not how happy we are but how holy.[100]

The apostle Paul compared the pursuit of holiness to physical exercise. "Exercise [train; practice; condition] yourself toward godliness" (1 Timothy 4:7). Most effective exercise routines are habitual, repetitive, demanding, and exhausting. To gain strength, each muscle group is isolated for several reps with weights or resistance. Such constant conditioning makes the muscles stronger. The more we exercise, we force our strength and stamina into peak performance.

Imagine our spiritual strength if we applied the same rigor in our pursuit of Christlikeness.

- It's interesting that happiness isn't listed with the fruit of the Spirit. The traits of a Spirit-filled, godly, Christ follower are love, joy, peace, patience, kindness, goodness, faithfulness, gentleness, and self-control (Galatians 5:22-23).

Let's apply these to the happy test. I can be loving yet not happy. At least not happy as most people consider it. In fact, loving the most difficult people can actually make us unhappy. I can be joyful in all things, yet still not happy. I can even be peaceful, patient, kind, good, faithful, gentle, and self-disciplined and still not be happy as we generally define happiness. Yet holiness encompasses all these traits.

The lasting joy of holiness far exceeds the fleeting feelings of happiness (Jude 1:24). The peace that holiness brings is beyond human understanding (Philippians 4:7). The kindness, goodness, and gentleness of holiness reflect Christ's disposition. All these confirm that this world's happiness can't compete with holiness.

The traits of Christlikeness may not always seem pleasant or agreeable from a humanistic standpoint. Loving my enemy doesn't make me happy. Neither does rejoicing in adversity. Pursuing peace in a hateful world is a struggle. Being kind to those who betray, falsely accuse, or manipulate me isn't high on my list of happy things.

But that's precisely what Jesus instructed us to do. "Love your enemies, bless those who curse you, do good to those who hate you, and pray for those who spitefully use you and persecute you" (Matthew 5:44-45). Such counterintuitive obedience is another distinction that separates true Christ followers from all others.

Holiness is Separation

The more I pursue holiness, the more God reveals what He wants to transform or remove.

Holy people separate themselves from *good* things so they can be separated to something or Someone far *better*. In both the Old Testament (Leviticus 20:26) and New Testament (2 Corinthians 6:17), God calls His followers to holiness and separation.

It's easy to understand separation from carnal desires and the sinful world. But we also need to separate ourselves from things and people—negative influencers, distractors, discouragers—those soul weights that slow our spiritual pace and drag us down. When running a race, excessive clothing and leg weights are cast aside (Hebrews 12:1). We run to win (Philippians 3:14).

Yeah but Nate, why such an intense focus on separation?

Because some things we'll never hear or learn in the presence of other people. We need time alone with God. Time to hear only His voice. Jesus often separated Himself from the crowd—including His disciples—to spend time alone in quietness and prayer with His Father. Only by withdrawing from the clamor of everyday life could He hear what He needed to hear. Only then could He have an undistracted conversation with heaven.

Many things and responsibilities clamor for our attention and involvement. The Devil subtly lulls people to spiritual sleep with busyness and enjoyments of the world. Even religious activities raise their voices for attention. Yet Scripture says much about being still and quiet in God's presence (Psalm 46:10). We hear His whisper only when we quiet all other voices—yes, even those inside our heads.

Separation to God requires discipline and commitment. Being still is difficult in today's frenzied world. We've grown accustomed to multitasking, filling every spare minute. Even white noise cascades the night's stillness to help us fall asleep. With all this going on, how can we ever expect to hear God's whisper?

> We who call ourselves Christians are supposed to be a people apart. We claim to have repudiated the wisdom of this world and adopted the wisdom of the cross as the guide for our lives. We have thrown in our lot with that One who while He lived on earth was the most unadjusted of the sons of men. He would not be integrated into society. He stood above it and condemned it by withdrawing from it even while dying for it. Die for it He would, but surrender to it He would not.[101]

The separation to holiness isn't a spiritual destination that, once attained, we stop the pursuit. It's a perpetual mindset. A lifestyle choice—complete surrender, consecration, and obedience to God. In the strictest sense, it's living every day in agreement with God's Word, under the direct influence of the Holy Spirit, while avoiding all known impurity from the world (James 1:27).

Even though we're created for, called to, and purposed for holiness, each person has the freewill choice to fulfill or reject that purpose.

Too many Christians want to enjoy the thrill of feeling right but are not willing to endure the inconvenience of being [living] right.[102]

Holiness—Personal Discovery

You can tell a lot about people by their Bible(s) and what you find inside.

Shortly after my dad died, I sat at his desk looking through his Bibles, study books, lexicons, and reference materials. In 1993 he didn't have the modern technological advances we have today with multiple Bible translations, Hebrew-Greek lexicons, and commentaries all on one easy-access application. He had an entire library that took considerable time to study when preparing sermons or Bible studies.

In one of his well-worn Bibles, I found an article by A. W. Tozer titled, *Marks of the Spiritual Man*. When I first read it, I thought it was great material. I tucked it away in one of my Bibles, little knowing how it would affect me later in life.

After years of regrettable sloshing in the pigpen of sin, that article became real to me. In reading through those marks of a spiritual man, the Holy Spirit ignited a holy flame within me. I found myself longing to incorporate them into my life. I don't claim to have fully succeeded. But I continue to "press toward the goal" (Philippians 3:14).

I offer the steps from that article to encourage others in their pursuit of holiness. They are a few suggestions for the person who feels a "desire to make definite progress in the life of Christ."[103]

1. *Strive to get beyond mere pensive longing.* Every man is as holy as he really wants to be. But the want must be all-compelling.
2. *Put away every un-Christian habit from you.* If other Christians practice it without compunction, God may be calling you nearer than other Christians care to come.
3. *Get Christ Himself in the focus of your heart and keep Him there continually.* Only in Christ will you find complete fulfillment. All of God is accessible to you through Christ.
4. *Throw your heart open to the Holy Spirit and invite Him to fill you.* Make your heart a vacuum, and the Spirit will rush in to fill it.

5. *Be hard on yourself and easy on others.* Practice the presence of God. Cultivate the fellowship of the Triune God by prayer, humility, obedience, and self-abnegation.

In the next chapter we'll fully unpack these traits. But the first step is making the intentional decision to stop wishing and start pursuing spiritual maturity, holiness, and Christlikeness.

Get Beyond Mere Pensive Longing

> *Whatever a man wants badly and persistently enough will determine the man's character.*[104]

The pursuit of holiness is an all-compelling, passionate quest of the committed heart.

It's the "hunger and thirst for righteousness" (Matthew 5:6), an insatiable desire for God's heart. "As the deer pants [longs] for the water brooks, so pants [longs] my soul for You, O God" (Psalm 42:1). This pursuit reveals itself with "ever-present, deep-settled wants sufficiently powerful to motivate and control the life."[105]

We desire to be holy because the God we love, worship, follow, and obey is holy (Leviticus 11:44-45). We want to become like Him because we are His. Nothing can distract or pull the committed heart away from this quest.

Some people want to lose weight or get in shape. But few intentionally change their diets or commit to a healthy exercise routine. Other people want better paying jobs. But only a committed few invest in themselves to increase their promotability or marketability. In the same way, the journey of holiness involves more than wishful thinking.

> There's a difference between wishing for a thing and willing it. In a single hour we may wish for a hundred differing objects and forget them. But how different from this is the fixed determination, the settled purpose of the *will!*[106]

There's a direct link between loving and obeying. The *will* mandates an "I have to" mindset (legalism). The *mind* stipulates an "I ought to" mindset (religious duty). But the *heart* compels an "I love to" mindset and lifestyle (committed passion).

Hiding God's Word in our hearts, not our minds (Psalm 119:11), creates an urgency to obey Him. We obey not because we *ought* to or *have* to but because we *want* to. We want to please our Lord and Savior. We imagine putting a smile on His face every moment of every day.

Again, a life of holiness isn't a works-oriented religion. Such a religion provides no lasting value against the pampering of our carnal nature or cravings of fleshly desires. On the contrary, holiness is what God continues doing for, in, and through us.

> May the God of peace Himself sanctify [set apart; make holy] you completely; and may your whole spirit, soul, and body be preserved blameless at the coming of our Lord Jesus Christ. (1 Thessalonians 5:23)

Holiness impacts us spiritually, mentally, emotionally, and physically. It's not enough to *study* and *know* a lot about it. Reading and meditating are all pointless unless we actually put into practice what we discover. The mind, feelings, body—they all become holy. Holiness becomes a lifestyle. A mindset. Our identity.

Christ followers prioritize the desire to become Christlike. Like any other passionate pursuit, it becomes part of who we are. Avid golfers, hunters, bowlers, whatever the hobby may be, all get energized about what they love. Grandparents whip out pictures of grandkids. Parents boast about their children's achievements. Fishermen brag about the size of their latest catch. Golfers romanticize their sweetest golf shot. Teenagers gush about their love interests. Face it, we talk about and prioritize what we're passionate about.

Now imagine that level of energy for holiness. How would we approach it if our lives depended on it? How passionate would we be if holiness promised a lot of money? Of course, we'd prioritize it. We'd talk about it with everyone. Some of us might even leave our jobs to pursue the riches of holiness. How much more energized to do it for the Christ we follow—Who gives us eternal life and the wealth of heaven.

The desire after God and holiness is back of all real spirituality, and when that desire becomes dominant in the life nothing can prevent us from having what we want.[107]

Yeah but, Nate, it's not a very exciting topic. And it sounds like a lot of work.

From a worldly perspective, holiness isn't tantalizing. And yes, it's a lot of work. It's supposed to consume our hearts and possess our minds. It contains the stuff eternity is made of.

God created and purposed us for holiness. His goal is to "make your hearts … holy as you stand before God our Father" (1 Thessalonians 3:13, NLT). He wants us to get beyond just *thinking* about it and actually *incorporate* it into our daily lives. Every moment. In every situation.

Personal Reflection

God created, chose, called, and purposed His followers for holiness. All other pursuits are misuses of the time, energy, and resources God has entrusted to us. What will you do with this realization? Pursue personal happiness and the things of this world? Or pursue holiness, for which you were designed?

Chapter Twenty-Three

Disciplines of Holiness

In Your death, I will daily live. In Your life, I will daily die.[108]

The pursuit of Christlikeness is exciting and potentially risky. Once we move beyond mere thinking about or wishing for holiness, our quest intensifies. It's exciting to become more like Jesus. It's an applicable mindset and lifestyle change. We can do this! We were made for this.

But there are battles along the way. There are things to do and things not to do. Spiritual insight is a must to distinguish between the two. We must also be careful who and what shapes our world view.

> Watchfulness, prayer, self-discipline, and intelligent acquiescence in the purposes of God are indispensable to any real progress in holiness.[109]

We discovered that holiness involves intentional commitment. Let's continue the discovery process by looking at the disciplines of holiness.

Put Away Every Unholy Habit

Jesus said we are *in* the world but not *of* the world (John 17:14-16).

We live in a filthy, wicked world. Not a day goes by that we don't experience something unholy. Yet holiness is what separates and identifies God's people from the world—its culture, value system, agenda, and things. True followers of Christ don't accept or tolerate the world's unholy stains. We are called to holiness in every aspect of life.

Sadly, many *religious* people have "left their first love" (Revelation 2:4). Jesus is no longer as precious as He once was. Their pursuit of holiness has grown cold. Pervasive and invasive sin has desensitized the very hearts that should be ablaze with God's holy nature.

Many cannot see the world's nastiness because they don't view it through God's eyes.

> Until we have seen ourselves as God sees us, we are not likely to be much disturbed over conditions around us as long as they do not get so far out of hand as to threaten our comfortable way of life. We have learned to live with unholiness and have come to look upon it as the natural and expected thing.[110]

Television, movies, and online streaming desensitize against immorality. They slowly and subtly introduce progressive depravity that, should it hit all at once, we'd reject it outrightly. But they first present evil as short, humorous situations, and we laugh it off. Then it returns with less humor and more of the storyline. Before long, what previously was abhorrent is now in full view with little thought of rejection or moral outrage. It is moral erosion by degrees.

In a matter of minutes, murder, sexual immorality, adultery, robbery, nudity, betrayal, violence, rape, brutality, and a whole host of other impurities assault our sphere of holiness. Even God's name is used as profanity without making us cringe. Yet we absorb it all, excusing it as entertainment. We turn our heads ever so slightly instead of refusing exposure to it in the first place.

Our holy temple is under unholy attack. We must protect it.

> Denying [rejecting] ungodliness and worldly lusts, we should live soberly, righteously, and godly in the present age. (Titus 2:12)

What ever happened to saying *no* to sin?

Why do people who claim to be followers of Christ sniff every puff of vile air the world's disgusting machine belches out? Why do we justify or excuse worldly preferences with, "There is nothing wrong with it"?

Imagine the result if every genuine Christ-follower:

- Boycotted all entertainment that doesn't glorify God
- Rejected the world's ridiculous fashions and immodest styles
- Refused to attend or watch sporting events whose main sponsors are alcoholic beverage companies

- Ignored celebrities with abhorrent lifestyles
- Boycotted products from organizations that promote immoral tolerance and acceptance of all forms of perversity
- Championed and supported only the products, fashions, lifestyles, and agendas that honor God's holy standard
- Voted for candidates and legislation that align with God's moral standard instead of blindly following political alliances
- United as one holy front against the world's perverse agenda
- Promoted holiness as aggressively as the world promotes immorality
- Lived each day according to God's holy standard instead of accepting and adopting the world's norms

Think how the world would change if all genuine believers stopped justifying or ignoring even marginal sin and separated ourselves to holiness.

Yeah but, Nate, that would pretty much shut down every source of enjoyment. We'd have nothing to watch. Nothing fashionable to wear. Nothing much to do. Then what're we supposed to do? What kind of life is that?

It's a holy life.

Look at all the time we could use focusing on Christlikeness. That's our purpose, remember? Look at the extra hours we could devote to quiet time with the Great I AM. Imagine the extra time to ponder what Jesus did for us on Calvary. Think about the spiritual growth and development that would take place.

Consider how we could better use our resources for spiritual endeavors. Instead of season tickets, we could support missions. Build a new church. Start a Christian school. Support God-honoring charities.

Sometimes we don't hear God's whispers because the world's noise drowns out His voice. If we spend time in His presence, actively listening to Him, we just might learn a thing or two.

Personal holiness comes only by conscious effort.[111]

Unfortunately, Satan's intentional, subtle, moral erosion is achieving his goal of deceiving even those who claim to follow Christ. Holiness is something we place in the back seat to be worn only on Sunday mornings.

It's no wonder we struggle to be holy when we digest the world's filth without so much as a moral twitch. It's no wonder we have so little spiritual power, so few answers to prayer. Why would holy God intimately interact with unholy children?

Unsaintly saints are the tragedy of Christianity.[112]

We've lost sight of Eternal, Infinite, Omni-Everything, Sovereign, Almighty God. We've lost sight of the costly price of His precious blood shed for us. The world's filth blurs our vision so we no longer see Incarnate God beaten and bleeding on a rugged cross. We forget the Christ we follow is seated high in majesty and sees everything. We've breathed so much nasty air that we've forgotten the pure fragrance of heaven.

Oh, may we bow before Almighty God. May we confess our waywardness and apathy. Let's beg His forgiveness and cleansing. Then may we commit to walking before Him in righteousness. May we fulfill His call to holiness.

Let's surrender our hearts to the Holy Spirit's transforming work while rejecting the world's filth. May we become God's "chosen generation, a royal priesthood, a holy nation, His own special people" and exhibit the virtues of Him who called us out of darkness into His marvelous light (1 Peter 2:9).

May we put away every unholy habit and make Christ the focus of our hearts.

Make Christ the Focus of the Heart

A genuine Christ follower can't get enough of Jesus or Calvary.

Is Christ the object of my heart's affection? Can I say with King Solomon, "My beloved is mine, and I am his" (Song of Solomon 2:16)?

People in healthy, loving relationships naturally want to spend time together. They naturally yield selfish ambitions for the good of the relationship. A personal relationship with Jesus prompts the same response. Fellowship with Him. Willingly obeying His Word. Gladly surrendering to His perfect will. These are the natural outflows of a heart overflowing with love for Him.

True Christ followers *want* to be holy because Jesus is holy. We passionately *want* to be like Him. Jesus sacrificed His life so His Bride could consistently become more like Him. He deserves no less nor will He settle for less.

- Christ also loved the church and gave Himself for her ... that He might present her to Himself a glorious church, not having spot or wrinkle or any such thing, but that she should be holy and without blemish. (Ephesians 5:25-27)
- Having made peace through the blood of His cross ... to present you holy, and blameless, and above reproach in His sight. (Colossians 1:20-22)

A law of development runs through nature. Seeds germinate and grow into plants over time. Seedlings grow strong and tall over time. Relationships develop intimacy as trust and vulnerability grow over time. Notice the time element involved in growth and development.

Spiritual maturity happens by spending consistent, quality time with Jesus. He gave Himself *for* us so He could give Himself *to* us. Think of how much more like Him we'd become by spending more time with Him.

> No single encounter between God and a creature made in His image could ever be sufficient to establish an intimate friendship between them."[113]

Yeah but, Nate, I'm so busy. I don't have time to spend with Jesus.
Read that statement again. Slowly.

Genuine followers of Christ, who have Jesus at the center of their hearts and lives, make and prioritize consistent, quality time with Him. If other things crowd Him out of our calendars, be careful using them as excuses. Jobs. Career goals. Relationships. Children. Hobbies. Pets. Ministry. Whatever. God is the giver of every good and perfect gift (James 1:17). But He can also remove them (Job 1:21) to free up some time for Him. Hold His blessings loosely and give Him preeminence over it all. And get Him on your calendar.

Like any other valuable relationship, our time investment with Jesus must be undistracted, unhurried time. May we prioritize quiet, quality time with our loving Bridegroom.

At its core, holiness is oneness with God. Since He is holy, He always *is*, *wills*, and *does* what is supremely good and pure. He desires and bestows supreme good and purity in His people. He makes us holy as we surrender.

As we continually surrender to the Holy Spirit, Christlikeness becomes more evident.

If Christ isn't evident or real in my life, talking about Him or representing Him is pointless. If the *faith* I share with someone has no *power* or transformation in me, I'm just gossiping, not witnessing. At the scene of an accident, police talk to actual eyewitnesses to determine the truth of what happened. They avoid anyone who says, "See, what I *think* happened was …" In my relationship with Jesus, I can only witness to what's real.

When Jesus lives at the center of my heart and remains enthroned there, I'm drawn to my Beloved. It's in the heart where holiness takes root. The heart is where commitment and surrender reside. Where logic and willpower fail, love prevails.

With Christ as the focus of the heart, we have His peace of mind, joy of heart, and purpose of life. If anything properly motivates Christ followers regarding His rightful place in their hearts, let it be Galatians 6:14 (NLT).

> May I never boast about anything except the cross of our Lord Jesus Christ. Because of that cross, my interest in this world has been crucified, and the world's interest in me has also died.

Christ gave us His all in demonstrating His loving heart for us. How can we possibly give Him any less?

Filled with the Holy Spirit

There's a huge difference between the Holy Spirit's *indwelling* and His *filling*.

Jesus said, "No one puts new wine into old wineskins, or else the new wine bursts the wineskins, [and] the wine is spilled … New wine must be put into new wineskins" (Mark 2:22). This is how He introduced the reality of the Holy Spirit taking up residence in a regenerated heart. The *old* man can't handle it. He needs a supernatural change (2 Corinthians 5:17).

The *indwelling* of the Holy Spirit happens when a person is born from above (John 3:3). God inserts a new, divine nature within those who fully and genuinely accept Him (2 Peter 1:4). This new nature is what makes Christlikeness possible.

Just as in eternity God acted like Himself and when incarnated in human flesh still continued in all His conduct to be true to His holiness, so does He when He enters the nature of a believing man. This is the method by which He makes the redeemed man holy. He enters a human nature at regeneration as He once entered human nature at the incarnation and acts as becomes God, using that nature as the medium of expression for His moral perfections.[114]

The *filling* of the Holy Spirit happens when we yield completely to Him. He enters and possesses every room made available to Him in the human heart. Paul gave insight as to the overwhelming influence and power of the Holy Spirit. "Do not be drunk with wine … but be filled with the Spirit" (Ephesians 5:18).

Yeah but Nate, why would Paul link drunkenness and being filled with the Holy Spirit?

He did this to emphasize the powerful, possessive effect the Holy Spirit should have in our lives. When a person is intoxicated, he loses control of his normal faculties. He's under the complete control of the alcohol in his body. This is the way genuine believers should live under the Holy Spirit's complete control.

Keep in mind that all of God does all that God does. God the Father purposed and called us to holiness. The Holy Spirit indwells us and prompts us toward holiness. Jesus gives us freedom (John 8:36). Freedom from sin, its penalty, and its power (Romans 8:2). Freedom to walk in holiness. Freedom of spontaneous spiritual movement (John 3:8) while always moving us toward Christlikeness (John 15:26).

Jesus said the Holy Spirit guides us into all truth (John 16:13). We limit the Spirit's freedom to move and teach spontaneously by unsurrendered desires and resistance (1 Thessalonians 5:19). Even programmed reading plans and rigid prayer routines may prevent the Spirit from showing us what He wants to in the moment. Strict, regulated prayer time may forfeit the spontaneity of praying without ceasing (1 Thessalonians 5:17) and absorbing what God has for each moment. Some of my most spiritually insightful moments have been spontaneous.

Every Spirit-led saint knows that there are times when he is held by an inward pressure to one chapter, or even one verse, for days at a time while he wrestles with God till some truth does its work within him. He is in the hand of the free Spirit, and reality is appearing before him to break and humble and lift and liberate and cheer.[115]

By spontaneous, I don't mean a carefree, haphazard approach. We still need deliberate, undistracted time in God's presence with His Word. We "hide" God's word in our hearts (Psalm 119:11) so the Holy Spirit can apply its truth to our lives. The wisdom of God's Word and the illumination of the Holy Spirit reveal how to pursue and develop holiness.

The next step is to humbly receive and diligently act upon what we discover. When the Spirit pricks our hearts against gossip or slander, we stop gossiping and slandering. When He convicts against the sins of lust, adultery, or pornography, we forsake them and ask Him to re-wire our minds against them. When He reveals an area of life not fully surrendered to God, we surrender it. We immediately put into practice what God's Word says and what the Holy Spirit reveals.

The reason so many of us are not filled with the Spirit is, we're so stuffed full of ourselves, there's not room for Him.[116]

Being filled by the Holy Spirit means emptying myself of my agenda. Instead of bombarding God with personal desires, a person willing to be Spirit-led humbly asks, "What do You want to show me?"

Doing this throughout each day opens heart and mind to His surprising and necessary work. It exposes prevailing weak areas and enables spiritual development. It also awakens visions of God's majesty.

Yeah but, Nate, it's difficult being as holy as God demands. No matter how hard I try, I continue to fail. How can I pursue Christlikeness like this?

In our natural, unsurrendered state, it's impossible. Even when we die to self and surrender completely to the lordship of Christ, our *old* nature constantly raises its ugly head. But we continue taking up the cross and dying daily. We confess our failings and ask His forgiveness and cleansing. We take the next step. Above all, we don't quit because "in due season we shall reap if we do not lose heart" (Galatians 6:9).

Thankfully, God empowers what He calls and protects what He expects. He is "able to keep you from stumbling [failing] and to present you faultless [unblemished; blameless] before the presence of His glory" (Jude 1:24). The Holy Spirit empowers us to live holy lives. This is why we welcome Him, never grieving or quenching His efforts. Resisting His transforming work throttles His power.

When we think it's impossible to live in obedience and surrender to God's holiness, we find refuge in the Holy Spirit. We just need to get out of His way. In dying to self, in yielding to His all-knowing conviction, instruction, and direction, He transforms us into what we can't become on our own.

> [God] bestows upon us the Spirit who sanctifies us, who so renews our heart and inward nature and fills us with His holy and heavenly power that it becomes really possible for us to be obedient. The one needful thing is that we should recognize and trust in the indwelling of the Holy Spirit, and follow His leading.[117]

Pursuing holiness, in partnership with the Holy Spirit, positions us for the presence of God.

Practice the Presence of God

> *You hide them [those who fear God] in the shelter of Your presence.*
> *(Psalm 31:20)*

God is omnipresent, yet there is precious intimacy in His personal presence.

When in the presence of someone we love, our hearts glow. Our minds are aflame. We focus our interests on our object of affection. We radiate the wellness and wholeness of the shared love. In the same way, the person who loves God deeply and wholeheartedly is lifted into the rapture of His personal presence and captured by His heart.

Jonathan Edwards (1703-1758) pursued such a longing after God. An American pioneer and catalyst of the revival known as the Great Awakening, he was also one of the forerunners of the Protestant missionary expansion.[118] One of his journals revealed his passion in the pursuit of holiness:

> It was my continual strife day and night, and constant inquiry, how I should be more holy and live more holily ... I went on with my eager pursuit after more holiness and conformity to Christ. The heaven I desired was a heaven of holiness; to be with God, and to spend my eternity in divine love and holy communion with Christ.[119]

Practicing the presence of God is more than basking in His fellowship or even surrendering in obedience to Him. It's developing and pursuing an ever-deepening, intimate, loving relationship with Him.

I can enjoy fellowship with someone with whom I don't have a relationship. A perfect stranger on a business flight may share many commonalities with me. We may enjoy engaging conversation, but we're not in relationship. I may obey a work supervisor, even excel at whatever job performance he may require. Yet we're not in relationship.

Pursuing a life of holiness goes deeper than superficial interaction. It's living each moment in personal communion with the vibrant presence of God.

May we live in such a way that we readily acknowledge God's personal presence. May we live each day as if in the presence of a king. After all, He's the King of kings and Lord of lords (Revelation 19:16).

Imagine Him there during business meetings. When in the car, place your hand in the empty seat beside you and imagine holding His hand while talking with Him. Invite Him along wherever you go, to whichever event you attend. Ask Him what He thinks before making a decision. Express your heartfelt love and gratitude for Who He is, not just what He's done for you.

Actively live in His presence. It's what we'll do for eternity.

Summary

We pursue holiness by faith, obedience, and surrender.

Christ followers believe God's Word and apply it daily. We surrender to the Holy Spirit's influence as we meditate on God's Word. We love righteousness and hate sin (Proverbs 8:13). We look for ways to become more like Jesus and less like the world. We endear ourselves to what is true, pure, right, holy, friendly, proper, truly worthwhile, and worthy of praise (Philippians 4:8, CEV). We foster an intimate relationship with the Spirit of truth, righteousness, and holiness (John 14:16-17) and yield to His leading. We do all this to present ourselves "holy, and blameless, and above reproach" to our Bridegroom (Colossians 1:22).

May we passionately pursue holiness (Christlikeness) with all our hearts and affections. May we prioritize it until its transforming work becomes evident in our lives. May we fan its flames until it consumes us fully and influences us completely.

Personal Reflection

Which holy discipline will you begin incorporating into your life? What first came to mind regarding the removal of every unholy habit? That may be what God wants to remove. Will you surrender it? How precious is Jesus to you? Does the Holy Spirit have full access to your life? How would a mindset of "living in the presence of a King" transform your life?

Chapter Twenty-Four

The Priority of Eternal Significance

No one has power over the spirit to retain the spirit, and no one has power in the day of death. (Ecclesiastes 8:8)

How much time do you have left to live? Most people don't want to think about their deaths. Even completing a Final Will and Testament is a struggle. Yet death is a reality we all face. A proper perspective of eternity brings us face-to-face with the inevitability of our own mortality. As a friend used to joke, "No one checks out of this ride alive."

Maybe it's just my imagination, but it seems people are dying younger these days. No matter the age, they now face eternity with no further opportunity to change. Close friends and relatives, from all age groups, are passing into eternity.

Years ago, I started collecting funeral notices of people I've known. It's my way of honoring their memories while also facing my own mortality. As the years pass, that memorial folder has grown increasingly thicker.

I think of Stella, an infant born prematurely. She only lived three months, yet had an incredible impact on the lives of her family and hospital staff.

Daveen, a college friend, was four days older than me. After enduring a lifetime of various treatments for severe illnesses, she passed into eternity at the age of twenty.

More recently there was René, a friend who helped with my lawn maintenance. I expected his usual bi-monthly visit. Instead, his distraught wife told me he died shortly after the New Year, leaving her and their two young daughters to face life without him. He was only fifty-two.

Jeff was a humble, godly man who led worship music at several churches. His voice was as smooth as his sense of humor. I had the privilege of singing with him for many years. During the COVID pandemic, he became sick and was placed on a ventilator. When asked if he needed to say any last words to his family, he calmly replied, "No, they know what they need to know." He joined heaven's choir at the age of sixty-one.

In February of 2023, I learned of Chuck's passing due to stomach cancer. He worked for me years ago. We became friends who enjoyed seeing humor in just about every situation. He lived eighty-one years before entering eternity.

Then there was Cynthia, a lovely lady with an infectious smile, radiant spirt, and heart overflowing with the love of God. She was a ministry partner who served the singles at her church. Soon after enjoying a spirit-filled conference, she suffered a stroke. It wasn't long before she ran into Jesus' loving embrace at the age of fifty-four.

Lastly, two days before Thanksgiving of 2022, while enjoying a morning cup of coffee, my father-in-law, Jeff, quickly and unexpectedly slipped into eternity. He was only sixty-eight years old and in great shape. He ate right and exercised every day. He could outwork most people. The time between when he started feeling dizzy and when he embraced Jesus was about ten minutes.

Ten minutes.

We all face those final ten minutes. We have no forewarning of when they start. But everyone, from infants to the aged, face their reality.

Since the Fall in the Garden of Eden, death reigns. Scripture forewarns that death is the inevitable appointment we each have (Hebrews 9:27). God lovingly alerts us that our brief time on earth is like vanishing vapor (James 4:14). Our days are like a breath or passing shadow (Psalm 144:4).

For this reason, we pray with the Psalmist, "Teach us to number our days" (Psalm 90:12). May we come to realize how brief life is. "Make me to know my end and what is the measure of my days, that I may know how frail I am" (Psalm 39:4).

Yeah but Nate, what does this have to do with becoming like Christ?

Our time is too short to waste. Eternity is too long to get it wrong. May we live with an urgency about the approaching reality of eternity. May we pursue Christlikeness intensely every day that we have—starting with today.

Along with the reality of eternity comes the certainty of eternal significance.

Eternity must influence everything about life here on earth. Every thought. Every action. Every decision. If eternity awaits, what do we need to know about it? What should we do to prepare for it? How do our actions here impact our reality over there?

May the reality of eternity help us realize the significance of our work here for an investment over there.

Infinity Revisited

Although physical death strikes us as gloomy and final, there's a victory side.

As I write this, we're celebrating Resurrection Sunday. Christ's tomb stands empty. Jesus is risen and ascended on high. He defeated death and now sits enthroned in heaven.

Eternity has no beginning or end, no past or future. It is life independent of time—always a glorious and endless present tense. Infinite, immeasurable God dwells in eternity. He has no origin, no end. He remains in the eternal present tense of I AM. He exists from a vanishing point of eternity past to a vanishing point of eternity future (Psalm 90:2).

Since God created us as time-bound creatures, He gives us relatable associations to better understand His infinity and eternality. He is the First and the Last, the Alpha and Omega, the beginning and the end (Revelation 1:8, 11; 21:6; 22:13). We need time to understand God's chronological and appointed events. But infinite God steps in and out of time as He pleases. He's already lived all our pasts and foreseen all our tomorrows. Time is merely the pause button on God's eternal remote control.

God never hurries. As Sovereign, He doesn't have to as He never forgets or overlooks any detail. Nor does anything happen of which He is unaware. He does everything in the *fullness of time*.

- When the fullness of the time had come, God sent forth His Son. (Galatians 4:4)
- In the dispensation of the fullness of the times, He might gather together in one all things in Christ. (Ephesians 1:10)

God may not act or respond when we expect, but He's always right on time.

Time will one day run out. Time for a person to accept Jesus as Lord and Savior ends at death. Time as we know it ends after the thousand-year reign of Christ. Then the mechanisms by which we track time will no longer exist (Revelation 21:23, 25). After the Millennium, only eternity future awaits.

For unbelievers, the brevity of life and ultimate end of time creates a personal urgency to accept Jesus Christ while there's still time. For Christ followers, it creates an urgency to become Christlike and be about our Father's business while we still can. Jesus warned, "*The* night is coming when no one can work" (John 9:4).

We have today. Let's make it count for eternal significance.

Don't squander or trifle with spiritual matters. Jesus emphasized the urgency of being prepared for eternity in His parable of the rich man who planned to build bigger buildings to accommodate his growing wealth. "Fool! This night your soul will be required of you; then whose will those things be which you have provided?" (Luke 12:20).

Our final ten minutes eventually run out. We leave everything behind when we embrace eternity.

Life after Physical Death

This is the promise that He has promised us—eternal life. (1 John 2:25)

It seems every month or so someone publishes a new life-after-death story. As a skeptical person, I wonder about their reliability and motives.

Some speak about experiences that don't align with Scripture. It could be a person may receive divine insight only intended for his particular journey. I also realize many people today simply want to "tell their story."

But I'd rather hear the main story of history—the story of Jesus. He shared His life-after-death experience in His eternal Word. It was witnessed and verified. Having His story is sufficient truth for me.

Yet God, in His grace and mercy, allowed a life-after-death experience within my family. It was more than a story told. We lived it. I offer it here, not as another *story*, but to share how it affected my family's life.

My dad died when he was eleven years old.

On a hot, dusty day in 1938, he and his brothers were hauling a load of gravel in their father's farm truck. My dad rode in the back on top of the gravel. Unfortunately, the truck hit a bump, tumbling him over the side. One of his Overalls suspenders hooked on the truck's sideboard. This saved him from his initial fall. But it also swung him underneath the truck. His brothers heard him scream but couldn't stop in time. The full weight of truck and gravel instantly crushed his small body.

At a hospital about an hour later, the doctor examined him thoroughly. Both lungs were punctured from six broken ribs. Left hip, completely crushed. Profuse blood loss. Internal injuries. Rising fever.

Dad soon lost consciousness as his nurse recorded his weakening pulse.

The doctor met my grandfather in the hallway. "Your son's body is severely broken. He simply cannot live. There's nothing we can do but make him comfortable until he passes."

While Grandpa Stevens prayed, my dad died. But he later described in great details what happened to him.

He was whooshed up to a dazzling city, his feverish brow cooled by a refreshing breeze. Soft, calming music emanated from everywhere. Buildings seemed to pulsate with energy. A distinctly sweet incense permeated the air. He said it smelled like home.

Then he heard a voice telling him to go back.

Go back where?

Back in the hospital, the medical staff kept their vigil beside his broken, lifeless body. They waited for the doctor's pronouncement.

Wait, what's this? The attending nurse felt a slight flutter, weak at first but growing stronger with each heartbeat. The room exploded in a flurry of activity.

Pulsing with new life, Dad returned from his celestial visit to find himself trapped in that mangled shell with insufferable pain, wishing he could return to the beauty, tranquility, and supernatural health of his heavenly home. There, he was free, happy, and whole. Here, he was trapped, hurting, and crippled.

Dad's heavenly experience stirred longings that affected the rest of his life. He was here, but his heart was over there. A homesick look clouded his eyes when he talked about his after-death experience.

Occasionally he would say, "I smelled that smell again today." Each time, these momentary whiffs coincided with the death of a loved one, family member, or friend. Dad deeply inhaled these brief whiffs of "home" that escaped the spiritual dimension. He was alert to its fragrance.

My dad's longing for heaven affected his earthly life. He served God with heaven on his mind. He feared death no more than he feared crawling into bed after a hard day's work. We knew he didn't want to be here. His earthly trek is summed up by two powerful words on a small plaque he kept on his desk. *Perhaps Today.*

Fifty-four years after his childhood after-death experience, his permanent appointment with death arrived at the age of sixty-five. A sudden and massive heart attack ushered him into Jesus' embrace. No longer crippled or homesick, he's finally home.

He lived with one foot firmly planted on heaven's shore while the other remained here on earth. Every day, he was ready to shift his weight to the solid ground of heaven. He lived with what I call the urgency of the immediacy of Jesus.

Not everyone experiences such things nor are they blessed with such a legacy. But everyone does have God's Word that gives the assurance of Christ's resurrection and the certainty of life after physical death.

Jesus "abolished death and brought life and immortality" (2 Timothy 1:10). Hallelujah! Placing our faith in Him removes the fear from "the shadow" of death (Psalm 23:4). Shadows may seem scary. But they are, after all, only shadows.

From conception, each person is an eternal being made in the image of God (Psalm 139:13-16). We will spend eternity with or without Him. Just as Jesus dismissed His Spirit into His Father's hands, upon our deaths, our spirits return to Him too (Ecclesiastes 12:7). For a true believer, the soul, mind, memory, and complete consciousness are whisked immediately into the presence of Jesus (2 Corinthians 5:8). For an unbeliever, the soul, mind, memory, and complete consciousness awake in torment (Luke 16:23).

Engineered for Eternity

This world is not our permanent home.

We're only "strangers and pilgrims" (Hebrews 11:13) passing through. We've been engineered for eternity yet temporarily placed in time. Our time here on earth, though brief, is a proving ground or boot camp that prepares us for eternity. This is why an eternity-based perspective is critical.

The apostle Peter encouraged us to conduct ourselves during "the time of your stay [dwelling as resident aliens] here in fear" (1 Peter 1:17). The word *fear* is the Greek word *phobos* (φόβῳ) from which we get the basis for phobia.

It means during our brief time here in this world, we should be alert, on guard, or wary. In other words, act like a visitor, not a permanent resident.

When we visit another home or country, we're on our best behavior. As guests, we conduct ourselves according to the local rules, but we don't act like it's our home. We keep a low profile since we don't have the same protections or rights as citizens. There's a certain *fear*, an alertness, that reminds us we're not at home.

Yeah but, Nate, then why're we here? Aren't we supposed to enjoy ourselves— even as believers? If not, what's the point of our existence here?

The answer points us back to the ultimate purpose for true believers. We are to be conformed [shaped; molded] into the likeness of Jesus (Romans 8:29). During the earthly journey [boot camp] of becoming like Christ, we are to "bear much fruit" of eternal significance (John 15:1-8).

Jesus shifted the values, mindsets, priorities, and efforts of His followers from the earthly and temporal to the heavenly and eternal.

> Do not lay up for yourselves treasures on earth ... but lay up for yourselves treasures in heaven. (Matthew 6:19-20)

Paul redirected the perspective for true believers. "We do not look at the things which are seen, but at the things which are not seen. For the things which are seen are temporary, but the things which are not seen are eternal" (2 Corinthians 4:18). What we see and feel in this life is temporary. The unseen, invisible realm is eternal. It alone has lasting value and significance. This is why it's critical to maintain a mindset of eternal significance.

This is a bit difficult because we become attached to this tangible world and its things. But the things of this world, even though some are necessary and legitimate, don't really matter.

Sure, we need jobs for income to feed ourselves. We need cars to drive to and from jobs. We need homes in which to live. But they're all temporary instruments for our journey toward Christlikeness. They shouldn't become the objects of our affections any more than we desire the knife and fork more than the steak. They're merely *tools* that provide the ultimate outcome. And we leave all the *tools* behind upon entering eternity.

The man with the most toys still dies and leaves them all behind.

Both my dad and father-in-law were talented men. It seemed they could fix anything and had the tools to do just that. Dad had a rather large library of books he cherished and used in ministry. He also built houses and church buildings, wired electrical systems, and arranged water and septic structures. He could repair cars, fix broken reading glasses, and sew car seat covers, among many other things.

My father-in-law seemed to have every tool known to man and knew how to use them. He loved working in the yard, planting new trees and bushes, and landscaping it to accommodate all his storage sheds. He built a Land Rover from scratch, loved tinkering on an old tractor, and enjoyed leading and playing music in church.

But both men left behind everything they accumulated. The visible things of this life didn't transition with them into eternity.

> We brought nothing into this world, and it is certain we can carry nothing out. (1 Timothy 6:7)

This emphasizes the significance of eternity. God created us to spend eternity with Him. God "puts eternity in their mind."[120]

To prepare us for that destiny, He calls us to Himself. He made the way possible through Calvary. He gave us His Word and Spirit to enable the holiness necessary to live in His presence. On top of all that, He gifted us with the tools necessary for both realities. He gives us earthly resources of time, talents, wisdom, and money as tools for this life while investing (laying up treasure) in eternity.

Jesus revealed a great guide for identifying the priority eternal significance has in our lives.

> Where your treasure is, there your heart will be also. (Matthew 6:21)

Temporary Rental Versus Eternal

The heart identifies a person's primary passion and priorities.

These will dominate our time, attention, and values. If our passion and priorities are on things of this world, we're short-sighted with a skewed investment perspective.

The Priority of Eternal Significance

Yeah but, Nate, your view sounds rather fanatical. Wouldn't it make us so heavenly minded that we serve no earthly good?

Prioritizing the temporal things of this life while ignoring the permanence of eternity is to "chase the wind."[121] That's the meaning behind the phrase, "Vanity of vanities, all is vanity" (Ecclesiastes 1:2). It's allowing the *rental* status of the physical body or physical realm to override the spiritual and eternal.

If I rent a home, I know it's not mine. How foolish for me to consider adding on a room or installing a pool. I'd waste money and time as it still belongs to the landlord. I leave it all behind when I move. Should I vacation at a hotel on the beach or a quiet mountain rental home, it's equally foolish to "spruce up the place" and spend my entire time there making improvements.

Our earthly bodies are rentals. God's already told us our bodies are not our own—they belong to Him (1 Corinthians 6:19-20). Any emphasis to please or pamper ourselves in this life is simply fixing up the rental.

The prophet Isaiah reminds us where our focus should be. "Why do you spend money for what is not bread, and your wages for what does not satisfy?" (Isaiah 55:2). Through the Psalmist David, God asked, "How long will you love worthlessness?" (Psalm 4:2).

Inside the human heart resides an innate and insatiable hunger. God alone can fill that God-shaped vacuum. The sooner we accept and incorporate that truth into our lives, the sooner we can be filled (Matthew 5:6). God alone gives fulfillment and rest for our souls (Matthew 11:28).

> God made the soul a little too large for this world. We could possess the entire world and a void would still exist.[122]

As further encouragement to develop an eternity-based life view, God's Word warns against the tempting attraction and temporary satisfaction of the *things* of this world (1 John 2:15). The world is a sinful place filled with alluring entrapments and attachments. We may shun its major wickedness and perversity. But our hearts can easily fall in love with the world's things.

The apostle John knew a thing or two about love. The word he used in verse 15 is *agapate* (ἀγαπᾶτε), a derivative of *agapao*. This word involves "a direction of the will and finding one's joy in something."[123] It's generally

211

used of God's love toward us and vice versa. And yet we can extend this same sacred love to the temporary and deceitful resource-wasters of this life.

Peter drove the final nail in the coffin of earthly things. He warned of a coming day when "the heavens will pass away with a great noise, and the elements will melt with fervent heat; both the earth and the works that are in it will be burned up" (2 Peter 3:10). Then he jolted true believers back to the reality of their ultimate purpose and eternal significance.

> Therefore, since all these things will be dissolved [melted; destroyed], what manner of persons ought you to be in holy conduct and godliness. (2 Peter 3:11)

Let's not have attached hearts like Lot's wife who turned around to get one last fond look at her "stuff" as it all went up in flames (Genesis 19:24-26). Instead of focusing on the *things* that will burn up, let's turn our attention and priority on what will last. Things of eternal significance—holiness and godliness.

Which brings us full circle to Christlikeness.

We're all personally accountable before God for what He entrusts to us (Matthew 25:14–30). May we always be conscientious and wise about how we spend the time, talents, and resources God gives us. While here in our proving ground or boot camp, may we keep the main thing the main thing. Let's keep our minds and affections on things above, not on things of this earth (Colossians 3:2).

Like my dad, may we live each day so in tune with heaven's fragrance that we become spoiled for nothing less. Our final ten minutes arrive eventually. This world isn't our eternal home. All its counterfeit perfumes, trinkets, enticements, and standards don't, can't, and won't ever come close to the treasures of heaven. May eternal significance influence every moment of our lives.

Personal Reflection

What do you value more, the things of this world or the future investments of heaven? Knowing you'll leave everything behind, how does that affect your perspective? How can you change your life view to focus more on the eternal? What significant investment are you making for eternity?

Chapter Twenty-Five

Personal Accountability for Eternity

Those who sleep in the dust of the earth shall awake, some to everlasting life, some to shame and everlasting contempt. (Daniel 12:2)

Every person's soul is engineered for eternity. Everything in a person's life brings them to this point. We all face Calvary. We all face eternity. They are inseparable. Because we're made to live forever, Calvary and eternity intersect at the same destiny: personal responsibility.

This is the climax of each person's history. God holds us personally liable for our choice about Calvary. For those who accept and claim what Christ did there, He holds us accountable for our pursuit of Christlikeness.

To prepare for this inevitable appointment, every person faces critical, inescapable questions *before* facing God in eternity. How we answer determines our eternal outcome. I cannot overstate the urgency of answering in a way that's acceptable and pleasing to God.

Four Eternal Questions

1. *What have you done with Jesus?* This speaks to the salvation He obtained at Calvary. We either accept or reject Him. Our answer in this life determines our eternal destination in the life to follow. Only those who accept Jesus as personal Lord and Savior face the following questions.
2. *What are you doing with God's Word?* This speaks to sanctification—the lifelong process of becoming more Christlike. Allowing God's Word to fill us with all wisdom (Colossians 3:16) only happens with daily, quality time spent reading, studying, and then obeying it by applying its truth to our lives.

3. *What are you doing with the Holy Spirit?* This speaks to surrender. The Holy Spirit indwells every genuine believer and performs His work of holiness. His transformation and anointing are proportional to our surrender to Him.
4. *What are you doing with the resources God gives you?* This speaks to stewardship. We are accountable for our time, finances, witness, and opportunities. "That each one may receive … according to what he has done" (2 Corinthians 5:10).

Jesus—Eternal King

There is a King in heaven with nail-scarred hands.

These scars reveal His identity and His authority. There will be no mistaking, questioning, or doubting Him. Every person from every age, nation, and language will stand before Him. God the Father has given all authority and judgment to Jesus (John 3:35; John 5:27; Matthew 11:27; 28:18).

As the suffering Lamb, Jesus endured the agony of the cross. Because of His obedience even to death, God the Father exalted Him. One day soon, every knee will bow and every tongue will confess that Jesus Christ is Lord (Philippians 2:9-11).

Jesus, in righteous justice and moral equity, will reward or rebuke each person according to His righteous and holy standard. Scripture confirms His rule will be firm and righteous (Psalm 9:8). There are no legal loopholes, no miscarriages of justice in His kingdom.

In his heavenly vision, the apostle John saw "a Lamb as though it had been slain" (Revelation 5:6). John knew Who this was. He previously identified Jesus as the "Lamb of God who takes away the sin of the world" (John 1:29). But this is no longer the suffering Lamb. This is the ruling and reigning Lion of Judah (Revelation 5:5). He's the subject of heaven's anthems of adoration and praise that combine all His omni-everything, divine attributes.

> Worthy is the Lamb who was slain to receive power [omnipotence] and riches [omni-wealth/resources] and wisdom [omniscience], and strength [omni-authority] and honor [omni-respect] and glory [omni-splendor] and blessing [omni-praise]! (Revelation 5:12)

This awe-inspiring scene should give goosebumps of joy to every genuine Christ follower—and shivers of fear to every unbeliever. Why? Because this same Jesus is coming back. Soon!

After Christ's ascension into heaven, two angelic beings announced, "This *same* Jesus … will so come in like manner as you saw Him go into heaven" (Acts 1:11). Not someone *like* Him—but this same Person. This same beaten, scarred, mocked, humiliated, murdered, resurrected, and glorified Jesus is coming again. Jesus Himself gave a three-fold warning: "I am coming quickly!" (Revelation 22:7, 12, 20).

The inevitability of facing Him hinges on the certainty of death and the certainty of Christ's return. Whether we die or He returns, our fate at that moment is forever sealed.

Yeah but, Nate, people have been saying that for over two thousand years. Maybe it's just a fairy tale. Or maybe you're misinterpreting what He meant.

Jesus—His Return Assured

The apostle Peter forewarned of such a mindset.

> Scoffers will come in the last days … saying, "Where is the promise of His coming? … All things continue as *they were* from the beginning of creation." (2 Peter 3:3-4)

Peter also warned against complacency about Christ's return. "With the Lord one day *is* as a thousand years, and a thousand years as one day" (2 Peter 3:8). Moses also said a thousand years are like yesterday to God (Psalm 90:4).

May we never presume upon the economy of heaven or on Christ's loving patience.

Heaven's time is different than our calendars or stopwatches. Using Peter's and Moses' comparisons, Jesus has only been gone a little over two days. That makes a return trip rather quick. Secondly, God may be delaying Christ's return to give everyone ample time to make his choice for Him. He wants everyone ready to spend eternity with Him. But eventually, even divine, loving compassion comes to an end.

Until that time, He repeatedly and lovingly extends His invitation to all. The time to respond to His eternal salvation is *now*. Now, before God shuts that door of opportunity just like He shut the door of the Ark before the flood.

Heaven or eternal damnation depend on this most important choice. Until we die, the choice to accept or reject Christ remains before each person. It's not something we can put off. There's no neutral stance.

Nor can we pick some other option. God the Father already determined the eternal process by the counsel of His will (Ephesians 1:11). Jesus already shed His precious, costly blood. The Holy Spirit already bears witness to the truth of the matter. All Three are in agreement and have done all they can (1 John 5:7). The choice is now up to each person.

> Men do not become Christians by associating with church people, nor by religious contact, nor by religious education; they become Christians only by invasion of their nature by the Spirit of God in the new birth. And when they do thus become Christians, they are immediately members of a new race.[124]

Religious Self-Deception

There's no salvation by osmosis.

It doesn't soak into you from a Christian family, being raised in a Bible-believing home, going to church all your life, knowing about Jesus, giving money to a church, or even teaching Bible study classes.

That religious deception faces many people today. They've been around Christianity so much that they've grown familiar with the words but not the Living Word. They recite Bible verses and sing praises with arms uplifted. But if Jesus walked past them, they wouldn't recognize Him because they have no personal relationship with Him.

They know *about* Him, but they don't know Him personally.

At the end of every church service, should an invitation be given to come to Jesus, they leave early to beat the crowd, sing along absentmindedly, or look around at who they think needs to respond. There's no serious introspection or listening ear to the Holy Spirit's wooing. They think, "I already know all this," or "I used to teach that."

Some cling to the fact they prayed a short prayer as a child. Although they may have been sincere as a child, most are unaware that, while reciting words after someone else, they had little understanding of what such a decision meant or the lifelong commitment involved.

If your salvation experience was such, I recommend revisiting it to ensure you were truly "born from above" and a spiritual transformation occurred. I'm not discounting any childhood experience—simply suggesting you confirm it. The Bible plainly states, "Examine yourselves *as to* whether you are in the faith" (2 Corinthians 13:5). The high stakes of eternity motivates such introspection.

There's also a subtle spiritual danger for "morally good" unbelievers. These are unregenerated people who are acquainted with Jesus and have acquired a taste for the Christian life. They flirt with Jesus but aren't interested in a lifelong commitment with Him.

They appreciate Scripture and hang out with church folk. They approach religion like any other community or civic group. They love the clean morals and sometimes feel guilty for their sinful actions, habits, and lifestyles. Some may even wish they had the inner virtues and power they see in genuine believers.

But most often, they want the *fruit* but aren't interested in a changed *root*. As a result, they camouflage their lives with luscious leaves. But their *fruit* eventually exposes their true *root*. A cherry root will always bring cherry fruit. A thorn bush will always bear thorns. Jesus said, "You will know them by their fruits" (Matthew 7:16).

Being morally good is eternally different from being born into God's family. Morally good unbelievers may fool other people but they can't con an all-knowing God.

This may be why some people struggle with unchanged behaviors, inner unsettledness, and unanswered prayer. They may ask God to change their *fruit*—immoral actions, addictions, unbridled passions, impure thoughts, unrighteous behaviors. But God won't do that for several reasons. First, they aren't yet His children. Secondly, He won't override their free will. Third, He won't override His law of nature. They must first ask Him to change their *root*, their sinful nature, that which produces the diseased *fruit*.

Religious self-deception will ban some people from the very heaven to which they think they belong. God's Word is clear. Until or unless someone has a genuine encounter with Jesus where, in brokenness, repentance, and surrender, he yields all he is, all he has learned, and all he thinks he has to offer, and personally accepts Jesus as Lord and Savior, he remains in his deceived, lost state.

Even praying the easy-believism prayer of, "I accept you, Jesus," doesn't help unless they are reborn "from above" (John 3:3). Such spiritual rebirth is evidenced by a genuine, supernaturally changed nature and behavior.

Actually, it doesn't matter what we *believe*. The Devil and demons believe in Jesus and know exactly who He is (James 2:19). They even recognize His authority and power (Luke 8:26-33). Yet their belief does them no good. No, heaven is only for those with new natures—regenerated, transformed, holy hearts.

Let's now look at the eternal destinations for both unbelievers and authentic followers of Christ. The place depends on each person's choice for or against Jesus. We look first at those who are not reborn spiritually.

Eternal Destiny for Unbelievers

Unbelievers include those who reject Christ, simply know *about* Him, or have been deluded into thinking they are in a personal relationship with Him when in fact they are not.

Yeah but, Nate, who are you to judge? Only God knows the condition of a person's heart. Maybe more are in such a relationship than you think.

God does know the condition of each person's heart. He also says we can tell the *root* by the *fruit*. It isn't judgmental or harsh to say a peach tree has peaches. It's making an assessment based on observable facts. Jesus told us, "Do not judge according to appearance, but judge with righteous judgment" (John 7:24).

For someone to say they are "in a relationship" with God without the accompanying evidence of such a transformational and spiritual rebirth reminds me of how some people approach dating. When two people begin enjoying shared interests together, they develop commonalities. They become better acquainted. They share more time together. But often, one person presumes the relationship is deeper or more exclusive than it is. That presumption results in an awkward conversation that pretty much ruins the friendship. "But I thought we were ..." is the way I believe many people will start their conversation with Jesus in the hereafter. Jesus gave an example of how that conversation will go.

Many will say to Me in that day, "Lord, Lord, have we not prophesied in Your name, cast out demons in Your name, and done many wonders in Your name?" And then I will declare to them, "I never knew you; depart from Me." (Matthew 7:22-23)

In essence, Jesus will tell them, "We were never in an exclusive relationship."

Even though they'll claim they believe in Him, prayed a sinner's prayer, served in church, or taught Bible studies. Whatever other claim they have, the result will be the same. "We were never in a personal, experiential, intimate relationship."

Oh, the horror for a person to falsely believe he's on his way to heaven, then face the terrors of eternal damnation in the lake of fire. This may sound overly dramatic and scary. But the reality is even worse.

If you minutely suspect you may have missed something regarding your eternal destination, I encourage you to toss all preconceived notions, clear your vision, and do something about it now.

Yeah but Nate, I have faith. Why are you questioning that?

Let's look at the word *belief* or *faith*. Two Greek words for this are *pisteuo* (πιστεύω) and *pistis* (πίστις). Their meaning goes beyond mere knowledge, mental persuasion, or personal belief. A far better meaning is "reliance upon, not mere credence."[125]

I can have all the faith and belief in a chair to support my weight. I can measure its dimensions and calculate how much weight it can support. I may love the chair. It may even be in my home. But until I sit in it, entrusting my full weight to it, relying on it to support me, my faith and belief are pointless.

Beware of presuming that you are saved. If your heart is renewed, if you hate the things you once loved, and love the things you once hated; if you have truly repented; if there is a thorough change of mind in you; if you have been born again, then you have reason to rejoice: but if there be no vital change, no inward godliness; if there be no love to God, no prayer, no work of the Holy Spirit, then saying "I am saved" is but your own assertion, and it may delude, but it will not deliver you.[126]

Just because I believe something doesn't necessarily make it true or real to me. Just because I'm familiar with Jesus and know what the Bible says about Him doesn't make an eternal difference for me. I must completely surrender to and rely upon Christ's sacrificial death on Calvary. In repentance for my sin, I accept Jesus as Lord and appropriate His blood so I can be reconciled to God. Such spiritual reliance must be on Jesus and Him alone.

As outlined in the Bible, here are the steps through that decision:

1. *Admit your sin.* "There is none righteous, no, not one. All have sinned and fall short of the glory of God." (Romans 3:10, 23)
2. *Acknowledge God's free gift of salvation.* It's the only option against sin's destiny of eternal damnation. "The wages of sin is death, but the gift of God is eternal life in Christ Jesus our Lord." (Romans 6:23)
3. *Accept Christ as your personal Lord and Savior.* "If you confess with your mouth the Lord Jesus and believe in your heart that God has raised Him from the dead, you will be saved. For with the heart one believes unto righteousness, and with the mouth confession is made unto salvation." (Romans 10:9-10)
4. *Place your complete faith and trust in Jesus.* Acknowledge Him as the only way to reconciliation with God and assurance of eternity in heaven. "Believe [fully trust; fully rely] on the Lord Jesus Christ, and you will be saved." (Acts 16:31)
5. *Pray and invite Him into your heart and life.* "Whoever calls on the name of the LORD shall be saved." (Romans 10:13)

When a person does this honestly and sincerely, Jesus said a spiritual rebirth happens that infuses him with God's divine nature (John 3:3, 7). The evidence of this new birth is twofold. First, it recognizes Jesus as Lord with full authority over his life. Salvation involves personal surrender to Jesus. Secondly, genuine salvation produces spiritual *fruit*. The Holy Spirit now living inside results in changed behavior and a new family resemblance.

Until or unless such a new birth takes place, a person is destined to eternal damnation. That's not judging; that's scriptural.

Yeah but, Nate, isn't hell just a scary idea to frighten people into being good?

The Reality of Hell (Lake of Fire)

Jesus talked more about the place of eternal damnation than any other biblical author.

What most people refer to as hell is called the "lake of fire burning with brimstone" (Revelation 19:20). It's a place of eternal, non-stop torment (Revelation 20:10). And it's the final dumping place of Death, Hades, and all unbelievers (Revelation 20:14-15).

Jesus vividly described it and warned of its horrors. He said it's a place of torments (Luke 16:23) and unquenchable fire with undying worms (Mark 9:44, 46, 48). He called it a furnace of fire where people wail in anguish and grind their teeth in regret (Matthew 13:42). It's a place of eternal torment, flames, and no return (Luke 16:19–31).

Jesus compared it to Gehenna (Matthew 10:28). In ancient Jerusalem, Gehenna was a trash dump outside the walls where people burned their garbage. It was where fire perpetually smoldered. Imagine the stench and choking smoke. The flies, maggots, and nasty rodents. Since Jesus described and warned about the reality of such a place, we can believe it's real.

Other biblical authors also warned about its reality. Paul referred to it as a place of "everlasting destruction from [away; apart] the presence of the Lord and from the glory of His power" (2 Thessalonians 1:9). The writer of the book of Hebrews called it a place of damnation or destruction (Hebrews 10:39). Both Peter and Jude referred to it as a place of eternal darkness (2 Peter 2:17; Jude 1:13). The apostle John called it "the second death" (Revelation 2:11).

Definitely a place to avoid at all costs.

And lest we falsely believe God viciously created such a place for people, Jesus said it was prepared, not for people, but for the Devil and his fallen angels (Matthew 25:41). God takes "no pleasure in the death of the wicked" (Ezekiel 33:11) and is "not willing that any should perish" (2 Peter 3:9). The lake of fire is simply the choice and consequence of people rebelling against God and rejecting Jesus.

Some people joke, "I don't mind going to hell because all my friends will be there." That mindset is misguided. There's no love, affection, or even friendship there because God alone is love (1 John 4:8). Whatever God is, eternal damnation is the opposite.

Even secular historian Flavius Josephus alluded to its reality and torment. As a Pharisee, he confirmed they believed the wicked would suffer eternal punishment in a perpetual prison.[127] He further described it as perpetual darkness with a lake of unquenchable fire where the unjust are "dragged by force" and "driven by violence," a noisy place with hot vapor, disease, distemper, fiery-undying worms, never-ending grief, and sleeplessness.[128] If he didn't accept Jesus as his Lord and Savior, he's in that place now, experiencing worse than what he described.

Yes, the lake of fire is a real place, with real torment, that will last for eternity.

Great White Throne

To understand what happens to unbelievers after death, we must look again at the last book of the Bible. Here's what John the Revelator described.

> And I saw a great white throne ... I saw the dead, great and small, standing before God; and The Books were opened, including the Book of Life. And the dead [unbelievers] were judged according to the things written in The Books ... And Death and Hell were thrown into the Lake of Fire. This is the Second Death. And if anyone's name was not found recorded in the Book of Life, he was thrown into the Lake of Fire. (Revelation 20:11-15, TLB)

There's no way to sugarcoat this horrific place and time. I can't imagine standing before such a majestic, frightening throne knowing full well the ultimate fate of all who are brought there.

To hear our loving Creator sadly yet firmly say, "Depart from me into the lake of fire prepared not for you, but for Satan, his demons, and his fallen angels. How I longed for you to accept Me. I patiently waited for your response to My gentle knocking at your heart's door. But you spurned every attempt. You rejected every gentle nudge of the Holy Spirit. I gave you numerous opportunities to accept Me, accept My love, appropriate My blood. But you ignored Me. If only you would've acknowledged Me as Lord and Savior and surrendered your heart and life to me. Now it's too late."

This is what awaits all who thumb their nose at God's love. Those who ignore or reject Christ's sacrificial death on Calvary. Those who continue on in unbelief. There will be no negotiating. No plea-bargaining. No asking for leniency. The conviction and sentence will be final.

The only way to avoid such a dire summons is to accept Jesus Christ today (John 14:6). Today, this precise moment, is the only guaranteed time you have. In view of the certainty and finality of death—and the reality of an eternity without God—I urge you to not delay another moment. Invite Him into your heart and life right now.

Yeah but, Nate, what if hell isn't real? What if when we die, we just simply cease to exist?

I accept your genuine skepticism. Believing God's Word does require complete trust. However, here's the deal. If *you* are right and I've lived a moral, upstanding life, when I die, I have nothing to lose. I will have left a good legacy, treated others with respect, and did what I could to benefit my fellow man. If *you* are right, my vanishing from the time continuum simply leaves me with a good reputation and legacy.

But …

If *I'm* right and you're wrong, you have everything to lose. Knowing that all previous Scripture prophecies have been fulfilled should lead to trusting what it says about the future will happen.

Eternal Destiny for Genuine Believers

How blessed is the journey for true followers of Christ who move from initial faith to acceptance of Jesus Christ as Lord and Savior. Who obey His Word and fully surrender to the Holy Spirit's transforming influence.

We aren't perfect people. Rather, we acknowledge our imperfections and weaknesses and rely completely on God's strength (2 Corinthians 12:10). We reckon ourselves crucified with Christ (Galatians 2:20), dead to sin, and apathetic to this world's temporary pleasures and treasures. We're alive to God (Romans 6:11). We embrace the Holy Spirit's indwelling and prioritize the journey toward Christlikeness.

Jesus promised, "In My Father's house are many mansions … I go to prepare a place for you. I will come again and receive you to Myself; that where I am, there you may be also" (John 14:2-3).

Hallelujah! He promised He "has prepared a city for them" (Hebrews 11:16).

While we're still on this earth, we anxiously long for our reunion with Him. With eyes fixed on Him, let's maintain a constant view of the majesty and splendor of God.

> May each genuine believer live with the knowledge that a nail-pierced hand holds over his head a crown of righteousness.[129]

May all followers of Christ faithfully represent on earth the One who faithfully represents us in heaven. May we faithfully live and witness to others of His love, grace, mercy, patience, and open arms. Let's shine His light through our lives so others may see it and be drawn to Him (Matthew 5:16). Let's surrender each and every day to His absolute authority—then walk in that surrender in all aspects of life. May we be so filled with His Spirit that people see Jesus in us.

But one word of caution. The closer we get to Jesus, the thinner the crowd.

Few are the followers of Christ who surrender all to Him. Those who live each day for Him. Who long for the day when they rush into His embrace.

Few daring souls turn their backs on what this world offers to pursue His eternal riches. Few soldiers of the cross willingly shoulder their own crosses, die to self, and follow Him. Jesus said this journey is narrow and difficult. He also said only a few would find it (Matthew 7:14). May we be part of that few.

Judgment Seat of Christ

Why is following and becoming like Christ important?

Under the direction and inspiration of the Holy Spirit, the apostle Paul alerted every believer of a future accountability before Jesus Himself.

> We shall all stand before the judgment seat of Christ. (Romans 14:10)

This is heaven's performance evaluation for every believer. Nothing we do is hidden from God's eyes. He rewards or punishes as we deserve (Jeremiah 32:19, CEV). Paul confirmed true believers will be liable for what we've built on the foundation laid by Jesus Christ (1 Corinthians 3:9-10).

It's here we will be held accountable for what we've done, "whether good or bad" (2 Corinthians 5:10). Jesus forewarned that our conduct as His followers will be thoroughly tested by fire (Mark 9:49). This isn't the judgment of hell because Christ already paid that penalty for us on Calvary. This judgment is an assessment of what we've done since being spiritually reborn (Romans 14:12).

The word translated "bad" (or "evil" in some translations) means worthless, harmful, or wicked. In that sense, believers still have the capacity to sin after salvation. This is why we have forgiveness and cleansing (1 John 1:9). So the "bad" here could be any unconfessed, unforsaken sin. Secondly, since we are "created in Christ Jesus for good works" (Ephesians 2:10), this "bad" includes all works, activities, passions, priorities, everything that is worthless, harmful, or not contributary to God's kingdom.

The *what* and the *why* will be important here. Motives will be scrutinized. Were our actions done in love (1 Corinthians 13)? Were they done for God's glory (1 Corinthians 10:31)? Or were they done in pride, a sense of duty or competition, or grudgingly? All will be revealed.

When summoned before Jesus, believers will have their entire lives placed on the altar of God's refining fire. The good works Paul refers to aren't simply good deeds. They are lifestyle actions motivated by creation purpose and love for Jesus. Every deed, thought, motive, priority, opportunity, attitude, mindset—everything will be tested by that fire.

There will be only one of two outcomes—rewards or rebukes.

> Now if anyone builds on this foundation [Jesus] with gold, silver, precious stones, wood, hay, straw, each one's work will become clear ... because it will be revealed by fire; and the fire will test each one's work, of what sort it is. If anyone's work ... endures, he will receive a reward. If anyone's work is burned, he will suffer loss; but he himself will be saved, yet so as through fire. (1 Corinthians 3:12-15)

The surviving gold, silver, and precious stones will be evidenced by "faithfulness, self-discipline, generosity beyond the demands of the law, courage before our detractors, humility, separation from the world, cross-carrying, and a thousand little deeds of love."[130] In essence, everything that results from the disposition of Christlikeness.

Everything consisting of insignificant, temporal, and worldly things—the wood, hay, and straw—will be burned up by God's everlasting flame. Those in this situation will experience heaven but will have no lasting reward to give back to Jesus who gave His all for them. Sadly, they will have saved souls but wasted lives.

Those with rewards will gratefully have something of eternal value to lay at Jesus' feet. We see the twenty-four elders casting their crowns before Christ's throne as an act of deep reverence and worship (Revelation 4:10). Oh, to join them!

This is why true followers of Christ turn their backs on things of this world. We don't have time to squander on such cheap, consumable trinkets. Keeping this throne room in mind gives clarity and strength when we're tempted to invest in worldly things.

I've had far too many years of wood, hay, and straw. With my remaining time, may God grant me the wisdom, clarity, and strength to pursue things of eternal significance. His gold, silver, and precious stones. May all Christ followers join the journey so we can "have confidence and not be ashamed before Him at His coming" (1 John 2:28).

Personal Reflection

To which heavenly courtroom will you be summoned? If you haven't yet placed your trust in Jesus, what prevents you from doing so? If you're a true Christ follower, what do you want Him to find you doing when He returns? How does His unknown but imminent return motivate you to leverage your time and resources being about our Father's business? Are you investing in heavenly rewards or worldly trinkets?

Chapter Twenty-Six

The Waste of Insignificant Things

Earth draws and holds as if it were made out of gold and not out of dirt; as though it were covered with diamonds and not with graves.[131]

One of the biggest obstacles to Christlikeness is the temporary "things of this world" (1 John 2:15).

Since we will all stand before Jesus Christ one day, it is wise to plan for that event. For unbelievers, that involves accepting Him as personal Lord and Savior. For true Christ followers, that involves the commitment to the journey toward Christlikeness.

An undenied, uncrucified self always looks for fulfillment apart from Christlikeness. It loves distractions and thrives on busyness and entertainment. It is hyper impulsive—seeking anything to fulfill its insatiable desires and impatient urges.

When those who claim to follow Christ take our eyes off Him, we become distracted by the world's noise and attracted to its shiny trinkets. Once in the world's deceptive grasp, we act like we have spiritual attention deficit and hyperactivity disorder. "Oh, look at this shiny object! Ah, look at that time-consuming opportunity!"

Being still and quiet with God's Word becomes a struggle. Finding time for God in overbooked schedules is difficult. The temporary, insignificant tentacles of this world encircle us, choking off the breath of eternity.

Since worldly things are temporary, they deserve little of our precious time, energy, and resources. Yet how appealing, distracting, and consuming they are. Once we commit to the journey of Christlikeness, it's interesting how *things* throttle our progress.

Heavenly Wealth

On a mission trip to Eleuthera Island in the Bahamas, I saw the vast difference between a contented, "thing-less" life, and a cluttered, distracted life.

The local missionary and I visited one of his church members. At the crest of the island, surrounded by stunning ocean beaches, stood a small mud hut. It belonged to an elderly lady who greeted us, beaming with the joy of the Lord.

She had raised eleven children there and made her living baking various breads in a nearby mud kiln. I told her how blessed she was with such a breathtaking view. Luxury resorts would pay top dollar to build there. Still smiling, she said, "God is good." In the midst of poverty by the world's standards, this woman had eternal riches and fulfillment this world cannot give.

Because of Calvary, our love for Christ should supersede all selfish desires and worldly pleasures. The fuller the heart, the less need for external things. A satisfied heart has no competition from what this world offers.

Even a casual friendship with the world identifies a person as an enemy of God (James 4:4). After all, it was the world who murdered Jesus, so why get cozy with what it has to offer. We either hold His nail-scarred hand or the world's bloodied hand.

Competing Against Christ

Believers can get caught in the world's subtle riptides.

The book of 1 John was written primarily to genuine believers. In it, John cautioned against anything the world promotes, flaunts, initiates, or influences as potentially captivating for a follower of Jesus. If something is a source of pleasure for the world, true Christ followers should approach it cautiously.

Jesus warned that the "cares of this world and deceitfulness of riches" choke out His Word and kill any spiritual fruit (Matthew 13:22). Peter confirmed the day is coming when the world and everything in it will burn up and fade away (2 Peter 3:11). This echoes an Old Testament theme that referred to earthly things as empty and unprofitable.

Do not turn aside from following the LORD, but serve the LORD with all your heart. And do not turn aside; for then you would go after empty things which cannot profit or deliver, for they are nothing. (1 Samuel 12:20-21)

Yeah but, Nate, I work hard for my possessions. It's taken a long time to accumulate them. Shouldn't I be able to enjoy them? What's the harm in that?

Luke 18:18-25 reveals a rich, young man who came to Jesus in a similar situation. He boldly asked, "Good Teacher, what shall I do to inherit eternal life?" This man wanted to *do* something—to work for his eternal life. He wanted a guarantee based on his *works*.

But when confronted with complete self-denial, self-sacrifice, and the removal of all earthly possessions, he walked away in sorrow. The loss of his temporal, earthly possessions grieved him more than the uncertainty of eternal life.

This doesn't mean Christlikeness requires complete poverty. It's a matter of priorities. Jesus lovingly pierced the part of that man's heart that valued his stuff more than investments in the world to come. This reveals the incredible power and influence the material possessions of this world can have if not kept in their proper context as mere *tools*.

Jesus gave this young man the same invitation He gave to His disciples—to follow Him. The disciples welcomed His invitation and responded immediately. But this man walked away. Worldly possessions gripped his heart. Giving his possessions to the poor would free him from many earthly obligations and give him the opportunity to invest in heavenly treasures. But his visible, temporal stuff blinded him from invisible, eternal riches.

It's interesting that the invitation to follow Jesus came only after the surrender of possessions. There must be a surrender of what we hold dear before we can fully and faithfully follow Jesus. He doesn't want anything competing with Him.

If anything is dearer to us than Jesus, our obedience will suffer. Our passion will dim. Our love will fade. Even worse, like this man, we won't surrender to His Lordship and closely follow Him.

> Man's service for God consists in the sacrifice and consecration of himself and all he has to God.[132]

Personal Challenge

Actually, 1 John 2:15 still challenges me.

When studying Scripture, I try to keep it simple. *What does it say? What does it mean? How does it apply?* I know what this verse says and I understand the underlying meaning. But the Holy Spirit keeps nudging me to dig deeper. I fully understand the evilness of the present world and I readily reject it. But what about those *things*? "Do not love the *things* in the world."

I need to define them before I can determine my association with them. If I'm attracted to or attached to them, I need to plan how to disentangle myself from their grip. How can I truly pursue Christlikeness with eyes darting elsewhere and hands full of stuff?

The *things* ... What are they? What do they include? Are they bad? Sinful? Or could they include something legitimate that has subtly overgrown my heart?

> A thing looks morally better because we want it. For that reason, our heart is often our worst counselor. We must surrender our hearts to God so that we have no unholy desires.[133]

A natural law of human behavior shows how knowledge leads to an emotional response which, in turn, prompts an associated action. Eyes are a primary portal of actionable knowledge. Jesus said, "The lamp of the body is the eye" (Matthew 6:22). Seeing something begins the process of gaining knowledge. It arouses feelings and prompts action.

Eve looked at the forbidden fruit and found it appealing. Thinking it would be good, she took it. Lot couldn't resist the sight of Sodom. It ended up costing him everything. King David recognized Bathsheba's beauty as he stared at her bathing. That knowledge led to strong, lustful feelings, which then motivated his subsequent adultery and murder.

According to Jesus, "whoever looks at a woman to lust for her has already committed adultery with her in his heart" (Matthew 5:28). If a mere look holds such persuasive power, imagine the influence of a life filled with this world's stuff.

The behavioral pathway remains the same: knowledge to feelings, feelings to action.

Sometimes our *wanter* is stuck in the wide-open position. We want and want and want—we simply can't get enough. This is why God tells us to guard our hearts (Proverbs 4:23), control what we see (Proverbs 4:25), and keep our eyes on Jesus (Hebrews 12:2). This is also why we must be content with what we have (Hebrews 13:5).

Minds are susceptible to what we *see*. Feelings are impressionable by what we *know*. Actions are vulnerable to what we *feel*. From this progression, we discover how much sin, heartbreak, and grief we can avoid by keeping our eyes on Jesus, not the things of this world.

The Nature of the World

John described the *nature* of the world by defining what is *in* the world.

> For all that is in the world—the lust of the flesh, the lust of the eyes, and the pride of life—is not of the Father but is of the world. (1 John 2:16)

First, we have the lust of the flesh—what appeals to the carnal body. This is the strong craving for what feels good. One of the world's mantras is, "If it feels good, do it."

Then we have the lust of the eyes—what appeals to carnal sight. It's the strong desire for what looks good. And yet with all the appealing things of this world, "the eyes of man are never satisfied" (Proverbs 27:20).

Finally, we have the pride of life—what appeals to status in this evil world. This pride promotes a look-at-me-I-am-somebody mindset. It includes anything that pulls us away from God, distracts us from His Word, quenches His Spirit, and opposes His eternal purpose and kingdom.

But here's the distinction for Christ followers. God separates His people from the world and sets them apart for consecration, holiness, and godliness. This involves rejecting any societal norms and cultural values conflicting with His interests and purpose. Christlikeness directly opposes the world.

> Consecration is … the separation from worldly, secular, and even legitimate things, if they come in conflict with God's plans, to holy uses. It is the devoting of all we have to God for His own specific use.

It is a separation from things questionable, or even legitimate, when the choice is to be made between the things of this life and the claims of God.[134]

Strangers in a Foreign Land

God's Word says true followers of Christ are strangers and pilgrims passing through this world, not driving down deep stakes (Hebrews 11:13).

> As temporary residents and foreigners ... keep away from worldly desires that wage war against your very souls. (1 Peter 2:11, NLT)

Christ followers are missionaries living in a foreign land. We are strangers here on temporary assignment. Our mission isn't to assimilate and accumulate. It's to seek first His kingdom, proclaim the gospel of Jesus Christ, make disciples, and become Christlike.

That's our purpose, remember?

This leaves little time or desire for the pleasures, politics, possessions, or pursuits of this foreign place. We have no business attaching ourselves to this world or its deceptive, distracting, and ultimately disappointing things. As our mission field, how can we have any association with its anti-God, anti-Christ, anti-Holy Spirit, anti-truth, morally relative, depraved agenda?

Yeah but, Nate, I don't see the world as such a dreary place as you're implying. This all sounds normal to me.

Here's what God says about this world. It is fallen, sinful human life and society as ruled and organized by Satan (1 John 5:19). He's the "prince of the power of the air" (Ephesians 2:1-2). His world promotes whatever looks good, feels good, and appeals to our carnal nature—there are no moral boundaries.

Sinful nature screams, "Please me. Adore me. Applaud me." All three components transformed dazzling Lucifer into the Devil himself (Isaiah 14:12-16; Ezekiel 28:12-19). In his blazing hatred for humans, he strategically inserts his evil agenda in the world. It's interesting how the humanistic, self-centered mindset of, *Me, Me, Me*, mimics Lucifer's *I, I, I* rebellion against God.

To love such a world is to love its ruler, Satan. To love the *things* of his world is to love what he offers. Such love is evidenced by willful acceptance of bondage to sin and willful rejection of all that is Christ (Mark 9:40).

Scripture plainly states that world followers are the enemies of Christ who "mind earthly things" (Philippians 3:18-19). To *mind* implies not only our thoughts but also affections, will, and moral considerations. The danger is that entire beings, decision making criterion, heart desires, and value systems can get attached to the things, values, and priorities of this world. God identifies such people as enemies of the cross of Christ.

This may be harsh to hear much less admit.

Maybe that's because we've acclimated and assimilated with the world. Quite possibly, it has a stronger hold and influence on us than we realize. Self-examination, under the Holy Spirit's guidance, will reveal how much the world has infiltrated our lives.

How grateful to know Jesus frees us from such a dark, tangled world. It underscores the urgency of our mission to shine the light of the glorious gospel while we're here. Yet how tragic to know some who claim to know Christ gleefully skip along hand-in-hand with such a world.

> If ever I become so one with the world, so tolerant of its spirit and atmosphere that I reprove it no more, incur not its hatred, rouse not its enmity to Christ—if the world can find in me no cause to hate me and cast me from its company, then I have betrayed Christ and crucified Him afresh.[135]

The Passing Nature of Things

To set your mind at ease, I don't dislike everything about this world. Nor am I advocating total isolation from it. I realize it holds many amazing aspects.

I've been incredibly blessed by the tender love and affection of my fantastic wife. I've enjoyed the wonderful smell of my children's heads while snuggling them to sleep when they were babies. Making sweet harmony with different church groups. Writing impactful lines. Socializing with stars and celebrities.

Amazing sunsets. Majestic mountains. A refreshing paddleboat ride on a smooth, snow-melt lake. Listening to snow fall. Living in foreign countries. Swinging in hammocks on Caribbean beaches. Hot-tubbing in the snow. Amazing, faith-building trips to Israel. Trekking the quiet trails of the Appalachians. Vacationing in an over-water cabana in the Polynesian Islands. All-inclusive resorts with incredible swim-outs.

Yep, all too cool. I get it. Countless wonderful experiences.

But I also recognize their temporary usefulness and eventual finality. Eternity beckons. We leave it all behind. Eventually it all burns up.

> Love of the world means the forgetfulness of the eternal future by reason of love for passing things."[136]

Becoming enamored with temporal, insignificant, worldly things pulls my heart away from eternal, significant, heavenly things. As a follower of Christ, I must guard against anything even slightly tainted by the world. This isn't extremism, it's scriptural.

Paul encouraged the surrender of even *legitimate* things. He wouldn't allow even what's permissible to gain the mastery over his life (1 Corinthians 6:12).

We have much at our disposal. But we must discern between *good* and *best* options.

Not everything is beneficial spiritually or eternally. Some things may be tempting distractions or temporary tools. To help differentiate, here are some candid questions. "How much will (fill in the blank) set me back on my spiritual journey? How will it look in the light of eternity? Does it help me glorify God? Does it help fulfill God's purpose for me?"

Yeah but, Nate, not everything in the world is bad or sinful. As you say, many things are at our disposal as tools. Entertainment is fun. Dancing is exercise. Golfing is a way to let off steam. Worldly music is cool—I grew up listening to it. Why shouldn't we accumulate as many "tools" and enjoy as much as we can?

The answer lies in the value and priority we give them. Their value becomes clear by our inner struggle if Jesus asks for their surrender.

Should anything gain more mastery over me, or demand more time, thoughts, and passion than God, His Word, and His eternal purpose, it becomes an idol. Something to be surrendered and avoided.

Water and fire are both great tools in their own environment. Water refreshes and cleans while fire warms and purifies. But should they escape their useful boundaries, they will drown and destroy. In their rightful place, the things of the world are useful tools. However, by their intrinsic nature, they have a sticky way of attaching themselves to our hearts.

This world and everything in it will pass away (1 Corinthians 7:31).

Instead of latching on to or prioritizing the temporal, it's wise to use it as God's momentary blessings to sustain our earthly existence. With the right mindset, we honor God and invest in His eternal kingdom.

Redeeming our Time

Both Ephesians 5:16 and Colossians 4:5 refer to "redeeming the time."

The word *redeeming* is an interesting choice in the context of time. The base Greek word is *exagorazo* (ἐξαγοραζό). It means to ransom or rescue from loss or waste. To fully leverage or make use of something. It generally means not allowing a suitable moment or opportunity to pass by unheeded.[137]

Rolling that into a concise, crisp nugget brings us to, "Don't waste your life on temporal, insignificant things!" This includes wasting our time, energy, and resources. God gives us all we need for our journey, not to waste but to fully leverage on what truly matters. As we've found, our ultimate purpose is what matters.

I'm either pursuing Christlikeness or I'm not.

Either I am overcoming the world or it's overcoming me.

By whom a person is overcome, by him also he is brought into bondage. (2 Peter 2:19)

Yeah but, Nate. Many things in the world aren't necessarily sinful but are actually quite fun. Are you saying Christlikeness is about having no fun at all?

For every *yes* there's an opposing *no*.

We cannot wholeheartedly and faithfully follow Christ while holding hands with the world. We deceive ourselves by pledging love and loyalty to Jesus while maintaining wandering eyes for the world. That's as ridiculous as keeping a dating profile active after marriage. When we commit to a lifetime with Jesus, we stop flirting with the world.

Marriage vows often include the phrase, "Forsaking all others." This implies not just rejecting other suiters but also anything potentially threatening to or distracting from the relationship. It's ludicrous for a spouse to continue accepting flowers and gifts from former love interests.

Saying "Yes" to Jesus means I turn my back on the world and what's distracting and potentially threatening. Jesus said, "No one can serve two masters; for either he will hate the one and love the other, or else he will be loyal to the one and despise the other" (Matthew 6:24). There's no divided allegiance in a healthy relationship.

> We need a holy temperance in regard to things not absolutely imposed upon us by God. Let us watch even in lawful and necessary things against the wondrous power these have to keep the soul so occupied, that there remain but little power or zest for fellowship with God.[138]

Personal Reflection

What things (even legitimate things) of this world have attached themselves to you? What worldly desires, passions, or priorities distract you from fully pursuing Christlikeness? If Jesus asked you to surrender your dearest worldly possession, fiercest passion, or ambition, how would you respond?

Chapter Twenty-Seven

Hindrance of Worldly Influence

One of Satan's vilest tricks is to destroy the best by the good.[139]

Most trails worth hiking involve challenging uphill climbs. Yet we climb slowly and steadily until we reach the summit.

The journey toward Christlikeness is narrow and difficult (Matthew 7:14). As we mature spiritually, we increasingly discover the challenges of self-denial and surrender. No longer are they simply great spiritual terms of a lofty ideal. They affect us personally as we apply them to our lives. But we keep climbing. We remain committed to the journey.

We can do this!

As I consider my life and how subtle things influence my behaviors, choices, and mindsets, I encounter uncomfortable truths from God's Word and the Holy Spirit's insight. And they remain uncomfortable.

That's the point. Nate has to constantly surrender to Jesus. I have to remove my hand [quenching and resisting] from the Holy Spirit's scalpel. Like any surgery, pain is necessary for spiritual health. I have to unclench my fist and release everything hindering the journey. If I truly want to become more like Christ, I have to "lay aside every weight" (Hebrews 12:1). The question before me and every Christ follower is: *How badly do you want it?*

A clear view of, and appreciation for, the cross of Calvary helps break any infatuation with the world. When I get a clear view of the suffering and sacrifice of the cross, then the world and what it offers no longer fascinate me. Seeing Jesus hanging on Calvary for my carnal, worldly desires motivates a priority shift. The cross stands between me and this world. As a result, the world won't find me appealing either.

> Since the world slew Christ, and hates God, its whole ambition and passion and swagger, its popularity and pleasure—yea, its ten thousand

enchantments all contradict the Cross and exclude "the love of the Father."[140]

From that standpoint, let's look at some subtle influences that captivate and hinder those who would become more like Jesus.

Lack of an Eternity Perspective

Chasing the temporary things of what feels or appears good now sacrifices the eternal.

The world distracts true Christ followers from spiritual growth and investment in eternity. This distraction hinders our earthly mission and reduces our heavenly rewards.

For one bowl of stew, Esau sacrificed his birthright and future destiny (Genesis 25:29-34). As the first-born son, he was entitled to a double portion of his father's estate. Yet he forfeited it for a temporary appetite.

God's Word encourages us to prioritize the unseen, eternal things over the seen, temporary things (2 Corinthians 4:18). Helen Lemmel summed it up wonderfully in her hymn, "Turn Your Eyes Upon Jesus."

> Turn your eyes upon Jesus, look full in His wonderful face,
> And the things of earth will grow strangely dim, in the light of His glory and grace.[141]

Oh, may all true Christ followers live each day with eternity in full view.

Indifference Against Sin

Affection for the world promotes infidelity with our "first love" (Revelation 2:4).

Our first love must always be Jesus. We can't serve two masters. If my eyes are firmly fixed on Jesus, the world fades from view. If the world attracts me, it distracts me from Jesus.

The world does a phenomenal job at desensitizing us. It generally positions what it offers as morally relative. What may be offensive to some may be acceptable to others. The mantra is, "Everyone has his own inner truth." The world calls this being progressive. But it's simply a retread of a previous immoral age when "everyone did what was right in his own eyes" (Judges 21:25).

With such moral anesthesia, *professing* Christ followers shrug or laugh along—all while our spiritual Enemy uploads his garbage to their minds. Instead of boycotting everything and everyone who endorses what Scripture describes as immoral, they try to fit in.

Let's not forget that we don't get to define what is or isn't sin. God has already defined it. We don't have the authority to excuse or justify sinful habits and preferences simply because we want them. And we can't change God's mind about sin, its destructive effect, or ultimate judgment.

The only option we have is to accept God's view about sin and His remedy for it. May God instill in us the courage to passionately protect our spheres of holiness. Instead of trying to fit in, may we stand up and stand out for Jesus. After all, He stood up and stood out for us.

Indifference Toward Heaven

Imagine our impact if we used our resources for the cause of Christ.

Keep the main thing the main thing. His name. His cause. His brand. His mission. His kingdom. Jesus is preparing a place for us (John 14:1-3). Let's invest our resources in His building program.

May we pray as David Brainerd,

> My desires seem especially to be after weanedness from the world, perfect deadness to it, and that I may be crucified to all its allurements. My soul desires to feel itself more of a pilgrim and a stranger here below, that nothing may divert me from pressing through the lonely desert, till I arrive at my Father's house.[142]

Christ followers are looking for a city whose Builder and Maker is God (Hebrews 11:10). Let's keep our heavenly home foremost on our minds. May this question motivate our eternal investments: *What type of home can God build for me with the investments I make there?*

Lack of Concern for Unbelievers

Getting cozy with the things of the world blinds us to the eternal doom of unbelievers.

One would think faithfully telling others and bringing them to Christ would be our grateful response for Him saving us. Yet it seems most are still hesitant to share their faith. Political correctness has scared us from sharing the most precious, eternally significant news.

Yet Jesus commanded His followers to "Go" spread His gospel throughout the world (Matthew 28:19-20). It wasn't a suggestion. It was and is a battle cry. As soldiers of the cross, we are called to battle. We armor up (Ephesians 6:10-18), stand strong, and allow no enemy influence to infiltrate our lines.

A spiritual battle rages for the souls of men. Satan and his forces have an aggressive, devious war strategy. They never stop, never take breaks. They never easily yield any lost soul or any spiritual ground.

Even when a person accepts Christ, evil forces increase their assault to prevent any spiritual growth or fruit by the new recruit. Yet Christ's commission includes everyone. No true follower of Christ is excluded from making disciples. Imagine the spiritual impact if we spent our leisure time praying for and witnessing to our unbelieving family, friends, work associates, or random strangers.

God promises eternal rewards for engaging in His work. But I don't recall any rewards for chasing after the world. Jesus said, "I chose you and appointed you that you should go and bear fruit, and that your fruit should remain" (John 15:16). As we've seen, each person will receive his own reward for his own work (1 Corinthians 3:8).

Let's live in this world anticipating the world to come. Let's be about our Father's business of bringing people into His kingdom. Let's focus on what will remain after this world is no more.

Entanglement with the World

"No one engaged in warfare entangles himself with the affairs [transactions; negotiations] of this life, that he may please him who enlisted him as a soldier" (2 Timothy 2:4).

That's our battle strategy for the ongoing spiritual warfare. We please the One who enlisted us and gave His life for us. As Christ followers, let's recognize the temptation of the world as a call to battle. Let's recognize the world's arousing aroma as yet another means of the Enemy to dull our spiritual senses and distract us from pleasing our Commanding Officer.

We're in the middle of the battle. From the moment of salvation, we don the colors of eternity. We are wise to put on the whole armor of God and do everything we can to stand firm in the day of battle. "Take up the whole armor of God ... having done all to stand" (Ephesians 6:13).

Jesus prayed that His followers would be kept *from* the world (John 17:11, 15-16). A boat may be in the water, but it rides above it. It remains safe so long as no water gets inside. Once water rushes in, the boat is doomed unless safety measures are quickly taken.

Paul said, "We have received, not the spirit of the world, but the Spirit who is from God" (1 Corinthians 2:12). True believers don't have the spirit, mindset, value system, or priorities of this present world. We have the indwelling Holy Spirit who teaches us all truth. God's Word is truth (John 17:17). His Spirit is truth. That's our mindset and standard.

Worldly, unregenerate man can't understand the things of God. Only true believers can climb the peaks of the mind of Christ (1 Corinthians 2:16) and the things of God. The mindset of Christ runs counter to the mindset of the world. Loving the world is as unnatural for a Christ follower as understanding and loving the things of God are to an unbeliever.

Let's keep our minds firmly fixed on Jesus., not tangled up with this temporary, immoral world.

Misguided Affections

Sometimes even our best intentions can reflect a worldly mindset instead of God's purposes.

On one occasion when Jesus told the disciples He must die and rise again, Peter had an issue with this. He didn't want to hear about Jesus, his kindhearted Master, being treated that way. So he scolded Jesus. But Jesus sharply corrected Peter for his worldly thoughts. "Get behind Me, Satan! For you are not mindful of [setting your thoughts on] the things of God, but the things of men" (Mark 8:33).

Spiritual danger awaits those who assimilate to this world's influence. Only the safety measures of constant repentance and daily surrender bring us back to spiritual soundness. Only by facing Jesus can we turn our backs to the world.

> Once the Cross lays hold upon the [Christ follower], he realizes how completely unhinged he has become from the whole of this present world.[143]

With eyes full of Jesus, the things of this world with their importance and influence fade from view. In the pursuit of Christlikeness, may we act, react, think, talk, decide, and live like Him. May we commit ourselves wholly to God. "*One thing* I have desired of the LORD" (Psalm 27:4, italics added). Let's not simply think and talk about being Christ followers (Mark 7:6). May we be wholly His.

Personal Reflection

Are you overcoming the world or is the world overcoming you? Are you becoming more Christlike or more worldly? Do people see Jesus in you or does your life more reflect the world's characteristics, nature, behavior, values, motives, and decisions?

Chapter Twenty-Eight

Hindrance of Worldly Associations

How many people know Christ because they know me?

There's a big difference between being *in* an environment and becoming *part of* it.

Christ followers should interact within the world without it affecting our primary allegiance to God. The challenge is to safeguard our associations within the world. Association implies fondness, an attachment of the heart. It's where attraction and affection shift from superficial acquaintance to dear friends.

> He who would walk with God is called to separate himself from unholy associations and the fellowship of the mixed multitude … who are unholy in walk and unsound in faith.[144]

That's the subtle sway of the world. Just when we think we can handle being close with it, the trap springs and we're ensnared. This is why God's Word counsels against such friendship. It warns against becoming soulmates with the world. To do so cheapens our relationship with Christ. It weakens our witness for Christ. And it deadens our separation to Christ.

Yeah but, Nate, you're making it sound like Christ followers are freaks. Aren't we supposed to have friends? How are we supposed to win the lost if we don't associate with them?

Yes, Christ followers find ways to lead the lost to Christ and help the hurting. But that interaction is different than becoming friends with all things worldly. Unfortunately, the worldly friend usually affects the believing friend more than the other way around. The world has no qualms about offending a Christ follower. Yet, most professing believers tiptoe around tough topics to not offend their worldly friends. A rotting apple decays the apples around it. Aside from miraculous intervention, good apples don't slow the decay of rotting apples.

Abraham's nephew, Lot, struggled with worldly associations. In reading his story in Genesis chapters 13-14 and 18-19, we notice his slow, subtle move toward Sodom, then finally into the city itself.

Lot had a godly uncle and much personal wealth. As part of Abraham's family, God's favor rested on Lot too. Their combined flocks became too much for the same pastures, so Abraham gave Lot first choice of the entire countryside.

Lot followed his eyes.

He moved toward the luscious Jordan plain. Then he moved to the outskirts of Sodom. As time passed, the appeal of city life got the better of him, and he eventually moved inside the city. Finally, we find Lot sitting in a position of authority at the city's gate.

He's a prime example of what Psalm 1:1 says *not* to do.

> Blessed is the man who walks not in the counsel of the ungodly, nor stands in the path of sinners, nor sits in the seat of the scornful.

Notice the negative progression: walking, standing, sitting. Like Peter who warmed his hands by the world's fire (Luke 22:55), Lot's spiritual testimony and resolve for Christ faltered.

When the destroying angels arrived, guess who met them in his position of worldly authority? Lot. Even worse, when God's judgment fell, guess who lost everything because he lived too close to the fire? Lot.

Lot had no business associating with Sodom. He had his own wealth and wide-open space in the Jordan plains. Sodom was a perverse, disgusting place. Yet it attracted him. Every visit to town attached his heart a little more to its people, merchandise, and energy.

Sadly, Sodom's wickedness also rubbed off on Lot. We see not only his assimilation into Sodom but also his growing indifference with its perverse environment. Unbelievably, he offered his virgin daughters to the despicable men of the city who came to molest the destroying angels Lot invited into his home.

Assimilation and apathy are the dangers of association.

Here are some examples of how worldly association can slowly lure distracted Christ followers into its deceitful, destructive web. The journey toward Christlikeness helps safeguard against these traps while still empowering a godly witness to the world.

Worldly Priority

When we're busy chasing the things of the world, we have little time left for God's kingdom and His righteousness.

Far too often I've heard, *Nate, I just don't have time to devote to reading and studying God's Word. And I'm too busy to get that involved in church or ministry.*

If we're too busy for God, then we're too busy.

This world isn't our home. It's completely under Satan's control (1 John 5:19). Yet its influence creeps in and steals our precious time and resources that ultimately belong to God. We're here on special, short-term assignment. Let's keep God's eternal kingdom the main focus instead of getting caught up in this world's distractions and resource wasters.

It's a matter of priorities.

Worldly Passion

Our passions energize us.

I find it intriguing how a person who claims to be a follower of Christ screams and jumps around at sporting events yet claims his faith is a "private matter." We act like fools at the world's events but go dark and silent when it comes to the One who gave His life for us.

Seriously?

Assessing the reactions [fruit] of both situations reveals the passion [root] or lack thereof. Pursuing the look, feel, smell, and behavior of the world for pleasure is to walk in opposition of God's call to separation. Followers of Christ are a chosen generation, royal priesthood, holy nation, special people, the people of God (1 Peter 2:9-10).

God created, chose, called, and commissioned us for Christlikeness. He sanctified and set us apart for His glory. The Omni-Everything, Infinite I AM loves us and sacrificed His life for us. We will stand before Him one day and live in His presence eternally.

That must be our driving passion.

Worldly Promotion

Covetousness is wanting what we don't have.

The apostle Paul said he learned to be content in whatever state he was (Philippians 4:11). Notice, it's something we can *learn*. An "I-want-more" mindset typically isn't content with what God has given us or where He's placed us (Hebrews 13:5).

Coveting, which breaks the tenth commandment (Exodus 20:17), is "the longing of the creature which has forsaken God to fill itself with the lower objects of nature."[145] Keep in mind, promotion (Psalm 75:6-7) and every good and perfect gift (James 1:17) all come from God.

In Christ's parable of the talents, two talents netted only two more (Matthew 25:15, 22). Yet human nature, driven by greed, asks for more. But God won't grant requests for more if we haven't been faithful in what He's already given. How can we ask for His blessing or promotion when we squander His financial favor on the things of this world?

Why do we spend so much time and money on this world's frivolous, temporal things? When we stand before Him to give account as stewards of God's favor, how will we respond? Bigger houses? More property? Fancier cars? Larger investment portfolios? The latest technology gadgets? Bigger televisions? Where does it end?

The world's insatiable mantra of "more" so invades our lives we forget that none of it matters for eternity. We leave it all behind. When will we stop and ask, *Why am I spending time and money on (fill in the blank)? How will it look in light of eternity and in view of Calvary's sacrifice?*

The promotions of this temporary world will appear very small on the threshold of eternity. When Jesus asks, "I did all this for you—what did you do for Me?", I suspect many things will quickly lose their appeal. But then it'll be too late for a shift in priorities.

Again, the things of this world are *tools* for our existence here. The secret is to balance our priorities and align them with God's perfect will for our lives. Let's use our time, resources, and opportunities to invest in God's kingdom.

Instead of asking for more temporary things, may we ask God for more of Himself. More of His anointing and filling. More of a complete union with Him. May we ask to become more like Jesus. May He find us faithful with what He's given us.

Worldly Profession

Even our work or business can become a *thing* of the world when out of its proper priority.

If we work to live, it's a means to an end. If we live to work, it becomes our master. Work is another resource God provides to meet our *needs*, not necessarily our *wants*.

When covetousness or greed drive a deeper focus on work, everything gets misaligned. Time with family decreases. Priorities get shuffled. We forfeit a deeper intimacy with God by focusing on climbing the corporate ladder to get *more*.

Working for a living is a legitimate need. It should be done like everything else for Christ followers—with all our might (Ecclesiastes 9:10) and to the glory of God (1 Corinthians 10:31). We are to work as if we worked for Christ Himself (Ephesians 6:5).

Imagine this paradigm shift. Focus on Christ's performance evaluation instead of our earthly supervisors' performance reviews.

Worldly Pleasure

Our society and culture are consumed by pleasure and entertainment.

Part of the meaning of the sin of lasciviousness is "no restraints" and "a readiness for all pleasure."[146] Today's society is certainly unrestrained in its pursuit of worldly pleasure.

We can rattle off the names of our favorite sports team members or the celebrities of our favorite shows. Yet we struggle to name the books of the Bible, the twelve disciples, or the twelve tribes of Israel. Memorizing large portions of Scripture is a thing of the past, yet entertainment magazines litter our homes. We chase the world's fashions, perfumes, sounds, music, movies, looks, appeal, status symbols, cultural norms, political agendas, narratives … all while being naïve about Satan's distracting deception.

In the days leading up to Christ's return to catch His Bride away, Scripture warns that people will be lovers of pleasure instead of lovers of God (2 Timothy 3:1-4). Let's not be part of that crowd. Instead, let's set our minds, hearts, and affections on things above (Colossians 3:2). When Jesus has the preeminence, earthly pleasures bow to His Lordship.

> People who are ruled by their desires think only of themselves. Everyone who is ruled by the Holy Spirit thinks about spiritual things. (Romans 8:5, CEV)

When Jesus is crowned Lord of heart, mind, soul, body, and life, when we've surrendered first place and priority to Him, everything else becomes a *tool*. Pleasing, honoring, and glorifying Him in everything becomes paramount.

Any pleasure hindering Christlikeness must be dethroned.

Worldly Power

"Power tends to corrupt, and absolute power corrupts absolutely."[147]

A spiritual conflict rages when we pursue power, status, and influence at the expense of imitating Christ, the suffering Servant (1 Peter 2:21; Isaiah 53). Satan uses everything to distract us from God and restrict the effectiveness of our witness—even promotions or influential positions.

Just because an opportunity presents itself doesn't mean God ordained it. Just because an attractive person crosses your path doesn't mean God orchestrated it. Just because a job promotion comes your way doesn't mean God appointed it.

> God has His best gifts for the few who dare to stand the test.
> His second choice He has for those who will not have His best.[148]

As with everything, our first consideration should be to ask God for His perspective—with unattached hearts. Seeking His will while accepting the job offer isn't seeking His *perfect* will. Praying for God's will while getting emotionally attached isn't seeking His *perfect* will. He may allow things through His *permissive* will, but I've learned the hard way that yielding to His *perfect* will is far better.

> [God] gave them their request; but sent leanness into their soul. (Psalm 106:15)

Without God's Word and the Holy Spirit's guidance, we're vulnerable to Satan's deceit. He dangles what we think we want, or the object(s) of our undisciplined, unsurrendered, uncrucified desires. Sadly, we often fall for his nonsense every time. He lies, deceives, discourages, misleads, and betrays to separate us from God's highest calling and true fulfillment.

This is why we need yielded spirits that pray, "God, not my will, but Thine be done." Even with our deepest desires. Allow God to provide your needs instead of shopping at Satan's store.

However God blesses with positions or professions of power, may we hold them loosely and perform them as faithful stewards. May we do all to His glory and for His Kingdom.

Worldly Persuasion

The world has become so churchy and the church has become so worldly, it's hard to tell them apart.

The world's mindset persuades many people to rely on logic, religious rituals, good deeds, and self for their spiritual journey. The pursuit of such *religion* is not the same as a personal *relationship* with Jesus.

Faith in Christ isn't a religious club or civic organization. Religious attendance and passion never substitute for a vibrant relationship with Jesus Christ. *Doing* is no substitute for *being*.

The world's approach can be extremely persuasive. But God warns against false teachers and apostates who seek to deceive and lead astray those not grounded in His Word. Even the wisdom of this world is foolishness with God (1 Corinthians 3:18-20).

Most things of this world simply don't matter and have no eternal significance or reward. Paul encourages us to forget what's behind, to reach for what's ahead, and "press toward the goal for the prize of the upward call of God in Christ Jesus" (Philippians 3:13-14).

Releasing the *things* of this world frees our hearts and minds to grasp the *things* of the future world. Everything in this temporary world pales in significance to surrendering it all to God, becoming more like Christ, and investing in His future kingdom.

The day is coming when this world and everything in it will be gone. Everything will be made new. It will all be back under God's righteous jurisdiction and authority. Oh, glorious day! Knowing this reality is fast approaching, it seems wise to divest and detach ourselves now of *this* world with its influence and persuasion.

Imagine how we can better invest our time and money. Growing in grace and the knowledge of God. Remaining steadfast in the faith. Equipping, encouraging, and exhorting each other to good works. Retraining our minds to dwell on things above. Supporting local churches, faith-based ministries, and global missions. Leading Bible studies and prayer groups. Being full-time employees in our Father's business.

It's really not optional (Titus 3:8).

As Rhea Miller wrote in her famous hymn, "I'd Rather Have Jesus," all the things of this world can't compare to Christ's "Well done, faithful servant."

I'd rather have Jesus than silver or gold;
I'd rather be His than have riches untold;
I'd rather have Jesus than houses or lands.
I'd rather be led by His nail pierced hand.[149]

Personal Reflection

Which has more of your heart: the things of this world or Jesus Himself? Are you loving like Jesus? Are you interceding like Jesus? Are you surrendered like Jesus? What distinguishes you from the world? What steps are you willing to take to become more Christlike?

Chapter Twenty-Nine

Satisfied at Last in His Likeness

Put on the Lord Jesus Christ. (Romans 13:14)

I love when God speaks unexpectedly and through ordinary things.

I spent almost an entire Saturday working in the yard. Filling in low spots with dirt. Sprinkling grass seed. Mulching the hedge beds. Pulling weeds here and there. Removing pine cones, branches, and other debris. Actually, this is my usual practice between Spring and Fall. But this day I did a *lot* of work.

Yet when I stepped back to admire my effort, I hardly noticed a change. In the grand scheme of things, nothing appeared any different. But I knew that, over time, what I'd done would be quite evident.

That's the way the Holy Spirit transforms us into Christlikeness.

He's constantly at work. Convicting me of sin here. Restoring a wound there. Infusing abundant life. Planting seeds from God's Word. Shaping my character. Renewing my mind. Strengthening my spirit. Emboldening my witness. Developing the fruit of the Spirit. As long as I don't grieve or quench Him, His work continues.

On a day-by-day basis, it may not seem like much. I may look at my life, and wonder if any spiritual progress is happening at all. I struggle with impatience. Anger flares up. Evil thoughts invade. Witnessing opportunities pass by unnoticed. Momentary apathy grips my heart. I need constant repentance and forsaking of sin (Proverbs 28:13). Every day I must die to self (1 Corinthians 15:31). In partnership with the Holy Spirit, I surrender to what He's doing to conform me into the likeness of Christ (Romans 8:29).

Yet, I need to give it time.

The Holy's Spirit's silent, unseen work is evidenced by spiritual growth and supernatural transformation. As the years pass, I can see where He's brought me from and trust where He's taking me. I can rest assured that

He who has begun a good work in me will complete it until the day of Jesus Christ (Philippians 1:6).

Here's a sober yet encouraging thought. The time and effort involved in becoming Christlike should motivate an earlier start. No matter where we are in our journeys, we can begin today. It starts with that first step. Then the next.

There's no easy path to Christlikeness. Only brief interludes between pressure points. This continues as we allow God to transform us or until such time as He takes us home. The maturity into His likeness depends on our willingness to surrender and follow.

Genuine Christ followers allow or "let" God have His way in our lives. Several Scriptures reference this. "Let the peace of God rule in your hearts" (Colossians 3:15). "Let this mind be in you which was also in Christ Jesus" (Philippians 2:5). "Let your light so shine" (Matthew 5:16). "Let a man examine himself" (1 Corinthians 11:28). Yes, there is much we can do on the journey. But we must also allow the Holy Spirit to do His work.

To that end, please understand there are no coincidences or random events with Omni-Everything, Sovereign God. Each new day, with its triumphs and failures, is an opportunity to become more like Jesus. Our choices along each day's path determine our proximity to that goal.

Jesus said the journey to Christlikeness is narrow and difficult (Matthew 7:14). Few brave souls dare travel the rocky path. There are twists and turns, potholes, sharp drop-offs, boulders, loose gravel, valleys and steep climbs. But with Jesus walking beside us and the Holy Spirit dwelling inside, the sunrise on the horizon is worth the climb.

And the view from the summit will be spectacular!

With each step we take, every day we live, we approach our final ten minutes. We draw closer to the sunrise. Every new surrender brings us closer to the goal. The more like Christ we become here and now, the closer our ultimate fulfillment and satisfaction.

Finally Satisfied

Imagine finally achieving Christlikeness. Being like Jesus. Completely holy.

We find the word *blessed* all throughout Scripture. Jesus used it in the Beatitudes (Matthew 5:1-12). He also promised blessedness as a reward for those who read, understand, and obey the things revealed in the Revelation of Himself and the end times (Revelation 1:3). James identified blessedness as the reward for those who remain steadfast and faithful in temptations and trials (James 1:12).

> Blessed *is the man* You choose, and cause to approach *You* ... We shall be satisfied with the goodness of Your ... holy temple. (Psalm 65:4)

At its core, the word blessed, *makarios* (μακάριος), means to be fully satisfied.[150] This is a growing satisfaction that supersedes mere happiness or joy. It's being fully content. Completely fulfilled.

We find the idea behind this in Psalm 23:1: "The LORD is my shepherd; I shall not want [lack]." In Him, we have everything we need. There's nothing lacking. We come to a place of contentedness where we want nothing more. We are fully satisfied.

> For I have satiated [fully satisfied] the weary soul, and I have replenished every sorrowful soul. (Jeremiah 31:25)

During the Christmas holidays when my children were younger, they complained about how hard it was to think of something for me as a gift. "Dad, what do you want for Christmas?"

I usually shrugged and said, "I don't need anything."

"C'mon, Dad, that's not fair. You have to give us some idea."

I explained that I have everything I need. But to let them off the hook, I'd suggest a good book. We can't have enough good books, right?

When we come to a place where Jesus is all we have, we find He is all we need. When Jesus is all we need, we will be truly blessed—fully satisfied. By indwelling us, God gives His followers full satisfaction, regardless of our circumstances. True believers may be in the world, but we aren't dependent on it for satisfaction or fulfillment. Our satisfaction and greatest fulfillment come from God alone.

What a glorious thought. There is coming a day of complete, heavenly satisfaction. King David revealed the final status of such satisfaction.

> I shall be satisfied when I awake in Your likeness. (Psalm 17:15)

The day is coming when I will bid this world goodbye and awake in Christ's embrace. I can only imagine the complete satisfaction of finally and fully being transformed into His likeness.

"We shall be like Him, for we shall see Him as He is" (1 John 3:2). The pursuit of Christlikeness will be fully complete. The purpose for which we were created, called, chosen, and commissioned fully realized. We will be blessed and satisfied indeed!

Until He comes, or takes us home, may we live in this growing satisfaction.

May we remove all spiritual familiarity. Let's toss aside all timidity and routine. Instead, may we live in the excited realization of being His children.

Along with that, let's surrender to His Spirit living within and experience His wondrous, ongoing transformation.

May we maintain a clear vision of our Triune, Omni-Everything God who is high and lifted up and seated in sovereign majesty.

May we cherish Calvary's precious, costly blood. Oh, may we appropriate it fully and walk in its divine power every day.

May we never lose sight of our Bridegroom, Jesus, seated at the Father's right hand. He loves us, died for us, redeemed us, reconciled us, intercedes for us, and sanctifies us. May we live each day with an urgent expectation of the immediacy of His return.

May we consistently yield to the sweet Holy Spirit who indwells us. May we never grieve or quench His influence and transformation, but fully surrender as He guides us into all truth.

May we spend quality time every day with God's precious Word, our instruction manual for holiness. Let's commit to hiding it in our hearts and minds and applying it to our lives.

May we live with eternity in mind and invest in things of eternal significance, while shunning the temporal things of this world.

May the rewards of heaven motivate us to serve our loving God with pure, grateful, heartfelt motives.

May we diligently and persistently pursue Christlikeness, our ultimate purpose.

Finally, may we anticipate the day we will be fully satisfied when we awake in His likeness.

Now may the God of peace Himself sanctify you [set you apart] completely; and may your whole spirit, soul, and body be preserved blameless at the coming of our Lord Jesus Christ. He who calls you *is* faithful, who also will do *it*. (1 Thessalonians 5:23-24)

Until then, enjoy the glorious journey!

About the Author

A lifelong student of Scripture, Nate Stevens has also enjoyed a forty-three-year banking career in a variety of leadership roles. He is the author of:

Matched 4 Life (book and workbook)
Deck Time with Jesus
Transformed: Until Christ is Formed in You
Conformed: Into the Likeness of Christ
Informed: Living by God's Absolute Truth
Surrendered: Yielding to God's Perfect Will
God's Secret Place
Accelerate Your Destiny

He is also a contributing author on several of the Moments Books series (*Billy Graham Moments, Romantic Moments, Divine Moments, Spoken Moments, Christmas Moments, Stupid Moments,* and *Broken Moments*).

He writes online articles for ChristianDevotions.us and KingdomWinds.com as well as several other ministries. Additionally, he co-founded and leads Fusion, a Christian singles ministry. A popular speaker and teacher at conferences, seminars and Bible study groups, he speaks on a wide variety of topics.

Nate has two adult children. He and his wife, Karen, live near Charlotte, North Carolina.

Follow Nate and find more resources at: www.natestevens.net.

Endnotes

1. *How U.S. Religious Composition has Changed in Recent Decades,* found at: https://www.pewresearch.org/religion/2022/09/13/how-u-s-religious-composition-has-changed-in-recent-decades , accessed July 20, 2023.

2. A. W. Tozer, *Of God and Men,* (Christian Publications, 1960), 13.

3. Vance Havner, quote found and accessed September 23, 2023 at: https://www.inspiringquotes.us/author/1504-vance-havner/about-christianity

4. A. W. Tozer quote found and accessed August 7, 2023 at: https://www.goodreads.com/quotes/1299807

5. D. L. Moody, *The Overcoming Life,* (Revell, 1896), 19.

6. Charles R. Swindoll, *So, You Want to be Like Christ?,* (Thomas Nelson, 2005), 91.

7. E. M. Bounds, *The Complete Works of E. M. Bounds – The Reality of Prayer,* (Pantianos Classics / Createspace, 2017), 142.

8. Spiros Zodhiates, Th.D., *The Hebrew-Greek Study Bible, King James Version,* Lexical Aids to the New Testament (AMG International, Inc. DBA AMG Publishers, 1991), 1549.

9. Charles R. Swindoll, *So, You Want to be Like Christ?,* (Thomas Nelson, 2005), xiv.

10. H. A. Ironside, *Holiness: The False and the True,* (Loizeaux Brothers, 1947), 139.

11. Thomas O. Chisholm, *O to be Like Thee, 1897,* found at: https://hymnary.org/text/o_to_be_like_thee_blessed_redeemer_this

12. H. A. Ironside, Holiness: The False and the True, (Loizeaux Brothers, 1947), 77.

13. Concepts excerpted from Nate Stevens' book, *Matched for Life,* (Createspace, 2017).

14. Andrew Murray, *The Blood of the Cross,* (Zondervan Publishing House, 1935), 49.

15. A. W. Tozer, *The Root of the Righteous,* (Christian Publications, 1955), 11.

16   Charles R. Swindoll, *Moses: A Man of Selfless Dedication,* (W Publishing Group, 1999), 270.

17   Author unknown

18   Charles R. Swindoll, *So, You Want to be Like Christ?,* (Thomas Nelson, 2005), 115.

19   Trinity definition as found at: https://www.merriam-webster.com/dictionary/Trinity, accessed March 23, 2023.

20   Trinity defined, *Council of Nicea Concludes,* as found at: https://www.history.com/this-day-in-history/council-of-nicaea-concludes, accessed March 23, 2023.

21   Spiros Zodhiates, Th.D., *The Hebrew-Greek Study Bible, King James Version,* Lexical Aids to the New Testament (AMG International, Inc. DBA AMG Publishers, 1991), 1734 (#3056).

22   *Purpose and Meaning of "Ego Eimi" in the Gospel of John – In Reference to the Deity of Christ,* found and accessed April 9, 2024 at: https://www.aomin.org/aoblog/general-apologetics/purpose-and-meaning-of-ego-eimi-in-the-gospel-of-john

23   Author unknown

24   *Presence,* Merriam-Webster.com Dictionary, Merriam-Webster, found at: https://www.merriam-webster.com/dictionary/presence, accessed March 25, 2023.

25   Vicky Sein, *What is the Speed of Light?* found at: https://www.space.com/15830-light-speed.html, accessed March 24, 2023.

26   Spiros Zodhiates, Th.D., *The Hebrew-Greek Study Bible, King James Version,* Lexical Aids to the New Testament (AMG International, Inc. DBA AMG Publishers, 1991), 1700 (#1097).

27   *Science,* Merriam-Webster.com Dictionary, Merriam-Webster, found at: https://www.merriam-webster.com/dictionary/science, accessed March 25, 2023.

28   The Average IQ: What It Is and How It is Measured, https://psychcentral.com/health/average-iq#:~:text=In%20general%2C%20an%20IQ%20score,IQ%20between%2085%20and%20115 accessed March 25, 2023.

29   *Potent,* Merriam-Webster.com Dictionary, Merriam-Webster, https://www.merriam-webster.com/dictionary/potent, accessed March 28, 2023.

Endnotes

30. https://www.paulandersonpark.org/about-paul-anderson, accessed March 28, 2023.

31. How Much Does Earth Weigh and How is This Measured? Found at: https://coolcosmos.ipac.caltech.edu/ask/61-How-much-does-Earth-weigh-and-how-is-this-measured, accessed March 28, 2023.

32. Keith Chen, *How Much Does the Sun Weigh?* found at: https://jacksofscience.com/how-much-does-the-sun-weigh, accessed March 28, 2023.

33. Matt Pelsor, *The Star Arcturus*, found at: https://www.wfyi.org/programs/weekend-sky-report/radio/The-Star-Arcturus , accessed March 28, 2023.

34. Joe Rao, *See the Bright Yellow Star Arcturus in the Night Sky,* found at: https://www.nbcnews.com/id/wbna42723273 , accessed March 28, 2023.

35. John Philips, *Exploring the Gospel of John*, (Kregel Publications, 2001), 181.

36. *Sovereignty*, Merriam-Webster.com Dictionary, Merriam-Webster, found at: https://www.merriam-webster.com/dictionary/sovereignty, accessed March 29, 2023.

37. A. W. Tozer, *The Knowledge of the Holy*, (HarperOne, 1961), 8.

38. Nate Stevens, *Deck Time with Jesus*, (CreateSpace, 2018), 60-61.

39. Spiros Zodhiates, Th.D., *The Hebrew-Greek Study Bible, King James Version*, Lexical Aids to the New Testament (AMG International, Inc. DBA AMG Publishers, 1991), 11614 (#2654).

40. Warren Wiersbe, as quoted in John Phillips' book, *The View from Mount Calvary*, (Kregel Publications, 2006), 7.

41. Jennie Evelyn Hussey, *Lead Me to Calvary*, 1921, found at: https://hymnary.org/text/king_of_my_life_i_crown_thee_now, accessed March 31, 2023. Public domain.

42. John Phillips, The View from Mount Calvary, (Kregel Publications, 2006), 130-131.

43. John Phillips, *Exploring the Gospel of Matthew*, (Kregel Publications, 2005), 503.

44. *The Passion of The Christ*, (2004) directed by Mel Gibson; screenplay by Benedict Fitzgerald and Mel Gibson; produced by Bruce Davey, Mel Gibson, Stephen McEveety; Icon Distribution. Beverly Hill, CA, 20th Century Fox Home Entertainment.

45 *What Does Blood Do?* National Library of Medicine, found at: https://www.ncbi.nlm.nih.gov/books/NBK279392, accessed March 31, 2023.

46 Andrew Murray, *The Blood of the Cross*, (Zondervan Publishing House, 1935), 65.

47 Spiros Zodhiates, Th.D., *The Hebrew-Greek Study Bible, King James Version,* Lexical Aids to the New Testament (AMG International, Inc. DBA AMG Publishers, 1991), 1654-1655 (#6918, 6942).

48 Spiros Zodhiates, Th.D., *The Hebrew-Greek Study Bible, King James Version,* Lexical Aids to the New Testament (AMG International, Inc. DBA AMG Publishers, 1991), 1680-1681 (#40, 53).

49 Spiros Zodhiates, Th.D., The Hebrew-Greek Study Bible, King James Version, Lexical Aids to the New Testament (AMG International, Inc. DBA AMG Publishers, 1991), 1680-1681 (#38).

50 John Phillips, *Exploring the Minor Prophets,* (Kregel Publications, 2002), 226.

51 *Atonement*, Merriam-Webster.com Dictionary, Merriam-Webster, found at: https://www.merriam-webster.com/dictionary/atonement, accessed March 31, 2023.

52 Andrew Murray, *The Blood of the Cross*, (Zondervan Publishing House, 1935), 55.

53 Charles R. Swindoll, *So, You Want to be Like Christ?,* (Thomas Nelson, 2005), 170.

54 John Phillips, *Exploring the Book of Daniel*, (Kregel Publications, 2004), 168.

55 Isaac Watts, *When I Survey the Wondrous Cross*, 1707, Public Domain, lyrics found and accessed May 17, 2024 at: https://hymnary.org/text/when_i_survey_the_wondrous_cross_watts

56 Nate Stevens, December 23, 2022.

57 *The Meaning and Definition of the Word "Excruciating"*, found at: https://symbolgenie.com/origin-of-the-word-excruciating, accessed February 29, 2024.

58 *The Roman Scourge*, Bible History, found at: https://bible-history.com/past/flagrum, accessed April 2, 2023.

59 John Phillips, *Exploring Philippians,* (Kregel Publications, 1995), 135.

60 *Love*, Merriam-Webster.com Dictionary, Merriam-Webster, found at: https://www.merriam-webster.com/dictionary/love, accessed July 25, 2023.

Endnotes

61 F. B. Meyer, *The Christ-Life for the Self-Life*, (Bible Institute Colportage Association, 1897), 47.

62 Greek word *Sunecho*, Bible Study Tools, found at: https://www.biblestudytools.com/lexicons/greek/kjv/sunecho.html , accessed April 2, 2023.

63 Charles Wesley, *And Can It Be, That I Should Gain*, 1738, Public Domain, lyrics found and accessed May 17, 2024 at: https://hymnary.org/text/and_can_it_be_that_i_should_gain

64 Nate Stevens, December 31, 2022

65 Frances Havergal, as quoted by Robert Morgan in *Then Sings My Soul*, (Thomas Nelson, 2003), 191.

66 L. E. Maxwell, *Born Crucified: The Cross in the Life of the Believer*, (Moody Press Chicago, 1945), 165.

67 Spiros Zodhiates, Th.D., *The Hebrew-Greek Study Bible, King James Version*, Lexical Aids to the New Testament (AMG International, Inc. DBA AMG Publishers, 1991), 1680-1681 (#37).

68 H. A. Ironside, *Holiness: The False and the True*, (Loizeaux Brothers, 1947), 56.

69 A. W. Tozer, *That Incredible Christian*, (Christian Publications, 1964), 40, 42.

70 Lewis E, Jones, *Power in the Blood*, 1899, found at: https://hymnary.org/text/would_you_be_free_from_the_burden_jones, accessed April 3, 2023. Public Domain.

71 John Phillips, *The View from Mount Calvary*, (Kregel Publications, 2006), 257-258.

72 Andrew Murray, *The Blood of the Cross*, (Zondervan Publishing House, 1935), 85.

73 Andrew Murray, *The Blood of the Cross*, (Zondervan Publishing House, 1935), 45.

74 C. I. Scofield, *The New Life in Christ Jesus*, (The Bible Institute Colportage Association, 1915), 19-20.

75 John Phillips, *Exploring the Gospel of Luke*, (Kregel Publications, 2005), 221.

76 Margaret Mauro, *The Young Christian*, found at: https://www.wholesomewords.org/poetry/youngchr.html, accessed April 7, 2023.

77   Joseph A. Alexander, *The Doomed Man*, 1837, Public Domain, accessed March 20, 2024 at: https://hymnary.org/text/there_is_a_time_we_know_not_when

78   Spiros Zodhiates, Th.D., *The Hebrew-Greek Study Bible, King James Version*, Lexical Aids to the New Testament (AMG International, Inc. DBA AMG Publishers, 1991), 1620.

79   John Phillips, *Exploring the Book of Daniel*, (Kregel Publications, 2004), 160.

80   A. W. Tozer, *The Root of the Righteous*, (Christian Publications, 1955), 62-64.

81   Augustus M. Toplady, *Rock of Ages*, 1776, Public Domain, accessed July 20, 2022 at: https://hymnary.org/text/rock_of_ages_cleft_for_me_let_me_hide

82   Charles Spurgeon, quote found and accessed August 10, 2023 at: https://quotefancy.com/quote/785402

83   L. E. Maxwell, *Born Crucified: The Cross in the Life of the Believer*, (Moody Press Chicago, 1945), 26.

84   A. W. Tozer, *Culture – Living as Citizens of Heaven on Earth*, (Moody Publishers, 2016), 76-77.

85   A. T. Pierson, as quoted by L. E. Maxwell, *Born Crucified: The Cross in the Life of the Believer*, (Moody Press Chicago, 1945), 63.

86   Nate Stevens, *Surrendered: Yielding to God's Perfect Will*, (Kingdom Winds Publishing, 2023), 7.

87   L. E. Maxwell, *Born Crucified: The Cross in the Life of the Believer*, (Moody Press Chicago, 1945), 156-157.

88   Adelaide A. Pollard, *Have Thine Own Way, Lord*, 1906, Public Domain, accessed April 14, 2024 at: https://hymnary.org/text/have_thine_own_way_lord

89   E. M. Bounds, *The Complete Works of E. M. Bounds – Prayer and Praying Men*, (Pantianos Classics / Createspace, 2017), 243.

90   John Phillips, *Exploring the Epistle of James: An Expository Commentary*, (Kregel Publications, 2004), 157.

91   Croft M. Pentz, *Zingers*, (Tyndale House Publishers, 1990), 10.

92   F. B. Meyer, *The Secret of Guidance*, (Fleming H. Revell Company, 1896), 10.

93   F. B. Meyer, *The Christ-Life for the Self-Life*, (Bible Institute Colportage Association, 1897), 82.

94 Andrew Murray, *Andrew Murray on Prayer – The Prayer Life*, (Whitaker House, 1998), 212.

95 A. W. Tozer, *That Incredible Christian*, (Christian Publications, 1964), 82.

96 Andrew Murray, *Andrew Murray on Prayer – Abide in Christ*, (Whitaker House, 1998), 91.

97 Spiros Zodhiates, Th.D., *The Hebrew-Greek Study Bible, King James Version*, Lexical Aids to the New Testament (AMG International, Inc. DBA AMG Publishers, 1991), 1680-1681 (#37, 38, & 42).

98 John Phillips, *Exploring Revelation*, (Kregel Publications, 2001), 179.

99 *Happiness*, Merriam-Webster.com Dictionary, Merriam-Webster, found at: https://www.merriam-webster.com/dictionary/happiness, accessed 5 Apr. 2023.

100 A. W. Tozer, *Of God and Men*, (Christian Publications, 1960), 45.

101 A. W. Tozer, *Culture – Living as Citizens of Heaven on Earth*, (Moody Publishers, 2016), 76-77.

102 A. W. Tozer, *The Root of the Righteous*, (Christian Publications, 1955), 52-53.

103 A. W. Tozer, *Man: The Dwelling Place of God*, (Wilder Publications, 2009), 27.

104 A. W. Tozer, *The Root of the Righteous*, (Christian Publications, 1955), 116.

105 A. W. Tozer, *That Incredible Christian*, (Christian Publications, 1964), 110.

106 F. B. Meyer, *The Secret of Guidance*, (Fleming H. Revell Company, 1896), 59.

107 A. W. Tozer, *The Root of the Righteous*, (Christian Publications, 1955), 117.

108 Andrew Murray, *With Christ in the School of Prayer*, (Pyramid Publications, 1953), 444.

109 A. W. Tozer, *That Incredible Christian*, (Christian Publications, 1964), 54.

110 A. W. Tozer, *The Knowledge of the Holy*, (HarperCollins, 1961), 103.

111 Spiros Zodhiates, Th.D., *The Hebrew-Greek Study Bible, King James Version*, Lexical Aids to the New Testament (AMG International, Inc. DBA AMG Publishers, 1991), 1154.

112 A. W. Tozer, *Of God and Men*, (Christian Publications, 1960), 75.

113 A. W. Tozer, *That Incredible Christian*, (Christian Publications, 1964), 25.

114 A. W. Tozer, *Of God and Men*, (Christian Publications, 1960), 59.

115 A. W. Tozer, *Of God and Men*, (Christian Publications, 1960), 71.

116 Adrian Rodgers, *Learning to Possess Your Possessions: Love Worth Finding*, found at: https://www.oneplace.com/ministries/love-worth-finding/read/articles/learning-to-possess-your-possessions-17359.html, accessed April 6, 2023.

117 Andrew Murray, *The Blood of the Cross*, (Zondervan Publishing House, 1935), 86.

118 Jonathan Edwards, *Encyclopaedia Britannica*, found at: https://www.britannica.com/biography/Jonathan-Edwards, accessed April 6, 2023.

119 Jonathan Edwards, https://graceonlinelibrary.org/biographies/personal-narrative-of-jonathan-edwards-by-jonathan-edwards accessed August 6,2022.

120 Ecclesiastes 3:11, *The Israel Bible*, First Edition 2018, English translation adapted by Israel365 from the JPS Tanakh, (Jewish Publication Society, 1985), 1839.

121 John Phillips, *Exploring Ecclesiastes*, (Kregel Publications, 2019), 27.

122 Dwight L. Moody, Goodreads Quotable Quotes, found at: https://www.goodreads.com/quotes/10218193-god-made-the-soul-a-little-too-large-for-this , accessed April 11, 2023.

123 Spiros Zodhiates, Th.D., *The Hebrew-Greek Study Bible*, *King James Version*, Lexical Aids to the New Testament (AMG International, Inc. DBA AMG Publishers, 1991), 1680 (#25).

124 A. W. Tozer, *Culture – Living as Citizens of Heaven on Earth*, (Moody Publishers, 2016), 126.

125 W. E. Vine, *Vine's Dictionary of Bible Words* (Thomas Nelson Publishers, 1997), 56.

126 Charles Spurgeon quote found at: https://www.azquotes.com/quote/565664, accessed and paraphrased February 13, 2024.

127 William Whiston, *The Works of Josephus: New Updated Edition*, *The War of the Jews 2.8.14-15*, (Hendrickson Publishers, 1987), 608.

128 William Whiston, *The Works of Josephus: New Updated Edition*, Extract out of the Discourse to the Greeks Concerning Hades (Hendrickson Publishers, 1987), 813-814.

129 C. I. Scofield, *The New Life in Christ Jesus*, (The Bible Institute Colportage Association, 1915), 66.

Endnotes

130 A. W. Tozer, *Of God and Men*, (Christian Publications, 1960), 50.

131 E. M. Bounds, *The Complete Works of E. M. Bounds – The Reality of Prayer*, (Pantianos Classics / Createspace, 2017), 139.

132 Andrew Murray, *The Blood of the Cross*, (Marshall, Morgan, & Scott, Ltd., 1935), 37-38.

133 A. W. Tozer, *The Root of the Righteous*, (Christian Publications, 1955), 117.

134 E. M. Bounds, *The Complete Works of E. M. Bounds – The Essentials of Prayer*, (Pantianos Classics / Createspace, 2017), 62.

135 L. E. Maxwell, *Born Crucified: The Cross in the Life of the Believer*, (Moody Press Chicago, 1945), 38.

136 Dwight L. Moody, *The Overcoming Life*, (Fleming H. Revell Company, 1896), 24-25.

137 Spiros Zodhiates, Th.D., *The Hebrew-Greek Study Bible, King James Version*, Lexical Aids to the New Testament (AMG International, Inc. DBA AMG Publishers, 1991), 1714 (#1805).

138 Andrew Murray, *Andrew Murray on Prayer – Abide in Christ*, (Whitaker House, 1998), 89.

139 E. M. Bounds, *The Complete Works of E. M. Bounds – The Purpose in Prayer*, (Pantianos Classics / Createspace, 2017), 172.

140 L. E. Maxwell, *Born Crucified: The Cross in the Life of the Believer*, (Moody Press Chicago, 1945), 33.

141 Helen Howarth Lemmel, *Turn Your Eyes Upon Jesus*, 1922, Public Domain, accessed July 28, 2022 at: https://hymnary.org/text/o_soul_are_you_weary_and_troubled.

142 David Brainerd, *Inspiring Quotes*, accessed August 25, 2022 at: https://www.inspiringquotes.us/author/3211-david-brainerd

143 L. E. Maxwell, *Born Crucified: The Cross in the Life of the Believer*, (Moody Press Chicago, 1945), 95.

144 H. A. Ironside, *Holiness: The False and the True*, (Loizeaux Brothers, 1947), 72.

145 Spiros Zodhiates, Th.D., *The Hebrew-Greek Study Bible, King James Version*, Lexical Aids to the New Testament (AMG International, Inc. DBA AMG Publishers, 1991), 1749 (#4124).

146 Spiros Zodhiates, Th.D., *The Hebrew-Greek Study Bible, King James Version*, Lexical Aids to the New Testament (AMG International, Inc. DBA AMG Publishers, 1991), 1695 (#766).

147 Lord Acton quote, found at: https://www.acton.org/research/lord-acton-quote-archive , accessed April 14, 2023.

148 L. E. Maxwell, *Born Crucified: The Cross in the Life of the Believer*, (Moody Press Chicago, 1945), 176.

149 Rhea F. Miller, I'd Rather Have Jesus, 1922, Public Domain, accessed August 18, 2022 at: https://hymnary.org/text/id_rather_have_jesus_than_silver_or_gold

150 Spiros Zodhiates, Th.D., *The Hebrew-Greek Study Bible, King James Version*, Lexical Aids to the New Testament (AMG International, Inc. DBA AMG Publishers, 1991), 1735 (#3107).

Printed in Great Britain
by Amazon